GW00720582

ALI AKBAR KHAN, General Editor

THE MUSIC OF THE BABA ALLAUDDIN GHARANA
AS TAUGHT BY ALI AKBAR KHAN
AT THE ALI AKBAR COLLEGE OF MUSIC

BOOK ONE

INTRODUCTION TO THE CLASSICAL MUSIC OF NORTH INDIA

Volume One

The First Years' Study

Notation and Explanatory Text by
GEORGE RUCKERT

EAST BAY BOOKS

WORLDWIDE AGENTS AND DISTRIBUTORS:
MMB MUSIC, INC.
Contemporary Arts Building
3526 Washington Avenue
Saint Louis, Missouri 63103

The Series *The Music of the Baba Allauddin Gharana as Taught by Ali Akbar Khan at the Ali Akbar College of Music* is published by East Bay Books by arrangement with Laureate Music Press, whose performing rights are vested with Broadcast Music, Inc., 320 West Fifty-Seventh Street, New York, New York 10019.

Library of Congress Catalog Card Number 91-072251

ISBN 0-930997-02-6

ISSN 1057-0934

East Bay Books: SAN 678-8939 MMB Music, Inc.: SAN 210-4601

This book has been typeset by George Ruckert on a MacIntosh SE20. The main body of the text is set in PALATINO, and the sargam (pitch notation) in HELVETICA BOLD. The text underlay to the songs is set in TIMES INDIAN ITALIC, designed and distributed by George Hart of the Department of South and Southeast Asian Studies at the University of California, Berkeley. The Devanagari letters are set in JAIPUR, and the transliterations directly below them in HINDUSTAN, both designed and distributed by Kenneth E. Bryant of the Department of Asian Studies at the University of British Columbia, Vancouver.

The cover is by Kathryn Stark Design, Pacific Grove, California, and reproduces Hallie Gene King's watercolor *Rag Bhimpalashri*, painted for Ali Akbar Khan and used by his and the artist's permission.

Printed in the United States of America
Off-Campus Books

OCB

THIRD EDITION
4 6 8 10 9 7 5 3

The First Years' Study

Ustad Ali Akbar Khan

Photo by Betsey Bourbon

TABLE OF CONTENTS

Photographs

Most of the photographs in this book have been taken from the personal collection of Ali Akbar Khansahib and that of the Ali Akbar College of Music. Many of these are old, and the photographer unknown.

The frontispiece and several of the more recent photographs are used with the generous permission of the photographers, Betsey Bourbon (2215R Market Street, Suite 194, San Francisco, CA 94114) and Faustin Bray (P.O. Box 2111, Mill Valley, CA 94942). Individual credit is given below their photographs.

Preface

This is a book of and about the classical music of North India, among the oldest continual musical traditions of the world. Presented here is a small part of the musical legacy of one of the foremost families which has preserved and collected this ancient music and developed it to the highest standards: the Baba Allauddin Gharana of the Seni tradition. This volume introduces the great richness and variety of the different styles of music as taught by one of this century's greatest musicians, Ali Akbar Khan.

Preparing a book on Indian music in the name of perhaps its foremost practitioner has not been an easy task. Even though I have studied with Ustad Khan for twenty-five years, every time I wrote a word, I felt I had either all India or all Music looking over my shoulder. Indeed, Khansahib (as Ali Akbar is known to friends and students) represents both: he is at once an embodiment of India's great musical tradition (and all that this incredible music and cultural legacy represent), as well as an individual musician of towering eminence. His language is not just Hindi or Indian or American or highbrow or raga-and-tala: it is just music, and cannot be obfuscated or dimmed by the grasping possessiveness of any one cultural, artistic, or social group. It speaks to everyone with or without experience of India or special musical initiation. In the rare and lofty heights to which we are taken by this great artist, most people are usually stunned to silence.

This awe has certainly been a stumbling block in proceeding, for although it has been nearly fifteen years since Khansahib requested this beginning book, I have had to realize that the project ever required a larger book but at the same time a simpler one. Many people around the world look to Khansahib for musical guidance, and the book has had to address the needs of students of many backgrounds and cultural attitudes.

For Khansahib, and most musicians of this classical tradition, music is a *process,* a way of thinking about a divine intermingling of sound, art, and life—like some other kinds of music to a certain degree, but also unique. To represent it only as a *product* reduces it to something only partially viable—and this half-truth is difficult for "Indian" musicians to accept as a realistic representation of their tradition. Hence, the result: a great measure of humble silence, even reluctance to speak, by the musicians themselves in the face of the sacred immensities of music.

Over the centuries, this music has been used as a yoga, a spiritual discipline, practiced by musicians without idea of worldly reward. But it has also been a concert music in the splendor of court chambers, and more modestly in the homes of patrons in all walks of life. It has lived in the temples and in the tents of armies. It has been the vehicle for the divine expression of saints and of actors portraying sacred dramas. It has been subject to both the refinement and decadence of thousands of musicians in the service of both wise kings and foolish emperors. Through its millions of lives, it has developed freshness and preserved oldness—an incredibly rich artistic method of weaving sound patterns in which can be seen the many facets of the musical life of mankind, both public and private.

Our sages developed music from time immemorial for the mind to take shelter in that pure being which stands apart as one's true self. Real music is not for wealth, not for honors, or not even for the joys of the mind—it is one kind of yoga, a path for realization and salvation to purify your mind and heart and give you longevity.

Ali Akbar Khan

I hope that the quality and nature of the music to follow will reward everyone, from beginner to professional. Indeed, the scope alone of the musical styles represented is more complete than in any other published survey. But the form of presentation will naturally generate a number of questions: "Why didn't you put it in Western notation?" "Why are there no cassettes?" "Why haven't you put in more sitar music?" "Why did you choose Rag Marwa over Rag Bhupali in a beginning book?" I have attempted to answer some of these questions in the Introduction and text of the book. But another response is that this is the beginning of a larger project—the presenting of the music of Ustad Ali Akbar Khan in many volumes, which will include instruction manuals for particular instruments and a series of learning cassette tapes. But providing a background with the broadest viewpoint in mind was considered the best starting place, and this is the idea behind this first volume.

In trying to cover the great expanse of music history, style, and theory which are presented to us in this music, I have constantly been self-conscious of the superficial qualities of the descriptions; this is especially true in the omission of the immense personal contributions of so many of India's other great musicians. This book is written from the important, but decidedly non-Western, persepective of the approach from India's *guru-shishya* tradtition—that is, in pursuing the understanding of one guru's point of view, the disciple gets the lesson; in pursuing everything, the disciple gets nothing. I have tried, especially in the areas of vocabulary and terminology, to bring the reader into a basic awareness of the scope of what this great tradition embraces. For experienced students in India and elsewhere, I am sure they will feel that much has been glossed over—on the other hand, they may be rewarded with the simplicity of the way that one of their great musicians has presented his music (albeit with the warps in understanding that ever attend even the most earnest disciples).

This book comes out of many years' study with Khansahib at the Ali Akbar College of Music in California. In his weekly four days of teaching, Khansahib normally teaches a two-hour vocal class followed by a two-hour instrumental class. The music in this book was generated in these classes, and has been heard, sung, and played by many of his students. It was reviewed in subsequent lessons, and sometimes retaught later in alternative versions. The versions presented here are chosen for their beauty and simplicity, over other perhaps more highly ornamented or unusual ones. The music presented here is only a drop in the ocean of Khansahib's creative output at the College, which, when published, will require more than forty volumes.

The format of the book has been created with the practical musician in mind. In typesetting the music, choices have been made with the idea foremost of the student's sitting on the floor and reading from a slight distance, as would be normal in the practice of the music. After a brief explanatory introduction, the music itself comes first in the book's layout. The bulk of the text is in the back, where it is intended to be useful for reference. This is to reinforce the central idea that it is the music itself which will reveal its secrets, and that a knowledge of the theory and history is secondary.

Most of the titles of musicians have been left off in the text. For example, in India one would never refer to the eminently respected sitarist Ravi Shankar without a form of address or a title (in this case "Pandit," or "Panditji"), and similarly with other great musicians (see the chapter "Manners Among Musicians"). But in the West we say "Bach" and "Beethoven," or similarly, "Arturo Toscanini" or "Horowitz" without titles when they are referred to in print, while we would use other polite forms of address in person. This is the convention in this book, and I hope that Indian friends will recognize this as a literary convention rather than a lack of respect. Exceptions are made with Ustad Allauddin Khansahib and in the use alone of the name "Khansahib" for Ali Akbar Khan.

When Khansahib is speaking directly, his further words appear in italics without citation. All other quotes have their author's name appended.

George Ruckert
Ali Akbar College of Music
San Rafael, California
March, 1991

Acknowledgments

In the many years that it has required to assemble this book, I have had the good fortune of having the help of a number of friends and advisors without whom the project would never have come to fruition. They have assisted with graphic design, polished the Hindi, and proofread and examined the text and the music.

Many days have been spent in India trying to produce suitable English translations of the Hindi song lyrics. I am grateful to the ICCR and ISTAR in India, and the AIIS in the United States for sponsoring and helping to fund two research trips. Biresh Roy of Calcutta worked patiently on them and was able to come up with fresh, imaginative, and appealing translations of many of the songs. I appreciate his long labors, his inspiring musicianship, and the warm friendship he always extends.

With the help of the faculty in the Department of South and Southeast Asian Studies at the University of California, Berkeley, the critical literary aspect of this book was molded considerably. Usha Jain taught me Hindi for several years; Bruce Pray initiated me into the history of Indian languages, revealing much of their nuances, and taught me Hindi and Urdu; and Linda Hess unveiled Hindi poetry and culture and helped place the language in the context of its literary tradition. Professors Hess and Pray read parts of the manuscript, making valuable critical suggestions. George Hart helped with getting Devanagari and English diacritics into print. Despite all their patient assistance, the inevitable shortcomings of the book in this all-important area of language must not be attributed to them; rather, whatever success may have been achieved can be ascribed directly to their generosity.

Bonnie Wade of the Music Department at Berkeley has been also of prime importance in bringing this project to life. She assisted and directed some of the research projects which resulted in chapters of the book, and her own scholarship in Indian music is a beacon to many who write on the subject. Her warm and prodding teaching methods awakened awareness, and her thorough style of reading assisted the writing immeasurably.

Kathryn Bilotti-Stark has been especially helpful for her layout suggestions, criticisms, and overall contribution in getting the manuscript in and out of the computer. I spent many hours learning the ways of the MacIntosh computer under the expert guidance of Donley Smith and David Warkentin who were never too tired to drop what they were doing to walk me through yet another process.

The reason this book is not laden with footnotes is because of the way the material has been assimilated. Over the years at the Ali Akbar College of Music, there have been a number of teachers who have given their individual perspectives on history and theory. None was more persistent and important than Ali Akbar Khansahib himself, whose elusive theoretical perceptions I have tried to put into words—words of which he would be highly skeptical, to be sure. At his feet I have heard thousands of hours of music; I have listened to him talk about and read theory; I have read theory back to him, and have heard him reiterate over the years those ideas which he feels to be important. And yet I cannot claim to have captured the subtlety of his understanding. Other teachers have made notable impressions on me in this area, including Ravi Shankar, Jnan Ghosh, Shankar Ghosh, Zakir Hussain, Swapan Chaudhuri, Nikhil Banerjee, Sanjukta Ghosh, Indranil Bhattacharya, Laxmi G. Tewari, Prakash Wadhera, and Chitresh Das. Jnan Ghosh read an early version of the manuscript and made important suggestions.

Khansahib's family, especially his sons Ashish and Pranesh who both live in the United States, and son Dhyanesh and son-in-law Stanley Perera in Calcutta, have always given time and assistance to this project. Their patient help is warmly appreciated.

This book started in the 1970s and slowly went through cycles of emerging and disappearing. The manuscript was lost in shipment in 1984 and had to be entirely reconstructed. Throughout all this time, my guru brothers and sisters have helped keep me on track. Their "nameless and unremembered acts of kindness and of love" have been woven into this book without my knowing where or how. None has been more supportive of the Ali Akbar College than Daisy Paradis. My guru sister, Sisir Kona Dhar Chowdhury of Calcutta, went with me note by note through the music. Mimi Spencer created a version of the music on the typewriter, showing me how to begin. Bridget Conrad typed an early manuscript and made valuable criticism. Rod Blouin helped with the exercise portion and in a thousand other ways stood behind both the project and me. Ross Kent, Jim Kohn, Ron Nierenberg, James Pomerantz, Chris Ris, John Rothfield, Lynn Taussig, and Peter van Gelder all contributed suggestions. Huib Schippers and Ken Zuckerman have been especially helpful proofreaders. In the final days of preparation, Joep Bor, Swapan Chaudhuri, Bruce Hamm, Richard Harrington, Allyn Miner, Terry Pease, and Rajiv Taranath all read the manuscript and shared their invaluable insights. Hisayo Saijo, likewise a careful reader of the manuscript, has been a lifelong source of encouragement, and assistance.

My parents and brother Dave have been pillars of strength and support all my life—Dave's love of the word has helped considerably in manifesting my ethereal musings into "hard copy."

The supreme value of my wife Gretchen's many sacrifices as well as constant love and encouragement cannot be reduced to words.

Khansahib teaching an instrumental class at the Ali Akbar College of Music. The students, l. to r.: Geoffrey Lipner, Ron Nierenberg, Chris Ris, George Ward, Richard Harrington, Rick Henderson, John Rothfield, George Ruckert, and John Bell. Shyam Kane accompanying on the tabla. Photo by Faustin Bray.

Introduction

How do you learn Indian music? Or any music, for that matter? You hear it, practice it, and play it; or as the traditional Sanskrit expression goes, *shiksha, dīksha, parīksha*: learning, dedicated practice, evaluation. Since ancient times in India, all three have traditionally been supervised by a *guru* (teacher) whose musical authority was the final word. And in the past, the student lived with or near the guru. There was no recourse to other teachers' opinions, recordings of other artists, books of music—the entire musical life of the student revolved around the oral exchange of the music directly from the teacher. If a disciple happened to hear other music, the teacher was close by and could correct any confusions of rag or impurities of stylistic presentation. During long hours of daily practice, the teacher would be near enough to interrupt and say, "not that way," "do that ornament ten more times," or even, "that's enough for now." The teacher would give many short lessons every day, so as the disciple's capacity to memorize expanded gradually, a repertoire grew progressively. And in off-hours, the teacher would tell stories of the past which casually but firmly shaped the student's sense of style, history, vocabulary, and theory. This was the way for thousands of years.

There was no need for written music. How could any system of notation capture the evanescence of rag, or the subtlety of emotion and ornament, or the numberless variations of rhythm? It was never considered a possibility. In addition, musicians and families were noted for particular and personal repertoires, and writing parts of them down would have put the family treasures at risk.

Then came the dramatic changes of the modern world, the quickly vanishing older lifestyles, and the accessibility to Indian music all over the globe. The music was no longer the exclusive province of those few privileged to have a guru nearby. Neither could students afford to retreat from the world with their teacher for many years to get the training the music demanded. Individual music lessons became more infrequent and each session with the teacher became longer. Schools now taught the arts, subjects which were once the exclusive provinces of the individual exchange of *guru* and *shiśhya* (disciple). Primary lessons were expected to be learned before coming into the presence of the master artists, whose valuable time was too scarce to be spent going over and over the rudiments. Books and recordings now gave access to valuable materials which otherwise would have taken years to assimilate.

The life and music of Ustad Ali Akbar Khan spans these ancient and modern worlds of music. He was trained in the house of his father, Ustad Allauddin Khan, himself a musical giant of the twentieth century. He received his training in the old way: his father meted it out with the strictest discipline, teaching him daily and supervising his practice for more than twenty years. Early employment came in a royal court, just as an accomplished musician might have expected in centuries past. But the tale turned abruptly in the 1940s. World War II and the Independence movement disturbed everyday life in India. Shortly after India gained independence, his patron, the Maharaja of Jodhpur, died suddenly in an airplane accident. A new economic order severed all musicians from the age-old system of court patronage. A twentieth-century trend was accelerated: musicians went to the cities, and the music became accessible to the masses through recordings, concerts, films, radio, and in the schools. No performing artist was spared the changing course of events. The musician became a traveller, playing far and wide. Ali Akbar Khansahib first came to America at the invitation of Yehudi Menuhin in 1955. He began teaching in California in 1965, founding his College of Music there three years later. This book, then, emerges out of his teaching for more than twenty-five years in the West. He has always taken great pains to bring his basically traditional conceptions of music into fruition, and, at the same time, to lift it beyond the barriers of time and culture into this new world.

It is not a question of Indian music, or American music, like that: any music, in rhythm, in tune, gives you food for your soul.

Khansahib, as Ali Akbar Khan is known to friends and students, has dedicated his life mostly to teaching, although he has also maintained an impressive concert and recording career. He teaches to classes of students as in any school, but in the traditional style, composing anew for each class, and not relying on written materials to communicate this music. Hence a point of departure in this book: presenting the music in written form has never been his teaching method. The students, who come from all backgrounds and all levels of musical understanding, have become used to writing the music down as it is orally taught, and thus have a copy of a newly created composition for their weekly study and practice. In review sessions, elder students help younger ones understand and assimilate these lessons.

This book has been assembled at the request and under the supervision of Khansahib, so that learners all over the world might have a basic primer with which to work.

Give the basic compositions in the rags—sargam, dhrupad, dhamar, slow khyal, fast khyal, tarana, slow gat and fast gat, and include some light music, too. Show the different styles of variation—bolbant, boltan, vistar, tans, tora, lari, jhala, etc. Give an explanation of the notation and some exercises...what they need to get started. Of course you must include something about what sort of material we are teaching, but only explain the basic ideas of history and theory, for that is covered in other books. My father didn't think that theory was so important in learning music; he didn't teach that way.

Just what is a *rāga* (Hindi, *rāg*)? That is a difficult question, because rags can include a wide range of possibilites, from simple scales to complicated melodies. Even a short description would probably run several pages in length. A rag's essence is embodied in traditional *bandish*es (fixed compositions). These may be in a number of different styles, from the simple *sargam* to the old and stately *dhrupad*, the appealing and romantic *khyal* and *thumri*, a lively *tarana* or *gat*, and developmental added sections: *vistars* and *tan* s. Rags are not learned through the memorization of theoretical concepts, like ascending-descending melodic patterns, *vādī-samvādī* (pitch hierarchies), etc., although these may indeed help in the conceptual grasp of the rag. A basic knowledge of a rag comes with learning how it behaves in the context of the above named types of compositions: the durations of the notes, the slides, the shapes of the note patterns, and the ornaments. The compositions themselves are an inventory of the rag's configurations, and a student may have to learn hundreds of them in order to understand one rag thoroughly.

One can see, then, that *ālāp*, the slow abstract introductory movement of a rag, is not taught in the same way. Rather, one learns many compositions in a rag and then is able to reconstruct the rag in the abstract independently. Later, this picture of the rag is played to the teacher for corrections and additions.

Alap is like you go someplace nice for a visit—like you go to France for a vacation. Then you come home and write a letter or tell your friend about where you were—where you stayed, what you did, what you saw, what you ate—like that the memory of the compositions comes in the alap.

This musical picture of rag is what Khansahib teaches through compositions, and what this book represents. The ten rags chosen and presented herein are basic to the literature. They are the rags which are derived from the names of V.N. Bhatkhande's ten basic scales, or *ṭhāṭs* (see the chapter "Organization of Rag"). They are not the ten simplest rags, nor perhaps the ten rags which might otherwise be selected for their introductory qualities. But the North Indian musical world is now beginning to accept the controversial *ṭhāṭs* of Bhatkhande as a workable starting point, even though they have serious limitations as a system of theoretical frameworks. For instance, it is often pointed out that because there are so many more rags in Khammaj *ṭhāṭ* than in Marwa *ṭhāṭ*, it is hardly realistic to put them on an equal theoretical level. Also, relegating the huge repertoire of rags to just ten *ṭhāṭs* will inevitably be problematical, creating a great number of vague or ambiguous classifications. Many rags could be ascribed to more than one *ṭhāṭ*, and others would hardly belong to any *ṭhāṭ* at all. Finally, the *ṭhāṭs* all but ignore the imaginative, extramusical associations of rag—seasons, times, moods, and family groupings—all of which are essential to understanding the music.

In spite of these limitations, the *ṭhāṭs* turn out to be as good a place as any to begin. They give the student a practical overview of a variety of tonal combinations and also suggest some of the basic moods. They correspond to the basic fret settings on the sitar, and give the player of any stringed instrument a good start in studying a variety of fingering positions. Five *ṭhāṭs* are derived from morning rags and five from evening ones, so that a rough sense of traditional time feeling can be maintained. And with the possible exception of Rag Marwa, these rags and scales would definitely be included in any beginning survey of the music.

These, then, are compositions in rags of the ten *ṭhāṭs* learned in class from Ali Akbar Khansahib. Each one was taught and composed in a weekly two-hour lesson. Then, after practicing it for at least a week, the class performed the composition in the following lesson, during which the master sometimes made alterations or extensions. In addition, he reviewed each one again prior to its inclusion in this book. Some of them, especially the vocal compositions, have been taught over and over, and are an integral part of his repertoire. Others are traditional and well-known older compositions which Khansahib has reshaped to conform to his conception of the rag. Hence, in a few cases the lyrics of a song, or perhaps its first melodic line, might be familiar to many; but Khansahib's way of rendering the rag lends a unique and personal stamp to these compositions which may be popularly known in other versions.

My father learned from a great teacher, and we always keep the traditional thing—from father to son, son to grandson, teacher to student—like that. What my father learned, I don't want that to die. It must spread all over the world.

When teaching this traditional material, Khansahib would be hard-pressed to separate his father's music from his own, his memory from his invention, tradition from spontaneous expression. With most of these compositions, it would be as hard for him to say, "I composed this," as it would be to say, "My father composed this." He often says, "I don't know when I am composing something new or when I am remembering something old," which reveals his perspective on the flexible interaction of memory and creation. The students, eager to participate in this obviously cosmic dance, never impugn with the question, "Where did this come from, anyway?" In some cases, he volunteers the source of the composition as this or that *gharana* (musical lineage), that it was traditional, modern, or from such-and-such a person. Beyond these qualifiers, it would be reshaped by his memory and his conception of the rag, and therefore personalized.

Do you want to know what it is about Khansahib that is so great? It is his conception of rag. The picture of the rag is always so clear, and he is never casual about it. At the same time his intuition is so powerful that it seems effortless. This is from his training from his father, of course, but it is also his genius alone.

Shankar Ghosh

In presenting the material in a lesson, Khansahib generates a composition line by line, repeats it line by line, and finally asks for it to be repeated in its entirety. As often as not, a complete song may take two hours to compose, and an instrumental composition several lessons of two hours each. Many of these songs and compositions have appended developmental sections in various styles, from *vistārs* to *tāns* to *jhālās*. Since there can be from five to thirty students learning at once, often there is much variation in the versions of every line. He may repeat a line from ten to fifteen times, sometimes with slight changes of ornament or rhythm. If these variations are disturbing, Khansahib will appraise them, and select one version which he thinks best. If they are not offensive to his sense of the possible ways a line may go, he will allow more than one version to exist. He can be minutely exacting in his correcting and refining a melody and rhythm, or he can let himself go in his musical outpouring of variation after variation. In subsequent lessons, he may frequently change what he has previously composed, which exasperates the note-taker who is eager for a final version chiseled in stone. In fact, it is often hard for him to accept any written facsimile of the music at all, since he has a rigorous fidelity to the adjustability and mutability of these old and venerated melodic forms which comprise the essence not only of the rags, but of music itself.

The next chapter, "Getting Started," is followed by "Notation" and "Pronunciation"; then come the compositions. The five morning rags are given first, then the five evening ones. For the sake of practice, morning (which by the clock goes from midnight to noon) can also be thought of as 2 a.m. to 2 p.m., and similarly with evening, which can last until 2 a.m. Ideally, the rags should be studied in their appropriate time slots, but some flexibility is acceptable for learning and practice. On the other hand, there are limits. For example, it would never be correct to play Iman Kalyan in the morning, or Bhairav at two o'clock in the afternoon.

Each rag has its own mood and its own time, you see. If you play the rags in their proper times, that mood will come. Of course it will take some time, some practice. But if you play them at the wrong time, one day you will call for that mood, and it won't come. Just like your friend—if you treat him badly, will he come to visit you?

One composition can be concentrated on for a week at a time, and thereafter reviewed with other compositions in the same rag. An instrumental composition, such as that in Khammaj, can be studied over the course of many weeks. A thorough study of this material, then, could take about two years. Each composition should be memorized.

This book is not expressly designed as a do-it-yourself manual, but it will help a student to get started if a teacher is not at hand. Even though everyone is not so fortunate as to have Khansahib or other masters to study with, there are many experienced musicians who can lead one through this material. The most recommended way to learn is first to absorb the compositions by listening and then memorize them with the help of the notation. A teacher can help with the apportioning, balancing technique with music, and correcting rhythm, intonation, technique, pronunciation, and expression.

All the compositions can and should be sung, and most of the vocal materials can be effectively played instrumentally. The sargams and taranas work especially well as instrumental compositions, but the other songs can serve just as well as instrumental studies. A dhrupad would, in former times, be accompanied by a vina or a rabab, and today the violin, flute, and sarangi will play in the vocal styles of *khyāl* and *ṭhumrī*.

One time a powerful and wealthy king wanted to learn sculpting, so he went to a sculptor of repute. "I am a great admirer of your work," he said, and several of his retinue murmured and nodded in agreement. "I wish to learn this great art."

"Yes, I can teach you," said the artist. "Let me see some of your painting."

"No, no, not painting," said the king. "Sculpture. I want to learn the art of sculpting."

"Of course, of course. But painting is the preliminary training for the visual arts. Let me see some of your work."

"Well, I have not painted at all."

"Hm, I see. I can teach you that, I suppose. Let me see you dance."

"Dance? What has dance got to do with it?"

"Surely one who wished to portray the human form would have studied its graceful movement."

"I do not dance."

The sculptor was taken aback. "Very well, I will teach you some dance, also. Bring your instrument."

The king began to falter. "Instrument? What instrument?"

"Listen. I have indicated the importance of the study of painting and dance to sculpting. Surely you understand that the dance is done to music of instruments? How could you expect to dance without knowing something about instrumental music?"

The king admitted that he didn't know the first thing about playing an instrument.

"Well, no matter. I will teach you. Sing something."

"I can't sing."

*"You can't sing? You come here expecting to learn the fine art of sculpting and you cannot sing? Doesn't the study of all art begin with singing? We have much work to do. Let's see, we shall start with the note **sa**..."*

Traditional story

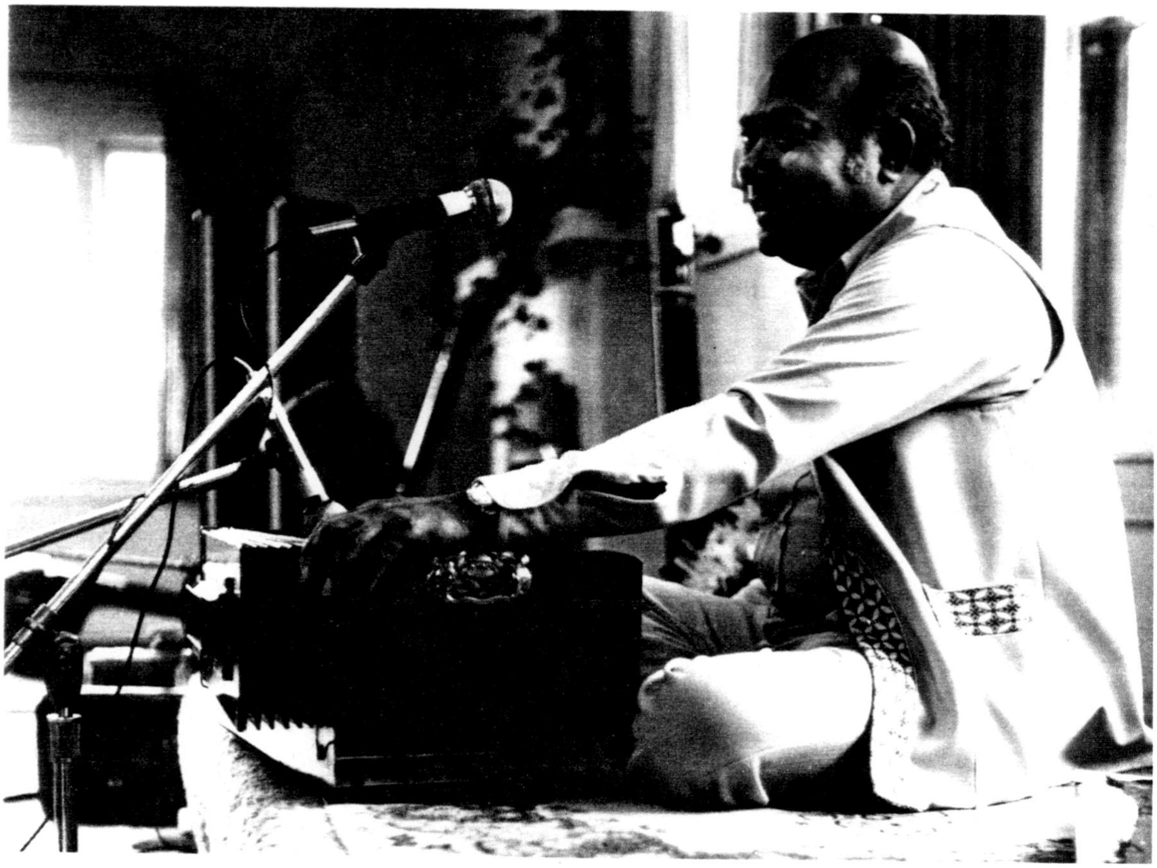

Khansahib playing harmonium and teaching class at the Ali Akbar College.
Photo by Faustin Bray.

Getting Started

The Teacher

The unique importance of the teacher in this music tradition is expanded upon elsewhere in this book, but for now let us just say that a teacher who can guide you through this book would be a great advantage in helping you break the materials down into lesson-sized portions and providing intermediate goals in your practice. And all musicians know that the embarrassment of facing the teacher unprepared is in itself an effective goad to inspire practice. Other aspects of music that a teacher can help with have been suggested too, especially in the chapter "Theory of Rag." A teacher need not always be a preceptor of your particular instrument or style. In the classical music of India, vocalists often teach instrumentalists, and vice-versa, and sarodists teach flute players and violinists. Of course, it is helpful to have a role model for your instrument or vocal style, but in the long run it is the music itself which will provide the guide.

Many people raise one common question about how we could learn sitar from a master whose medium of expression was the sarod. Baba (Allauddin Khansahib) had such an inexhaustible idea about the baj or style of playing every instrument that he could neatly distinguish between them and combine them as well for the best conceivable effect. One day he said to me, "Today I will teach you sitar after the style of Nawab Kutubadaulla Bahadur of Lucknow..."

Nikhil Banerjee

The Practice

It is good to have a regular time and place for practice. Naturally, that place should be kept clean and free from shoes, since when practicing it is customary to remove the shoes and sit on the floor. If possible, a special rug, mat, or covering should be placed down before practicing to provide a clean and comfortable area. If you can bathe before practicing, it will further enhance your mood. However, these things should not be thought of as barriers to your regular practice, but regarded as aids in putting you in the good frame of mind for classical music. In the long run, a regular practice (*riyāz*) in this manner can develop into a spiritual practice (*sādhanā*).

Choosing Your Sa

As each instrument has a tonic pitch where it sounds best, or from where the range of most music is best in focus, so each individual voice also orients itself better at different pitch levels. For male voices, the key note (**sa**) is usually chosen from Western A to D, and for female voices, from F-sharp to B. At the Ali Akbar College, B-flat is chosen as the vocal **sa**. But everyone is different, and to find out where your singing voice lies, sing a descending scale, "la, la, la...," from any pitch at all stepwise down to your lowest clear note. Call that low note **ma** (fa). Now you can sing ascending **ma pa dha ni sa**, and find your **sa** that way. Select a drone pitch according to that **sa**. This may take some time or the help of an experienced friend. But if you are in doubt, sing from B-flat until you find a permanent **sa**.

Using a Drone

The most common instrument used in classical singing is the *tānpūra* (also, *tamboura)*, the stringed drone. It usually has four strings, but occasionally has five or even six. Tune these open strings to a combination of **sa** and **pa** (sometimes **ma** or **ga** is substituted for **pa**, if the rag calls for it) and simply drone them over and over.

If your tanpura has four strings, carefully tune the two middle ones to **sa**. Once these are in tune, go on to the bass string, the fourth one called the *kharaj*, an octave below the two you have just tuned. After tuning this one, tune the first string to **pa**, between the two **sas**. If your instrument has more strings, tune them to middle **sa** with the others, keeping the outer ones for middle **pa** and low **sa**, as explained above. Tuning the tanpura can be a difficult job, and you may need some help at first, setting the *jawari* (buzzing sound) and getting the clearest sound. In the old days, it was said that everything about a musician could be judged solely from his tuning of the tanpura. It is important to take care with the tuning, and refocus your attention to matching the **sas**.

When you play the tanpura, try to bring out the glowing and atmospheric sound which hovers like a halo around the instrument. This is called the *ās* (or *āsh*, surround), and sets the atmosphere, background, and tonal reference for the music. Try to reduce the percussive effect of the finger sound, the rhythmic plucking of the strings. The right-hand plucking stroke should be a soft caress of the strings so that the *ās* is magnified. There is no "correct rhythm" for the tanpura. A slight pause left after the fourth or last string will help bring out the *ās*.

A *surpeti* (hand-pumped reed drone box), an electronic tone generator, or a guitar can also serve as drones. If a guitar or similar stringed instrument is used, the player need not tune or play all the strings, since it is the **sa** and **pa** tones which are necessary for the drone to be full.

Sitar student William Schwintz getting a lesson from Khansahib.
Photo by Betsey Bourbon.

Notation

The system of notation used in this book is derived from the letter notation used by the innovative twentieth-century musicians, Allauddin Khan, V.D. Paluskar, Vishnu Narayan Bhatkhande, and others. It has been somewhat adjusted and modified during twenty years of use at the Ali Akbar College in the United States. Although the Roman alphabet is used instead of the Devanagari script (i.e., Sanskrit/Hindi letters), and a few Western musical symbols are used for their convenience, the system is essentially the same. Western music notation, which may have the advantage of being more widely understood in the modern world, nevertheless cannot communicate certain of the essential musical relationships which are germinal to this and other modal music. In fact, it makes some of them equivocal when they are actually not so. Certain of the typical ornaments and rhythms of Indian classical music appear unnecessarily more complex when written in Western notation. In addition, Western notation can imply a whole tradition of tonal and rhythmic information, much of which is not useful for interpreting Indian music.

For example, pitch in the Indian system(s) is not absolute, like the 440 A of the West. The **sa**, or "tonic," of a sarod may be different from a sitar, or flute, and every vocalist may use his own individual **sa**. Staff notation can be used at the beginning to orient a student to the letter notation, but should not be substituted one for the other. The syllable names of the notes, which correspond to the western **do**, **re**, **mi**, **fa**, **sol**, **la**, and **ti** (**si**), are **sa**, **re**, **ga**, **ma**, **pa**, **dha**, and **ni**. These are the short forms of the words *sādja*, *ṛishaba*, *gandhāra*, *madhyama*, *panchama*, *dhaivata*, and *nishāda*. Modern Hindi pronunciation drops the final *-a* sound. Note that "**re**" is used as a syllable instead of "**ri**," even though the latter is also sometimes heard. The note for the tonic **sa** in the lowest register is also called *kharaja* (Hindi, *kharaj*).

Although **sa** can actually be placed anywhere in the Western system, for convention C is usually chosen. And if C *is* chosen for the tonic, then the twelve notes of the chromatic scale, each a half step apart, can be thus represented:

S	**r**	**R**	**g**	**G**	**m**	**M**	**P**	**d**	**D**	**n**	**N**
sa	**re**	**re**	**ga**	**ga**	**ma**	**ma**	**pa**	**dha**	**dha**	**ni**	**ni**

Which corresponds to Devanagari notation:

स	रि	रि	ग	ग	म	मं	प	ध	ध	नि	नि
sa	re	re	ga	ga	ma	ma	pa	dha	dha	ni	ni

Or, from the western C:

C	D♭	D	E♭	E	F	F♯	G	A♭	A	B♭	B

Note, too, that there is no change in the *vocalized* syllable for the *vikrit* (altered) notes, that is, the sharps and flats. There is one **sa** and one **pa**, but there are two **res**, **gas**, **mas**, **dhas**, and **nis**. The upper form of any note is written with an upper case (capital) letter; and the lower form is written with a lower case letter. **Sa** and **pa**, never altered, are always written in capital letters. This system is more convenient than placing lines above and below the notes, as is done in the Devanagari notation.

An unaltered (natural) note is called *shuddh* (pure). **Re**, **ga**, **dha**, and **ni** can be shuddh or made *komal* (flat, or "soft") by lowering them a half step. The lower form of **ma** is called *shuddh mā*, perhaps because of its inclusion in the "natural" scales (*Bilāwal*, and formerly *Kāfī*). Very rarely, it is called *komal mā*. The upper form is known as *tīvra* (sharp, high, bright) *mā*. It is the only note which is normally referred to as *tīvra*.

Chart of Pitch Notation

Note Name	Pronounced*	Written	Devanagari	From Western C
Sa	SA	**S**	स	C
Komal re	RE	**r**	रे (रि)	D♭/ C♯
Shuddh re	RE	**R**	रे (रि)	D
Komal ga	GA	**g**	ग	E♭ / D♯
Shuddh ga	GA	**G**	ग	E
Shuddh ma	MA	**m**	म	F
Tivra ma	MA	**M**	म॑	F♯ / G♭
Pa	PA	**P**	प	G
Komal dha	DHA	**d**	ध	A♭ / G♯
Shuddh dha	DHA	**D**	ध	A
Komal ni	NI	**n**	नि	B♭ / A♯
Shuddh ni	NI	**N**	नि	B

*A is pronounced broad, as in the English "father," **E** is long as in English "ray," and **I** is long as in English "see."

Register

There are three registers commonly used for classical music, and these can change according to one's voice or instrument. A male voice, for instance, might sound a given note an octave below a female voice, but they both sing "madhya Pa" notated the same way. The concept of the octave is represented by the word *saptak* which, interestingly, has its etymology in the root for "seven," instead of "eight" as in the West. The three registers (*saptaks*) are named *mandra* (deep), *madhya* (middle), and *tāra* (high pitched); or, simply stated, low, middle, and high.

The word *ati* (extreme) extends the range to the next level, and *ati-ati* to the next, but these are not so often encountered, except on instruments of wide range. Dots above and below the letters are used to indicate register:

Low (mandra)	Ṇ Ḍ P̣ ṃ
Middle (madhya)	S R G m
High (tara)	Ṡ Ṙ Ġ ṁ
Very low (ati mandra)	N̤ D̤ P̤ m̤
Very high (ati tara)	S̈ R̈ G̈ m̈

Ornaments

Ornaments, whose timing may not be fixed, are written with small superscript letters before or after the note which comes on the beat:

${}^{G}R$ ${}^{mGm}R$ $S^{\underset{.}{N}RS\underset{.}{N}S}$ ${}^{G}R^{GR}$

Most ornaments may be considered optional, and omitted altogether when learning a composition. Then, the largest pitch-letter, or the initial one, is usually considered the principal tone. Ornaments which clearly conform to a certain rhythm are written out.

Rhythmic Notation

The framework of bar-lines separating the divisions (*vibhāgs*) of the rhythm cycle (*tāl*) in which the composition is cast gives the matrix for writing the composition. They are always explicit in the beginning of a composition. If these bar lines later confuse the picture of the phrasing (which they often do in extremely fast or slow passages), they are sometimes omitted in order that the visual image be kept simple. Bar lines at the beginning and the end of a line are omitted for this reason. The numbering of the divisions is also occasionally omitted when the notation appears too crowded.

In the following example, the notes for a scale are substituted for the *theka* (drum syllables) for the rhythmic cycle *jhaptal* (2+3+2+3):

```
+        2                 o      3
Dhi  na |dhi  dhi  na |ti  na |dhi  dhi  na

+        2                 o      3
        |             |       |

+        2                 o      3
S    R  |G    —    m  |P   —  |D    N    Ṡ
```

The cardinal numbers above refer to the numbering of the divisions of the tal (the plus sign substitues for "1" and marks the *sam*, or downbeat). If a passage were to begin in the middle of a division, then ordinal numbers would be used to indicate the *mātra*, or beat (e.g., 2nd., 3rd., 15th., etc.).

If a note (letter) is written alone, it occupies one beat. A dash (written either - - or —) extends the duration of the note one beat, or up until the next letter. In the previous *jhaptal* example, **ga** and **pa** have two beats each, the others one beat each. If a rest, or silence, is specifically required (rare, but sometimes called for in ensemble music), it is written with two slashes after the note:

S// or **P// - - -**

In this second example above, note that the beat with **pa** is divided into four parts. Divisions of the beat are notated by dashes with loops underneath. A beat divided into two parts (e.g., eighth notes) is written:

Pm

which is equivalent to: 

three parts: **PmG** 

four parts: **PmGR** 

eight parts: **P - - m - - G -** 

In slower rhythms, the beat may be subdivided into loops to clarify the groupings:

SS - S RR - R 

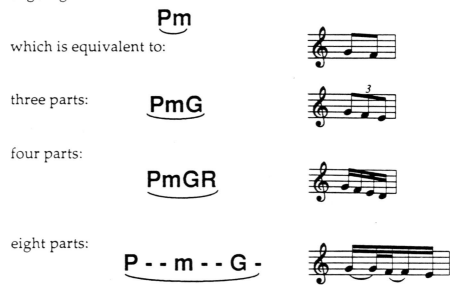

Signs and Symbols

A. Loops and slurs

1. In vocal music, a curved line over a group of notes indicates that the syllable below is sung over those notes:

SR Gm PDPm G -

san- gī- ta

2. In instrumental music, the same line indicates a *mīnd* or *mīr* (glide), which is a technique of slurring the notes that are bracketed with one pluck of the right hand:

SR Gm PDPm G -

I I –

3. Short loops are used for ornaments and are executed the same way as the longer slurs:

G R   mGm R   S NRSNS   G R GR

B. Apostrophes are used to separate phrasings, or to indicate places to take a breath (they have no rhythmic value):

SRG'RGm'GmP'mPD...

C. A wavy line over or after a note is used to show the slow undulation of a pitch, known as *āndolan:*

m g ~~~~

D. A sharp, saw-toothed line indicates *gamak:*

GGGGRRRR which is played:

RGRGRGRGSRSRSRSR

Repeats

A repeated section or complete line of a song is shown by the Western repeat sign at the beginning or end of the section. Slanted bars on the signs indicate the repeat of larger sections. The following passage would be played (sung) AAB AAB:

| ← A → | ← B → |

+ 2 0 3 + 2 0 3
[: S R | G -- m | P -- | D N Ṡ :|| Ṡ N | D -- P | m -- | G R S :]

A repeated fragment of a line, smaller musical unit, or *pala* (phrase) of a *tihāī* (three part rhythmic cadence) is shown with brackets and numbers to indicate the repeat scheme. Smaller repeated motives within a larger scheme would be shown with parentheses. Repeats only taken the first time through the composition are marked with words and arrows. The hierarchy of all repeat signs appears as follows:

{: ||: [( )] :|| :}

In the example below (in *rupak* tal, seven beats), the phrase begins on the 4th beat of the tal, and only the final **pa** comes to the *sam* (downbeat), which is indicated in parentheses:

4th (+)
[(SNSR)2x (GRGm)2x G m P] 3x

If a section or phrase repeats from the middle of a beat, the loop is extended under the repeat sign, and the repeated phrase is picked up from that next place in the beat. The repeated phrase is thus on the offbeat, as in this *tihāī* in tintal:

0 (+)
[SNSR GRGm PDP] 3x

The ∕. sign is used in a specific time-saving way in this notation. It can be translated as "in the same manner":

S̲N̲S̲R̲ R ∕. G ∕.

is played or sung:

S̲N̲S̲R̲' R̲S̲R̲G̲' G̲R̲G̲m̲

In the writing of instrumental *bol* patterns, it is used frequently to save time and space:

S̲S̲S̲'S̲S̲S̲'S̲S̲ R ∕.G ∕.
I - I I - I I -

is played:

S̲S̲S̲'S̲S̲S̲'S̲S̲ R̲R̲R̲'R̲R̲R̲'R̲R̲ G̲G̲G̲'G̲G̲G̲'G̲G̲
I - I I - I I- I - I I - I I- I - I I - I I-

Or, the ∕. sign might refer to the bols themselves:

S̲S̲S̲'S̲S̲S̲'S̲S̲ R̲R̲R̲'G̲G̲G̲'m̲m̲ P̲P̲P̲'m̲m̲m̲'G̲G̲
I - I I - I I-   ∕.   ∕.

In the notation of vocal music, the ∕. sign is used in a similar way to indicate verbal or melodic repetition:

Ṡ Ṡ Ṡ --|N ∕.|D ∕.
de re na

is sung:

Ṡ Ṡ Ṡ --|N N N --|D D D --
de re na   de re na   de re na

Bol Notation

Bols (words) are the words which describe the movements of the right hand in instrumental music. In a general sense, a *bol* could also be a word of a song, or a rhythmic drum stroke or syllable, or even a group of syllables in dance and drumming. However, in this situation, we are referring to the notation of music for stringed instruments.

1. **Da**, a downstroke, is notated: **|**
2. **Ra**, an upstroke, is notated: **–**
3. **Diri**, quick down- and upstrokes (tremolo), is notated: **∧**
4. **Chik**, the chikari stroke, is notated: ✓
5. A rest in bol notation is notated with a dot: **.**

For example, the bol

da - rada - ra diri

is notated: **| · – | · – ∧**

and *siddh* (straight) *jhala* is notated: **|** ✓✓✓

Metronome Marks

The metronome markings (e.g. **M.120**) are used to indicate the approximate speed of a composition. Although some of the faster pieces may have to be learned at a slower tempo before polishing them at the faster speed, the metronome markings are to be interpreted as a loose guide to the tempo at which the composition was originally composed. The number refers to the beats per minute, and as most metronomes do not go above 200, faster speeds should be set to half the tempo, and performed at double speed. **R** numbers at the top of each page identify each composition for purposes of performance and mechanical licensing.

Summary of Notation

In summary, the notation normally is written on three lines. The top line is for tal markings, the middle line for sargam (pitch and rhythm notation), and the bottom for bols, either instrumental strokes or song lyric. The middle line will also have articulation marks (slurs and ornaments) above the pitch notation, and loops below to indicate rhythm.

Here are two examples of vocal and instrumental music with some explanations and versions in Western notation:

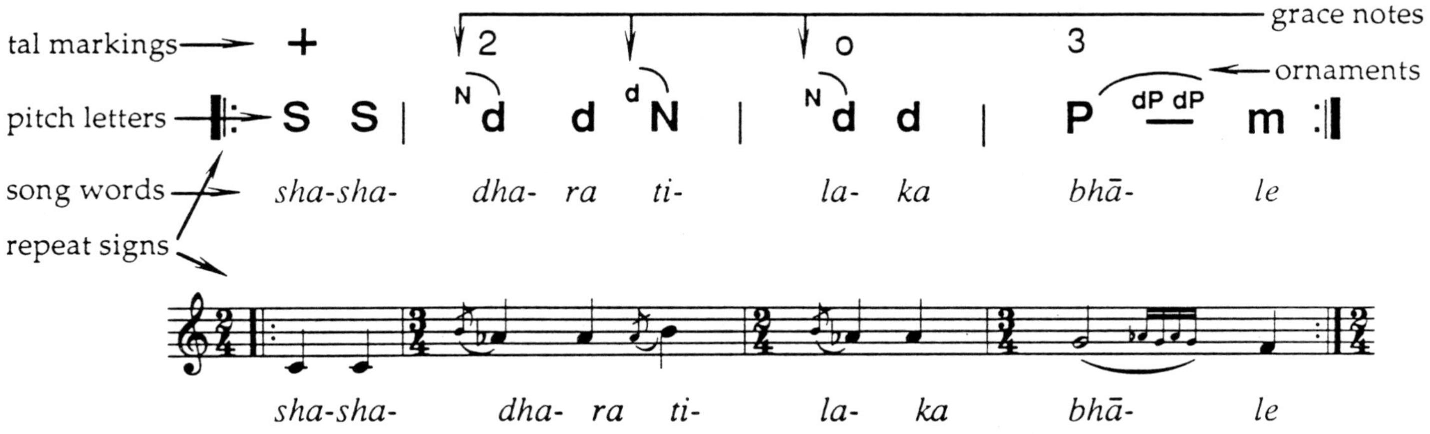

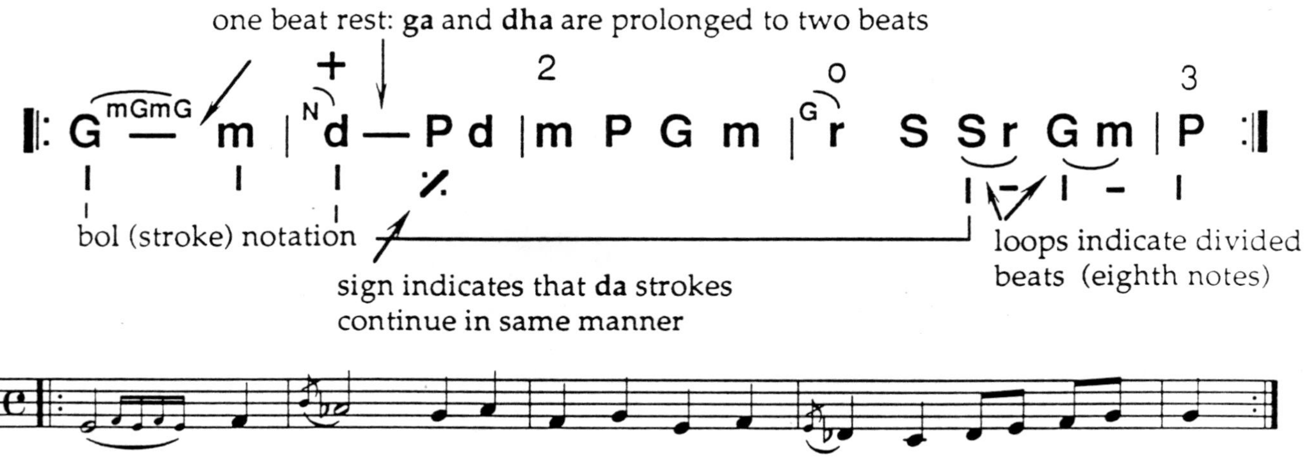

Khansahib teaching George Ruckert, violin, Rick Henderson, harmonium, and Daniel Karp, tabla. Photo by Faustin Bray.

GUIDE TO PRONUNCIATION

The Hindi language is written in the *Devanāgari* script, which is also the script used for the parent language, Sanskrit. The alphabet is systematic and easy to learn, and the pronunciation of the sounds of these letters is more or less straightforward, even considering the age of the language and geographical sprawl of the native speakers. It will be easy to pronounce most words, for there are few irregularities, at least in theory. Difficulties may arise when the many regional languages of India and their sounds are brought into the picture. These are compounded by the fact that several words have already crept into the musical vocabulary of the Western world in a somewhat corrupt form, making for some confusing spellings. This is especially true of names of places and some musical terms. *Ganga*, the name of the river, has come into English as "Ganges," and to try to wrestle with changing it here would make things more confusing than necessary. So it is with some of the rag names. *Alhaiyā Bilāval* has become *Alahīyā Bilāwal*. *Toṛī* has become *Todi*. *Sthāyī* has become *asthāī*, as it is pronounced in Bengali. Some *v*s have been interchanged with *b*s, as they are in Northeast India; and similarly, some *v*s with *w*s, as the sound of the two is very close in Hindi.

Therefore, in the orthography of this book, some of the now-common renderings into English have determined the spelling used in the text. In ninety percent of the instances, though, a classical form of the spelling is retained, and the pronunciation of the musical terms can be learned from the glossary. But students would be wise to check their pronunciations with a native speaker. With many terms, it would be best to ascertain how specific musicians may use some of them listed herein. Just as there are many different styles of music, so are there many differing interpretations of the meanings of words common to musical terminology.

In Sanskrit, all syllables are pronounced, whereas in modern Hindi, the final short *a* sound is dropped. This is the reason for the word *rāga* being shortened to *rāg*, and *tāla* to *tāl*, etc. But in song lyrics feminine endings are again the rule, the final short *a*s are traditionally kept, and thus in a song, *rāg* becomes *rāga* again! This is true of interior consonants as well. When words are first introduced in the text, the diacritical marks are inserted on the words in italics as an aid to learning the correct pronunciation. After this initial phase, however, they are omitted, and the word is printed in Roman letters. This is done to minimize the "foreign" nature of the vocabulary and to facilitate rapid assimilation of the materials. The glossary at the end of the book may be consulted as a pronunciation guide for specific words.

The following general guide to pronunciation of the sounds must be taken as introductory and not definitive, for there is quite a bit of discussion possible as to which dialect of Hindi one is comparing to which dialect of English. Use this guide as a directional tool to get started:

Pronunciation Guide to the Devanagari Alphabet

Letter		Transcription and Approximate English Pronunciation	
अ		a	cut
आ	ा	ā	father
इ	ि	i	pit
ई	ी	ī	feet
उ	ु	u	put, foot
ऊ	ू	ū	June, moon
ऋ	ृ	ṛi	retroflex **r**, as in river, + short **i**
ए	े	e	gate, rain
≤	ै	ai	between might and cat
ओ	ो	o	cold
औ	ौ	au	author, saw

क	k	kid
ख	kh	lakehouse
ग	g	goat
घ	gh	doghouse
ङ	ṅ	sung
च	ch	church
छ	chh	strong ch, as in achoo!
ज	j	join
झ	jh	sledgehammer
ञ	ṉ	bench
ट	ṭ	kettle
ठ	ṭh	no English equivalent
ड	ḍ	rudder
ढ	ḍh	no English equivalent
ण	ṇ	grind
त	t	boat
थ	th	anthill
द	d	damp
ध	dh	roundhouse
न	n	never
प	p	spin
फ	ph	uphill
ब	b	boat
भ	bh	clubhouse
म	m	mud

य	y	yellow
र	r	red
ल	l	lever
व	v, w	between very and wary
श	sh	shall
ष	ṣh	cushion
स	s	saint
ह	h	hay
ड़	ṛ	no English equivalent
ढ़	ṛh	no English equivalent

Rag Bhairav

Rag Bhairav is a principal rag which was also one of the six male rags in older *parivar,* or rag-family, systems of classification. *Bhairav* is one of the many names of Maheshwara, Lord Shiva, especially in his powerful form as a naked ascetic with matted locks and body smeared with ashes. The rag, while it may also have certain of these forceful masculine and ascetic attributes, is so vast that it allows a huge number of note combinations, and a great range of emotional qualities, from sadness to valor, peace to agitation. It is played in a devotional mood in the early morning hours, and has a number of related rags which are played before, during, and after sunrise.

Bhairav is hence acknowledged to be a basic rag, and one that is often taught first in the course of a student's training both in North and South India (where a similar mela is known as *Māyāmālavagaula).*

The vibrations of the notes in Bhairav clear your whole mind—like taking a shower in the morning. It is like yoga: once you can sing Bhairav and Bhairavi in the morning, and Iman Kalyan in the evening, in perfect tune, the other rags become your servants.

The notes of Bhairav are all strong, but be careful not to sing too much ***ma****, or else you will bring the effect of Rag Jogiya.*

Rag Bhairav

That: **Bhairav**

Jati: **sampurn**

Vadi: **d** Samvadi: **r**

Ang: **uttarang**

Time: **early morning (5-9 am)**

Mood: **gambhir, bhakti, vir, karuna, shanti**

Pakar: G m ᴺd

Arohi-Avarohi: S r G m P d N Ṡ Ṡ N d P m G r S

"More complete": S r G m P ' G m ᴺd P --m P ᴺd N Ṡ
Ṡ N d -- P -- P d P m mGPmGm ᴳr
r G m P G m ᴳr S

Chalan: S r G m ᴺd P -- P d m -- m P m G m ' G m r '
r G m P ' m G m r S -- ḍ Ṇ S r G m d P '
d m ' m P G m ᴺd P 'G m P G m ᴳr S

Antara m P ᴺd- N Ṡ ------- Ṡ ṙ Ġ ṁ ᴳṙ Ṡ -- NṠṙṠNṠ ᴺd P --
P d m ' PdNṠṙĠṁĠṙ -- Ṡ -- N Ṡ ᴺd P -- P d P m
mGPmGm G -- Gr mG PmGm Gr -- S --

Sargam in tintal M.80

Asthai

+ 2 0 3
‖: G m | ᴺd -- -- -- | P d P m | P -- -- -- | ᴾS -- :‖

+ 2 0 3
G m | ᴳr -- -- -- | -- -- G m | ᴳr -- -- -- | S --

Antara

+ 2 0 3
‖: m P | ᴺd -- -- -- | N -- -- -- | S -- -- r | S -- :‖

+ 2 0 3
‖: S r | G -- -- -- | -- -- mP Gm | ᴳr -- -- -- | S -- :‖

+ 2 0 3
-- -- | S -- N -- | d -- P -- | G m ᴺd -- | P --

+ 2 0 3
-- -- | r -- -- -- | ʳr -- G m | ᴳr -- -- -- | S --

Sharada Saraswati-- chautal

शारदा सरस्वती
सर्व कला समारा सर्वानी सर्गे
सरी-त्रयी रूप धरनी

खलनी-दलनी कंद करनी
विरद वेदपाल करनी
दीनन सुखदानी सरनी
असुर नेस्तार करनी
करनी भूमि भार महामोह हरनी

shāradā saraswatī
sarva kalā samārā sarvānī sarge
sarī-trayī rūpa dharanī

khalanī-dalanī kanda karanī
virada vedapāla karanī
dīnana sukhadānī karanī
asura nestāra karanī
haranī bhūmi bhāra mahāmoha haranī

Sharada, Saraswati,
Respository of all arts,
Appearing as Saritrayi,
Subjugator of the wicked;

Giver of fame and wisdom,
Of happiness to the poor,
Killer of monsters,

Destroyer of all sins and illusions.

Dhrupad in chautal M.72

Asthai

3 4 + o 2 o
‖: m G | m P | ᴺd -- | d d | d P | -- -- :‖
shā- ra - dā sa- ra- swa- tī
2nd d
sar-

3 4 + o 2 o
Pm P | mGP mGm | ᴳr -- | Gr mG | Pm Gm | ᴳr --
va ka- lā sa-

3 4 + o 2 o
r -- | ᴳr S | Ṡ r | G m | P d | N Ṡ ᴺʳṠᴺṠ
mā- rā sar- vā- nī sar- ge sa-

3 4 + o 2 o
ᴺd -- | d P | dP d | ᴾm -- | mGP mGm | ᴳr S
rī- tra-yī ru- pa dha- ra- nī

Antara

+ o 2 o 3 4
‖: P P | P ᴺd | d d | ˢṄ Ṡ | N Ṡ | Ṡ Ṡ
kha-la- nī da- la- nī kan- da ka- ra- nī

+ o 2 o 3 4
ᴺd d | d N | Ṡ Ṡ | ṙ -- | Ṡ NṠ | ᴺd P :‖
vi- ra- da ve- da - pā- la ka- ra- nī

+ o 2 o 3 4
P d | N Ṡ | Ṡ Ṡ | ᴺd -- | d ᴺd | ᴺd P
dī- na - na su- kha-dā- ni sa- ra- nī

+ o 2 o 3 4
m m | mGm ᴳr | GrmG P | m G | m ᴳr | ᴳr S
a- su- ra ne- stā- ra ka- ra- nī

+ o 2 o 3 4
S r | G m | -- m | P - | d ṙ | Ṡ --
ha- ra- nī bhū- mi bhā- ra ma- hā-

+ o 2 o
ᴺd -- | d -- | ᵈN d | Pd Pm
mo- ha ha- ra- nī

bhora bhayi - dhamari

भोरा भई सब जागो
राम नाम सुमिरन करो

प्रभु कृपा बिन कछु न होवे
राम नाम रटत रटत तब कछु कृपा पावे

bhorā bhayī saba jāgo
rāma nāma sumirana karo

prabhu kripā bina kachhu na hove
rāma nāma raṭata raṭata
taba kachhu kṛipā pāve

Awake!
It is dawn.
Call up the name of Rama.

Nothing is possible without God's grace.
Constantly repeating the Name
Brings this grace.

Song in dhamari tal (11 1/2 matras) M.72

Asthai

o 3 + 2
[|: m G m | Pm P/2 |^{N}d -- -- P -- | P m :|]
bho- rā bha- yī sa- ba

o 3 + 2
^{Pd}m -- ^{mP}G | mPG- m/2 |^{G}r -- -- -- -- | Ṡ -- :|]
jā- go

o 3 + 2
m -- m | mPG- m/2 | P -- -- P - | m P
rā- ma nā- ma su- mi- ra -na

o 3 + 2
d d -- | P- -/2 | d P d m P | G m
ka- ro

Antara

+ 2 o 3
[|: m m -- P P |^{N}d d |^{N}Ṡ Ṡ -- | - N d/2 :|]
pra- bhu kṟi- pa bi- na ka- chhu

+ 2 o 3
-- ṙ -- -- -- | Ṡṙ Ġṁ |^{G}ṙ -- -- | Ṡ - -/2
na ho- ve

+ 2 o 3
-- N Ṡ N Ṡ | NṠ ṙṠNṠ |^{N}d -- -- | P - -/2 :|]

+ 2 o 3
|: m -- m ^{mP}G -- | m m | P P P | d - d/2 :|
rā- ma nā- ma ra- ṭa - ta ra- ṭa - ta

+ 2 o 3
P d N Ṡ -- | NṠ ṙṠNṠ |^{N}d -- -- | P d m/2
ta- ba ka- chhu kṟi- pā pā-

+ 2
P G mP G m |^{G}r S
ve

Bolbants for dhamari song, concluded

1) mG mP d - - P - P' mG mP d - - P P'm Gm P/2 | d
bho- rā bha-yī sa- ba bho- rā bha-yī sa-ba bho- rā bha- yī

2) [mG mP d - PP Gm r - S] 3x mG mP d - P/2 | d
bho- rā bha-yi sa-ba jā- go bho- rā bha-yī bha- yī

3) ‖: P - PP d -' P - Pd - m P - mP md PN dP m/2 :‖
bho-rā bha-yī jā - go,jā- go, jā- go jā- go

P - dN S'S ᴺd - Pd - m P - mP md PN dP m/2
bho- rā bha-yī, jā - go, jā- go, jā- go jā- go

S - SS rS r - S - ' S - SS rS r - S'P - P P/2 | d
bho- rā bha-yī jā- go, bho- rā bha-yī jā- go, bho-rā bha- yī

shashadhara - jhaptal

शशधर तिलक भाले गंगे जटाजाल
कर धर त्रिशुल रुद्र के राजे

भष्म अंग छाये गरे रुद्रन की माला
भैरव त्रिनयन हर जोगी साजे

shashadhara tilaka bhāle gaṅge jaṭajāla
kara dhara trishula rudra ke rāje

bhashma anga chhāye gare rudrana kī mālā
bhairava trinayana hara jogī sāje

With the moon as a mark on his forehead,
The Ganges in the matted hair,
And trident in hand
Stands radiant Rudra;

Body smeared with ashes,
A garland of rudrana beads around his neck,
Bhairav, the yogi with three eyes,
Stands supreme.

Chhadra (jhaptal) M.70

Asthai

+ 2 o 3
‖: S S | ᴺd d ᵈN | ᴺd d | P ᵈᴾ ᵈᴾ -- m
sha- sha - dha- ra ti- la- ka bhā- le

+ 2 o 3
Gm r | G m P | mG PmGm | ᴳr ᴳr S :‖
gaṅ- ge ja- ṭa - jā- la

+ 2 o 3
S S | S ᴺʳˢᴺˢ ᴺd -- | d S | N r S
ka- ra dha- ra tri- shu- la

+ 2 o 3
S ᴳr | G m P | mG PmGm | ᴳr ᴳr S
ru- dra ke rā- je

Antara

+ 2 o 3
‖: m m | ᴺd -- d | ᴺS -- | S r S
bhash-ma an- ga chhā- ye ga- re

+ 2 o 3
S r | G m P | mG PmGm | ᴳr ᴳr S :‖
ru- dra- na kī mā- lā

+ 2 o 3
SN rSNS | N ᴺd P | ᵈN d | P m G
bhai- ra- va tri - na- ya- na ha- ra

+ 2 o 3
Gm N | d -- P | mG PmGm | ᴳr ᴳr S
jo- gī sā- je

jago mohan - **tintal**

जागो मोहन प्यारे
सांवरी सूरत मोरे मन भावे
सुन्दर लाल हमारे

प्रात समय उठ भानु उदय भयो
ग्वाल बाल सब बूपत ठाड़े
दरसन के सब मुखे प्यासे
उठियो नन्द किशोरे

jāgo mohana pyāre
sāṇvarī sūrata more mana bhāve
sundara lāla hamāre

prāta samay uṭha bhānu uday bhayo
gwāla bāla saba bhūpata ṭhāṛe
darasana ke saba mukhe pyāse
uṭhiyo nanda kishore

Rise, beloved Mohan,
Your lovely dark face enchants my mind.
Dear, beautiful child of ours!

It is morning, the sun has risen,
The cowherds are waiting
Eager to behold your face.
Awake, O child of Nanda.

Khyal in tintal M.132

Asthai

```
    o                3                 +                      2
‖: G m ᴺd -- | P -- ᴾd m | P -- mPd PmP | m -- G -- :‖
   jā-  go     mo-  ha- na pyā-              re

    o              3              +                  2
   G -- m G | m G m P | m G GmP Gm | ᴳr -- S --
   sāṅ- va- rī  sū-  ra- ta  mo- re ma-  na   bhā-   ve

    o              3              +          2
   S r G m | P d N Ṡ | ṙ -- Ṡ N | d P m G
   sun- da- ra  lā-  la ha- mā-           re
```

Antara

```
    o              3                +               2
‖: P -- P P | ᴺd -- N N | Ṡ -- Ṡ Ṡ | N Ṡ Ṡ Ṡ :‖
   prā- ta sa- may  u- ṭha bhā-  nu u- day  bha- yo

    o              3                +                2
  ᴺd -- d' N | Ṡ Ṡ Ṡ Ṡ | ṙĠ ṁ ᴳṙ Ṡ | N Ṡ^(NṙṠNṠ) ᴺd P :‖
   gwā- la  bā-   la sa- ba bhū-  pa- ta  ṭhā-          re

    o              3                +                     2
   G m P d | ᴺṠ -- d P | m G mGP mGm | ᴳr -- S --
   da- ra- sa- na  ke   sa- ba mu-  khe             pyā-  se

    o              3              +          2
   S r G m | P d N Ṡ | ṙ -- Ṡ N | d P m G
   u- ṭhi- yo  nan-  da ki- sho-          re
```

Tarana in tintal M.160

Asthai

```
     o              3            +            2              N
||: ᴺ d -- P d | -- P G m | ᴺ d d P d | m P G m :||
    dim   ta  dim    ta  na  na   ta  da  re  ta   da  re  da  ni

     o                            +            2
    rG mP Gm ᴳ r̂ | --ᴳ r̂ S S | - S r̂ G - r | G m - G m P
    dim              tom    ta  na  na   de re na   de re na    de re  na
```

Antara

```
     +                   2              o              3
||:  m  mm  mm  m | -- m' P PP | PP P -- d' | r r -- Ṡ :||
    na dere dere da     ni, tum dere dere da   ni,   ta  da    ni

     +            2            o                      3
||:  r̂ -- r r | -- r̂ S S | SrG m    - r - G | r -- -- Ṡ :||
    dim    ta dim    ta  da  re  ta        da  re  da       ni

     +                    2                    o
    r N S -' d d | P -' d m P - | asthai
    de re na      de re  na   de re na
```

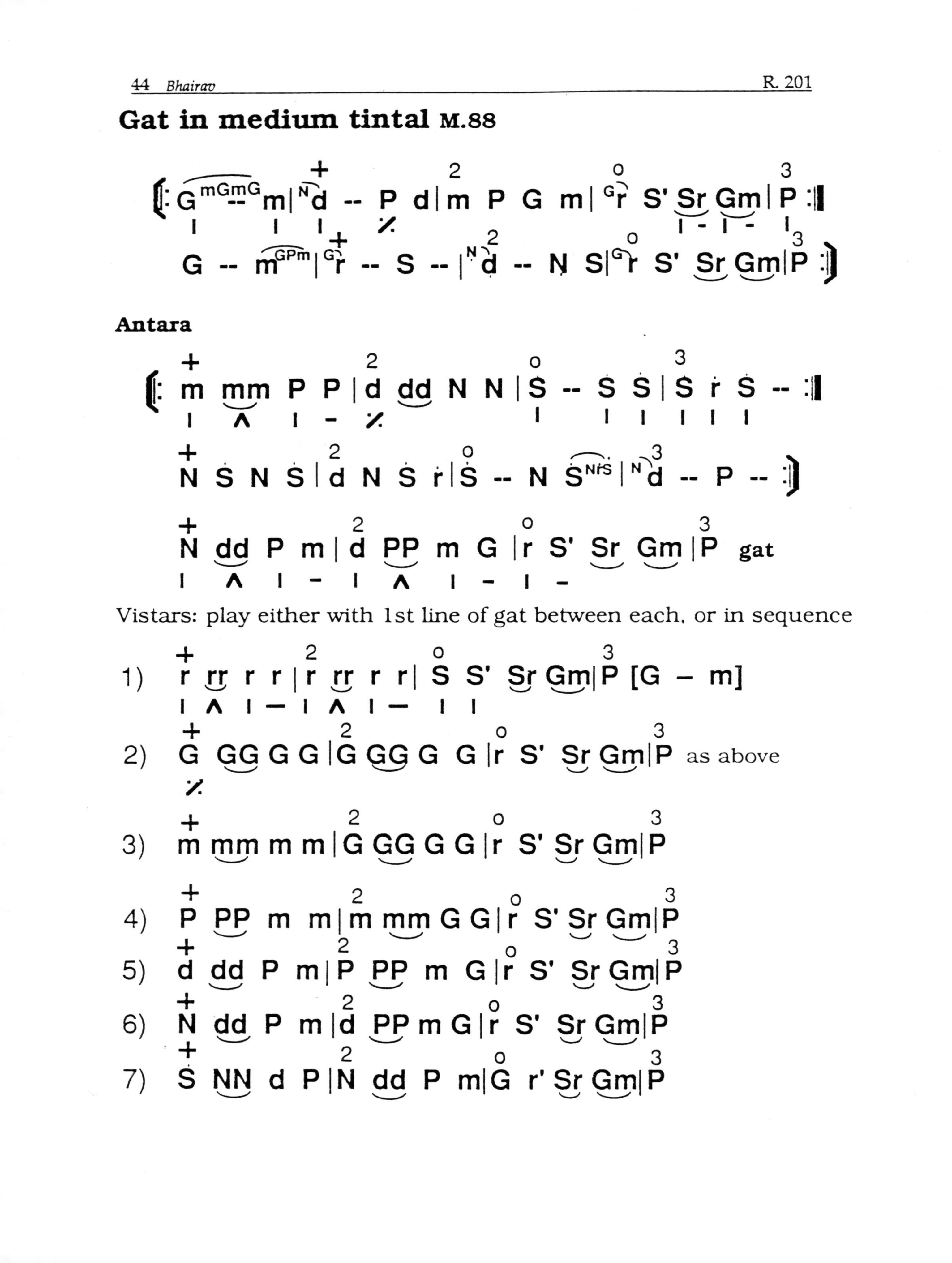

Gat in medium tintal M.88

+ 2 o 3
[: G mGmG -- m | N d -- P d | m P G m | G r S' Sr Gm | P :]
I I I ⁒ I - I - I

+ 2 o 3
G -- m GPm | G r -- S -- | N d -- N S | G r S' Sr Gm | P :]

Antara

+ 2 o 3
[: m mm P P | d dd N N | S -- S S | S r S -- :]
I Λ I - ⁒ I I I I I I

+ 2 o 3
N S N S | d N S r | S -- N S NrS | N d -- P -- :]

+ 2 o 3
N dd P m | d PP m G | r S' Sr Gm | P gat
I Λ I - I Λ I - I -

Vistars: play either with 1st line of gat between each, or in sequence

+ 2 o 3
1) r rr r r | r rr r r | S S' Sr Gm | P [G – m]
I Λ I — I Λ I — I I

+ 2 o 3
2) G GG G G | G GG G G | r S' Sr Gm | P as above
⁒

+ 2 o 3
3) m mm m m | G GG G G | r S' Sr Gm | P

+ 2 o 3
4) P PP m m | m mm G G | r S' Sr Gm | P

+ 2 o 3
5) d dd P m | P PP m G | r S' Sr Gm | P

+ 2 o 3
6) N dd P m | d PP m G | r S' Sr Gm | P

+ 2 o 3
7) S NN d P | N dd P m | G r' Sr Gm | P

Tans for gat in medium tintal

8) + dN S -- -- | 2 SN d -- -- | o dN S gat

9) + dN Sr -- -- | 2 rS Nd -- -- | o dN S gat

10) + dN Sr G -- | 2 Gr SN d -- | o dN S gat

11) + dN Sr Gm -- | 2 mG rS Nd -- | o dN S gat

12) + dN Sr Gm P - | 2 Pm Gr SN d - | o dN S gat

13) + dN Sr Gm Pd | 2 dP mG rS Nd | o dN S gat

14) + dN Sr Gm Pd | 2 Nd Pm Gr SN | o dN S gat

15) + dN Sr Gm Pd | 2 NS Nd Pm Gr | o SN dN gat

16) + Pd P- mP m- Gm G- rG r- o Sr S- gat

17) + Pd P'm Pm' Gm G'r Gr' Sr S'S o rG mP gat

18) + Pd dP' mP Pm' Gm mG' rG Gr' o Sr rS gat

19) + Pd Pd -'m Pm P-' Gm Gm -'r o Gr G- gat

20) + Sr Sr' Gr Gr' Sr S'r Gr' Sr o S'S rG gat

21) + Sr Gm P'S rG mP' S- rG mP' o S r G m P' G -- m | + d gat

22) + Sr Gm P'S -r Gm P'S - - r- o -G - - m- -P - -' G- -m - - | + d gat

23) + Sr Gm Pd NS rG rS Nd Pm Gr' Sr→r→r ⁒ S→S→ r ⁒

S→N→r' ⁒ S→d→r' ⁒ S→P→r' ⁒ S→m→r' ⁒

Sr Gr' | 3 Sr S'S rG mP | + d gat,2x, end

Shrī Shāradā Māyī in Maihar, Madya Pradesh. She is one of the manifestations of Saraswati, and her name means "giver of essence." This image is in the temple at the top of a hill near Allauddin Khansahib's home. The temple is a place of pilgrimmage for thousands of devotees who come to Maihar from all over India.

Rag Bhairavi

Rag Bhairavi is named for the *shakti*, or feminine aspect of the cosmic life force, which is personified as a consort of Lord Shiva. As these associations suggest, Bhairavi is a big, powerful rag, and filled with devotion and compassion—it is the quintessential song of the Earth Mother.

Shuddh (pure) Bhairavi, is presented in the rag definition following, but there are two other common traditions of Bhairavi presented also in the following compositions. One, **pa**-vadi Bhairavi (sometimes referred to as *Sindhu Bhairavi*), allows some borrowed notes—shuddh **re** and **dha**, and tivra **ma**—used judiciously:

Like you don't bring alcohol into church, you see; but when Communion is there, it is different; like that, in Bhairavi you bring the beauty with borrowed notes, very carefully. Otherwise it becomes Sindhi Bhairavi.

A third type is Sindhi Bhairavi, a folk-derived rag which may use all the notes except, usually, shuddh **ga**. Bhairavi is traditionally rendered as the last item on a program, for its unique fullness of sentiment, as well as its wide scope of the tonal combinations, are considered too rich to be followed immediately with other rags.

Rag Bhairavi

That: **Bhairavi**

Jati: **sampurn**

Vadi: m (P) Samvadi: S

Ang: **purvang**

Time: **morning, or as the concluding item in a program**

Mood: **bhakti, shṛingār, karuna, shanti**

Pakaṛ: S r g m --- P m g m r --- g m -- r g r S

Arohi-Avarohi: S r g m P d n Ṡ Ṡ n d P m g r S

"more complete" S r g m P m g m -- P d n Ṡ

Ṡ n d P m --- g m g r S

Sargam in tintal M.60

Asthai

```
  o           3           +           2
‖: S  d  P  d | m  P  g  m | n  d  --  r | --  g  m  P

  o           3           +           2
   r  S  --  r | S  n  ḍ  n | S  g  --  m | d  --  n  Ṡ

  o           3           +           2
   g̣  g̣  r  Ṡ | n  d  P  m | g  m  n  d | P  m  g  r :‖
```

Antara

```
  o           3           +           2
‖: S  g  --  m | d  --  n  Ṡ | g  g  r  Ṡ | n  Ṡ  g  ṁ

  o           3           +           2
   P  g  --  ṁ | g  r  Ṡ  n | d  --  n  Ṡ | n  d  --  n

  o           3           +           2
   d  P  m  g | m  n  d  n | d  P  m  g | m  g  r  S :‖
```

jo tu racho - chautal

asthai

जो तू रचो समान
दया सों नाना प्रकार
तो है न विसारो सादा
हर हर गुण गाय गाय

sanchari

जाकी माया निरङ्कार
लिखी न जात अप्रम्पार
सुर नर मुनि कर विचार
जाको शिव ध्याय ध्याय

antara

दुख सुख जी सहाय
अन्तर ना कछु उपाय
ओक्त जोक्त सम्पूरण
ध्यानांत्र लाय लाय

abhog

प्रेम दास सिरि निवास
पूरण घट घट प्रकाश
जल थल प्रभु बन विलास
रहे प्रभु छाय छाय

jo tū racho samāna
dayā so nānā prakāra
to hai na visāro sādā
hara hara guṇa gāya gāya

jākī māyā niraṅgkāra
likhī na jāta aprampāra
sura nara muni kara vichāra
jāko shiva dhyāya dhyāya

dukha sukha jī sahāya
antara nā kachhu upāya
okta jokta sampūrana
dhyānāntra lāya lāya

prema dāsa siri nivāsa
pūraṇa ghaṭa ghaṭa prakāsha
jala thala prabhu bana vilāsa
rahe prabhu chhāya chhāya

O Lord, thy love expresses itself through the multiplicity of all things; my mind will constantly dwell on thee and sing thy praise. I shall bear with whatever joy or sorrow falls to my lot. Formless art thou; words fail to describe thy majesty. Heavenly beings and sages, and even Shiva, meditate on thee. Premdasa says, "God manifests himself in all beings. He dwells everywhere on land and water. He is all-pervasive."

Dhrupad in chautal M.69

Asthai

+ o 2 o 3 4
‖: ˢm -- | -- ʳg | -- m | gr g | r S | -- S :‖
jo tū ra- cho sa- mā- na

+ o 2 o 3 4
‖: S r | n S | -- r | g -- | r S | -- S :‖ ← **1st time only**
da- yā so nā- nā pra- kā- ra

+ o 2 o 3 4
S d | d P | -- d | P m | m P | m --
to hai na vi- sā- ro sā- dā

+ o 2 o 3 4
S Sr | g g | g m | gr g | r S | -- S
ha- ra ha- ra gu- ṇa gā- ya gā- ya

Antara

+ o 2 o 3 4
[: d d | m d | -- n | Ṡ -- | ṙ Ṡ | -- Ṡ :‖ ← **1st time only**
du- kha su- kha jī sa- hā- ya

+ o 2 o 3 4
ġ -- | ġ ġ | ġṙṁġ ṙ | ṙ ṙ | ġ ṙ | -- Ṡ :]
an- ta- ra nā ka- chhu u- pā- ya

+ o 2 o 3 4
d -- | d P | -- d | P m | P -- | m m
ok- ta jok- ta sam- pū- ra- na

+ o 2 o 3 4
S Sr | g -- | m m | gr g | r S | -- S
dha- yā - nān- tra lā- ya lā- ya

dhrupad in chautal, continued

Sanchari

+ o 2 o 3 4
‖: S d | d P | -- P | n d | Pm P | m m
jā- kī mā- yā ni- raṅg- kā- ra
+ o 2 o 3 4
S S | r g | -- m | ^{g}r r | -- S | -- S :‖
li- kha na jā- ta a- pram- pā- ra
+ o 2 o 3 4
ṇ ṇ | ḍ P̣ | ḍ ṇ | S S | r S | -- S
su - ra na- ra mu- ni ka- ra vi- chā- ra
+ o 2 o 3 4
S -- | S r | g m | gr g | r S | -- S
jā- ko shi- va dhyā - ya dhyā- ya

go directly to abhog:

Abhog

+ o 2 o 3 4
‖: d -- | m d | -- n | Ṡ Ṡ | Ṡ Ṡ | -- Ṡ
pre- ma dā- sa si- ri ni - vā- sa
+ o 2 o 3 4
ġ -- | ṙ ṙ | ġ ġ | ṙ ṙ | ġṙ Ṡ | -- Ṡ :‖
pū- ra- ṇa gha- ṭa gha-ṭa pra- kā sha
+ o 2 o 3 4
S S | Ṡ Ṡ | ^{n}d d | P d | P m | -- m
ja- la tha-la pra- bhu ba- na vi- lā- sa
+ o 2 o 3 4
n d | -- ^{m}g | -- m | gr g | r S | -- S
ra- he pra- bhu chhā - ya chhā- ya

dhrupad in chautal, continued

Bolbant

+
1) S - - r - - g - - m - - g - - r - - n - - S - -
jo tū ra- cho sa- mā- na

+
2) S --| n gr |S S |Sn d |d n |S --
jo tū ra- cho sa- mā - na

+ +
m m |g P |m m |g g |m gr |g r |-- S
da- yā so nā- nā pra- kā- ra nā- nā pra-kā- ra

o +
S - rg mg r - r'n - S rg rS - S' PP P -
jo tū ra-cho samāna,jo tū ra-cho samāna,da-yā so

2nd (+)
[Pm gr - S - -] 3x
nānā prakā- ra

+
3) r - - r - - r - - r - -' SS -S' S - SS SS - S'
jo tū ra- cho sa-mā-na, jo ra-cho sa-mā- na

+
d -- | n -- | S -- | S --| r n| -- S
jo tū ra - cho sa- mā- na

+
dn dn Sn Sr Sr gr Sr Sr gr S - S - S -
jo tū ra- cho ra- cho sa- mā- na

+
dn dn nS nS Sr Sr rg rg g - m g r - S -
jo tū ra- cho sa- mā- na

+
S - - r - - g - - m - - ' r - - g - -
jo tū ra- cho jo tū

10th +
P - P - PP PP - P' m - m - mm mm - m'
jo tū racho samā-na, jo tū racho samā- na,

8th
r - r - rg rS - S
jo tū racho samā-na

dhrupad in chautal, concluded

+ o 2 o 3 4
4) ‖: P P | -- dP | m P | d -- | d d | -- d
da- yā so nā - nā pra- kā- ra
+
n d | P g | -- m | P -- | P P | -- P :‖
da- yā so nā- nā pra- kā- ra
+
P P P' P - - d - - P - m - m - m -'
da- yā so, to hai na vi- sā- ro
+
m - - P - - m - g - g - g -' g - - m - - g - r - S - S -
to hai na vi- sā- ro, to hai na vi- sā- ro

+
3
5) ‖: S - S SSS S - S' nn - g - r g - r S - S
jo tū racho samā- na dayā so nā-nā pra-kā - ra
m - m mmm m - m' P - m mm -
jo tū ra-chosa-mā- na jo tū ra-cho
+ o 2 o 3 4
3/2 3/2
P - d - m - | P g P | m m' r | r g g | m m P | P S -- :‖
da-yā so nā-nā pra- kā- ra, da-yā so nā- nā pra- kā- ra jo
+ (12th)
Sn dP | nd P'd | Pm gm | r-S' [P PPPP PP] 3x
jo tū racho samāna, jo tū racho samāna, jo tū racho samāna

***hori khelata* - dhamar**

होरी खेलत नंदलाल
ब्रज में धूम मची है

सब सखियाँ मिले गावत
नाचत दे दे ताली

horī khelata nandalāla
braja mẽ dhūma machī hai

saba sakhīyāṇa mile gāvata
nāchata de de tālī

The young lad Krishna is playing Hori,
In the land of Braj there is a great celebration.

All the gopis are singing together,
Dancing and clapping their hands.

Dhamar M.76

Asthai

o 3 + 2
‖: r ṇ S | g m P d | P -- P dP m | m --
ho- rī khe- la- ta nan- da- lā- la
o 3 + 2
P d n | d -- P -- | dP ᵐg m r g | r S :‖
bra- ja mē dhū- ma ma- chi hai

o 3 + 2
‖: g m -- | d n Ṡ ṙ | Ṡ Ṡ -- Ṡṙ g | ṙ Ṡ :‖
sa-ba sa- khī- yā- ṇa mi- le gā- va- ta
o 3 + 2
n n n | Ṡ -- Ṡ ṙ | n d P m gm | ᵍṙ S
nā-cha-ta de de tā- lī

***bansuri baja rahi* - tintal**

बांसुरी बाज रही
धून मधुर कन्हैया खेलत गावत होरी

जिन जाऊँ सखी उन संग गौरा
हट नट खट हैं ठठोली

bāṇsurī bāja rahī

dhūna madhura kanhaiyā

khelata gāvata horī

jina jāū̃ sakhī una saṅga gaura

haṭa naṭa khaṭa haĩ ṭhaṭholī

Krishna is playing charming
melodies on his flute,
Singing and playing the games of Hori.

But his way of dancing and his pranks,
Disrupts the gopis as they try to dance
together.

Rag Sindhi Bhairavi
Khyal in slow tintal M.80

Asthai

```
   3                    +          2              o
‖: r | n  S  gm Pd | P -- P P | P -- D n | P d P
   bāṇ- su- rī        bā- ja ra- hī  dhū-na ma-dhu- ra

           o              +                   n2                    o
   d |ᴾm  P  g  m | Pd nṠ  ġ Ṡ | d-Pm g  SgmP m |ᵍr̄ -- S :
   kan-hai-  yā  khe-  la-ta gā-        va-    ta  ho- rī
```

Antara

```
   o              3        +          2
‖:ᵐg  m  ⁿd  n | Ṡ -- ᵍr̄ Ṡ | n  n  Ṡ Ṡ | Ṡr nṠ  ⁿd P :‖
   ji- na  jā-  ū    sa-khī  u- na saṅ-ga gau-        ra

   o           3         +
   Ṡ  ġ  Ṡ  ṁ |ᵍr̄ Ṡ'  g  m | dn Ṡn Ṡ --
   ha-ṭa na-ṭa kha-ṭa hai ṭha-ṭho-    lī

   2                         o
   d-Pm g  SgmP m |ᵍr̄ -- S
   gā-     va-    ta  ho-  rī
```

Sharada - **tintal**
(Hymn to Saraswati)

शारदा विद्यादानी दयानी दुख हरणी
जगत जननी ज्वाला मुखी माता सरस्वती

सुदृष्ति कीजिये अलम पर अपनी
अपना गुण बकस दीजे
राग ताल तान कर सुहाग

shāradā vidyādānī dayānī dukha haranī
jagata jananī jvālā mukhī mātā saraswatī

sudṛiṣṭī kījiye alama para apanī
apanā guṇa vakasa dīje
rāga tāla tāna kara suhāga

Saraswati,
Giver of learning and mercy,
Remover of sorrow,
Mother of the universe,
Radiant-faced goddess:

Look lovingly at your servant, Alam;
Endow him with the gifts of
Rag, tal, and tan.

Khyal in tintal M.144

Asthai

+ 2 o 3

‖: Sr ṇ S | ⁿd -- -- P | -- n d Pm | g -- -- m | P n dP m

shā- ra- dā vi- dyā- dā- nī da- yā- nī

+ 2 o 3 +

g -- -- m | g r S' r | ṇ S g m | P -- Pnd Pm | g -- --

du- kha ha- ra- nī ja- ga- ta ja- na- nī jvā- lā

2 o 3

m^Pm | ^gr -- S r | ^rg ^rg r S | -- :‖

mu- khī mā- tā sa- ra- swa- tī

Antara

o 3 + 2

‖: g m ⁿd -- | n Ṡ -- Ṡ | Ṡ -- -- ^ṙn, n | Ṡ ṙ ġ ṁ

su- driṣ- tī kī- ji- ye a- la- ma pa- ra

o 3 + 2

ġ ṙ Ṡ -- | P P n d | -- P g g | m ^gr -- S :‖

a- pa- nī a- pa- na gu- ṇa va- ka- sa dī- je

o 3 + 2 o 3

‖: ^mg -- m ⁿd | -- n Ṡ -- | ṙ ^ṙġ ^ṙġ ṙ | n d m g :‖ r g r S | -

rā- ga tā- la tā- na ka- ra su- hā- ga

Tarana in tintal M.208

Asthai

o 3 + 2
|: -- gr S r | n S g m | P -- -- P | -- n d P
dim ta na na de re na dim ta na na

o 3 + 2
m g -- m | g r S -- | S -- P dP m | -- mg R g
de re ta de re na dim ta dim dim ta

o 3 + 2
m g -- m | g r S n | d --' d P | d n d P :|
na na ta na na de re na ta di ya na re ta

Antara

o 3 + 2
|: g gg mm m | m' d dd nn | n n' S -- | r n -- S
na deri deri da ni tum deri deri da ni ta re da ni

o 3 + 2
g R g -- | g' g R g | g' g R g | m g r S :|
di ya na re, di ya na re, di ya na re da ni

o 3 +
gR mg Rg r r S' nD Sn Dn D D m'
chum cha na na, chum cha na na,

2 o 3
dP nd Pd M M m' gR mg Rg r r S
chum cha na na, chum cha na na,

+ 2 o 3
gg gg gg mm mm mm dd dd dd nn nn nn | S r S --
tere kita taka, tere kita taka, tere kita taka, tere kita taka, ta na na

+
[Sg r n -- S' Pn d m -- P' Sg r n S] 2x
ta da re da ni, ta da re da ni, ta da re da ni,

3 + 2 o
Sg r n -- | S' Pn d m | P' Sg r n | S
ta da re da ni, ta da re da ni, ta da re da ni

Rag Sindhi Bhairavi

Tarana in fast tintal M.220

Asthai

```
      o              3              +              2
‖: -- P -- d | m P g m | P -- g m | g r S -- :‖
   dim    ta  na  na de re  na    ta  na de re na

      o      2nd: P ͡dP m          +              2
‖: S r g g | m -- -- -- | g m g r | S -- -- -- :‖
   ta na de re na              ta  na de re na

      o              3              +              2
 S͡ d P d | m P g m | D -- n Ṡ | n d P --
 dim  ta  na der der ta  na  dim   ta  na de re na

      o              3              +              2
 P d d͡Pm | m P P͡m g | g m m͡g r | S r S --
 de re na       de  re na    de re na     de re na
```

Antara

```
      o              3              +              2
‖: g -- m m | d -- n n | Ṡ -- Ṡ Ṡ | ṙ n Ṡ -- :‖
   dim    ta na dim   ta na dim   ta  na de re na

      o              3              +              2
 Ṡ ġ Ṙ ġ | Ṙ ġ Ṙ ġ | Ṙ ġ R͡ġm -- | ġ ṙ Ṡ --
 ta na na na na na na na na na    na       de re na

      o              3              +              2
 ġ ṙ Ṡ -- --' ṙ Ṡ n -- --' Ṡ n D -- --'
 de re na       de re na       de re na

      o    o         3              +              2
 n͡D S͡n d -- --' d -- M -- m' M -- m -- g'
 de re na       dim   dim   ta,  dim   dim   ta,

      o              3              +              2
 m -- g -- R' g -- r -- S'| S r g m | P d n Ṡ
 dim   dim   ta,  dim   dim   ta, ta na na na  na na de re
```

jo to racho - dadra

जो तू रचो, श्याम
तेरी लीला अपरमपार

तू जो सेवक दाता
तेरे बिना कोई ना अपनो

Jo tū racho, Shyāma,
Terī līlā aparampāra

Tū jo sevaka dātā
Tere binā koī nā apano.

O Creator, Shyam,
Infinite is your divine play.

You, who give to to those who serve you:
None is our own, save you.

Dadra M.98

Asthai

```
    +            o           +             o
||: m  --  --| ᵐg  --  P | mg  m  --  | gr  S   r :||
    jo           tū        ra- cho       shyā-  ma

    +            o              +           o
    P  P  --  | Pd  Pdn  --  | P  P  n | dP  mg  m
    te- rī       li- lā         a- pa- ram- pā-   ra

    +            o              +           o
    P  P  --  | gr  Ṡnd  P  | P  P  n | dP  mg  m
    te- re       li- lā         a- pa- ram- pā -  ra
```

Antara

```
    +            o              +             o
||: P  m  g | P  --  -- | P  d  nṠ | nd  P  -- :||
    tū          jo          se- va- ka   dā- tā

    +            o              +             o
||: P  d  n | Ṡ  --  -- | ṙ  Ṡn  Ṡ | P  ⁿd  P :||
    te- re bi- nā           ko- ī  nā   a- pa- no
```

Two gats in tintal

Slow tintal M.54

$$\overset{3}{\parallel}:\; Sr\,|\,\overset{s)}{n}\;\; SS\;\; g\,\underbrace{mm}\;\; \underbrace{Pd}\,|\,\overset{+}{P}\;\; P\;\; P$$

$$\overset{\wedge}{} \quad | \quad \overset{\wedge}{} \quad | \quad \overset{\wedge}{} \quad | \text{-} \quad | \quad | \quad \text{-}$$

$$\overset{gr}{\overline{SR}}\,|\,\overset{2}{g}\;\; \underbrace{PP}\;\; d\,\overset{sn}{n}\;\; \overset{n}{d}\,|\,\overset{o}{mg}\;\; rg\;\; rS\;:\parallel$$

$$| \text{-} \quad | \quad \overset{\wedge}{} \quad | \text{-} \quad | \quad | \text{-} \quad | \text{-} \quad | \text{-}$$

variation:
$$\overset{p}{\overline{M}}\,m\;\; g\widehat{RSr}\;\; S$$

$$| \quad \text{-} \quad | \quad \text{-} \quad |$$

Medium fast tintal M.176

$$\overset{+}{\parallel}:\; P\; \text{--}\; P\; d\,|\,m\; \underbrace{PP}\;\overset{2}{}\; d\; n\,|\,\overset{o}{d}\; P\; m\; P\,|\,\overset{3}{g}\; \underbrace{mm}\; P\; d\,:\parallel$$

$$| \quad \text{-} \quad | \quad \overset{\wedge}{} \quad | \quad \text{-} \quad | \quad | \quad | \quad \text{-} \quad | \quad \overset{\wedge}{} \quad | \quad \text{-}$$

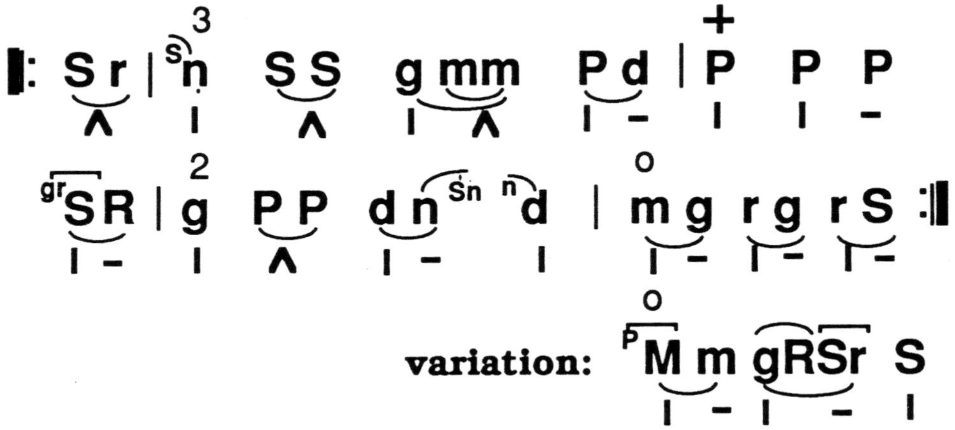

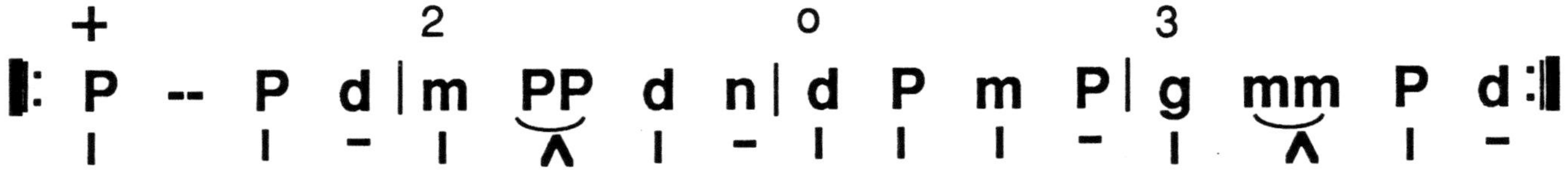

Bhairavi with Ragmala

Gat in medium rupak tal M.96

```
    o       1     2     o        1     2
‖: m  m -- | m -- | m -- | g  g -- | g -- | g --

   o       1     2     o        1     2
   r  r -- | g -- | m -- | g  r -- | S ṇ | S -- :‖

          o       1     2     o         1     2
2)     ‖: S  r -- | G -- | G -- | m  -- -- | m -- | m --
Bhairav   o                   o
          P  d -- | P -- | m -- | G  r -- | Ṇ -- | S -- :‖

          o                    o
Jogiya    S  r -- | m -- | m --- | P  P -- | d -- | Ṡ --
          o                   o
          N  d -- | P -- | m -- | G  r -- | S Ṇ | ḍ -- gat

          o                   o
3)     ‖: Ṇ  r -- | G -- | m -- | M  -- -- | m -- | m --
Lalit     o                   o
          M  d -- | N -- | d -- | M  d -- | M -- | m -- :‖

          o                   o
Malkauns  m  -- -- | d -- | n -- | Ṡ  n -- | d m | g  S
          o                   o
          ḍ  ṇ -- | S g | m -- | g  -- -- | g -- | Ṡ -- gat

          o                   o
4)     ‖: G  -- -- | M -- | D -- | D  -- -- | M G | S --
Hindol    o                   o
          Ṇ  Ṇ -- | Ḍ -- | Ṃ -- | Ḍ  -- -- | S -- | S -- :‖
          o
Dhanikauns                    o
          S  G -- | m -- | m -- | N  D -- | m -- | G --
          o                   o
          N  -- -- | D -- | D -- | G  m -- | G -- | S -- gat
```

Ragmala, concluded

Gunkali 5) ‖: S r m | P d | P m | r -- -- | S -- | S -- :‖

Durga ‖: m m -- | P -- | D -- | P m -- | P -- | P --
R m P | D -- | -- -- | m R -- | S D | S -- :‖

Kedara ‖: S m -- | G -- | G -- | P P -- | M -- | P --
M P -- | D -- | P -- | DP m -- -- | m -- | m -- :‖

Todi S r -- | g -- | g -- | M M -- | d -- | N --
d -- -- | P M | g -- | M g -- | r g | S -- gat

6) ‖: (Todi) S r -- | g -- | g -- | (Bhairav) r G -- | m -- | m --
(Kalyan) G M -- | P D | N -- | (Hindol) M -- -- | D -- | Ṡ -- :‖
(Ahir Bhairav) Ṡ n -- | D n | ṙ -- | (Khammaj) Ṡ n -- | D -- | P --
(Khammaj) G m -- | G -- | G -- | (Malkauns) m -- -- | g m | S --

Ustad Ali Akbar Khan in concert in San Francisco. Photo by Betsey Bourbon.

Asawari

Rag Asawari (*asāvarī, sāverī*) is an ancient rag in a larger family of rags which include some of the rags of the Todi group. The popular rag, Jaunpuri, is one of its closest, most frequently rendered, relatives. Asawari is full of *tyāg*, the mood of renunciation and sacrifice, as well as pathos. It is best suited for late morning. The notes are the same as the Western Aeolian mode, or natural minor scale. The very important evening rags, Darbari Kanra and others of the Kanra family, also use the notes of Asawari, and hence one must avoid bringing life to the shadows of these rags.

In some old forms of Asawari you have both shuddh and komal ***re****, but in our school we call this Komal Asawari. In khyal style they sing mostly Jaunpuri with shuddh* ***re*** *and ascending* ***pa dha ni sa****; but my father taught that this was Gandhari Todi and kept it separate from both Asawari and Komal Asawari.*

Rag Asāvarī

That: Asāvarī

Jati: aurav sampurn

Vadi: d Samvadi: g

Ang: uttarang

Time: late morning (9 am-12 noon)

Mood: shṛingār and karuna

Pakaṛ: S R m P d – P' m P Ṡ ⁿd – P

Arohi-Avarohi: S R m P d Ṡ Ṡ n d P m g R S

Chalan: S – R m P ˢ ⁿd -- P -- P d m -- m P n d P --

m P d m P ᵐg -- ˢR S --

Antara m P ⁿd Ṡ -------- Ṡ Ṙ ġ Ṙ Ṡ --

Ṙ n Ṡ Ṙ ⁿd P --- m P ġ Ṙ Ṡ --

P Ṡ n ṠṘnṠ ⁿd P -- P d m --

m P Ṡ ⁿd -- P d m P ᵐg ˢR S --

Sargam in tintal M.80

Asthai

3 + 2 o

‖: R m P n | ^{n}d -- P -- | m P d P | ^{m}g -- R S :‖

3 + 2 o

R S ^{n}ḍ P̣ | ṃ P̣ ^{n}ḍ S | R m P d | ^{m}g -- R S

Antara

3 + 2 o

‖: m P ^{n}d -- | Ṡ -- Ṙ Ṡ | ^{n}d -- Ṡ ġ | Ṙ n d P :‖

3 + 2 o

P ġ Ṙ Ṡ | Ṙ n d P | m P d P | ^{m}g -- R S

Komal Asawari

navariya **- dhamar**

नावरिया झांझरी आनपड़ी
मझधार, आनपड़ी मझधार

ना कोऊ पीर मिले
न कोऊ संग साथी
नाम लिये कर पार

nāvariyā jhāṇjharī ānapaṛī
majhadhāra, ānapaṛī majhadhāra

nā koū pīra mile
na koū saṅga sāthī
nāma liye kara pāra

My boat, full of leaks,
is in midstream.

I have not met any saint,
nor a friend, nor a companion.
Let your name take me ashore.

Rag Komal Asāwarī

Dhamar M.84

Asthai

3 + 2 o 3

‖: R m P P ^{m}P | ^{n}d -- -- d -- | P -- | dP m m | P --

nā- va- ri- yā jhāṇ- jha- rī ā- na- pa- ṛī

\+ 2 o

Pd mP | ^{m}g ^{g}r^{g} S R m | PdmP mP | ^{m}g ^{g}r^{g} S :‖

ma- jha- dhā- ra ā- na - pa- ṛī ma-jha- dhā- ra

Antara

o 3 + 2

‖: m -- m | P ^{n}d - - d - d | Ṡ -- -- -- Ṡṙ | nd P - :‖

nā ko -ū pī- ra mi- le

o 3 + 2

d Ṡ Ṡ | ġ -- ^{g}ṙ^{g} Ṡ | ^{s}ṙ n Ṡṙ ^{n}d -- | P -- :‖

nā ko- ū saṅ - ga sā- thī

o 3 + 2 o

ġ -- ġ | ^{g}ṙ^{g} -- Ṡ -- | ṙn Ṡ ṙ ^{n}d -- | P -- | ^{m}g ^{g}r^{g} S

nā- ma li- ye ka- ra pā- ra

Komal Asāwarī is very similar to *Asāwarī*, except for the use of slight komal **re** in descent. This note cannot be dwelt upon and, when approached from above, is quitted with a slight upward movement. These movements should be quick, small, while maintaining the stately manner of dhrupad.

***are mana samajha* - tintal**

अरे मन समझ समझ पग धरिये
अरे मन इस जग में नहीं अपना
कोई परछायी सों डरिये

दौलत दुनिया कुटुम कबील
इन सों नेहान कबहुन करिये
राम नाम सुख धाम जगतपती
सुमरन सों जग तरिये

are mana samajha samajha paga
dhariye
are mana isa jaga mē nahī apanā
koī parachhāyī so ḍariye

daulata duniyā kuṭuma kabīla
ina so nehāna kabahuna kariye
rāma nāma sukha dhāma jagatapatī
sumarana so jaga tariye

O my mind, watch your steps,
O my heart, none is your own in this
world,
Even your near and dear ones.

Remember the name of Rama,
The source of all joy,
And cross the ocean of life.

Khyal in slow medium tintal M.72

Asthai

2 | o | 3 | +

‖: m m P Ṡ | ⁿd P Pd mP | ᵐg R m m | P P P -- :‖

a- re ma- na sa- ma- jha sa- ma- jha pa- ga dha- ri- ye

2 | o | 3 | +

ᴾd m P P | ⁿd ⁿd ⁿd P | d m Pd mP | ᵐg ᵐg R S

a- re ma- na i- sa ja- ga mē na- hī a- pa - nā

2 | o | 3 | +

R -- S -- | ⁿS S ˢg -- | R S R n | ⁿd -- -- P

ko- ī pa- ra- chhā- yī so ḍa- ri- ye

Antara

o | 3 | + | 2

[: m -- P P | ⁿd d ⁿd -- | ᵈS S S S | S -- S -- :‖

dau- la- ta du- ni- yā ku- ṭu- ma ka - bī- la

o | 3 | + | 2

ⁿd d d -- | S -- S S | ˢᴿg g ˢR S | n RSRS ⁿd P :]

i- na sō ne- hā- na ka- ba- hu- na ka- ri- ye

o | 3 | + | 2

P d n d | -- P dm P | ᵐg -- R S | R ˢn S S

rā- ma nā - ma su- kha dhā- ma ja- ga- ta- pa- tī

o | 3 | +

S S ˢg g | ˢR -- S S | ˢR n ⁿd P

su- mi- ra- na sō ja- ga ta- ri - ye

"**are mana**", concluded

Vistars (sing ākār: "ah")

1)
2 o 3 +
^{m}R -- ^{P}m ^{P}m | P -- -- -- | d -- -- nd-- | P -- -- --
2 o 3 +
P m d P | n d -- P | d m P d | ^{m}g -- R S **asthai**

2)
2 o 3 +
d -- -- -- | -- -- -- m | ^{m}P -- -- -- | -- -- -- --
2 o 3 +
n -- d -- | m -- P -- | P d n -- | d -- m --
2 o 3 +
P Ṡ n d | m -- P -- | R -- m -- | R -- P --
2 o 3 +
m -- d -- | m -- P -- | R m Pd mP | ^{m}g -- R S **asthai**

3)
2 o 3 +
m P ^{n}d -- | n d ^{dP}m -- | P -- d n^{Sn} | d -- P --
2 o 3 +
m P ^{n}d ^{n}d | Ṡ -- Ṡ -- | ġ -- Ṙ Ṡ | Ṙ n d P
2 o 3 +
P ġ Ṙ Ṡ | Ṙ ^{S}n Ṡ -- | n -- Ṡ Ṙ | ^{n}d -- P --
2 o 3 +
R -- m -- | P -- n -- | d -- m -- | P d m P **asthai**

Boltans

1)
2 o 3 +
R m P P | ^{n}d - -^{n}d - - PP | Ṙn ṠṘ ^{n}dd P - | dm Pn dd P - **asthai**
a- re ma- na a- re ma-na sa-ma-jha sa-ma-jha pa-ga dha-ri-ye

2)
2 o 3 +
ṠṘ mP Rm Pn | dd PP P -' ṠṘ | nṠ dP' Pd | mP ġṘ'
a-re ma-na sa-ma-jha pa-ga dha-ri-ye pa-ga dha-ri-ye pa-ga dha-ri- ye
ṠṘ mm P - **asthai**
pa-ga dha-ri-ye

***baje re* - rupak**

बाजे रे बांसुरिया
माधुर माधुर सुर बाजे

मोरे नैन
बरसन लगे
सखी री

bāje re bāṇsuriyā

madhura madhura sura bāje

more naina

barasana lāge

sakhī rī

How sweet the tones of his flute.
My eyes begin to pour tears,
O my friend.

Khyal in rupak tal M.126

Asthai

```
   2        o              1    2        o              1
(: P  d |ᴾm  --  R |ᴿm  --  | P  Ṡ |ⁿd  --  -- | P  -- :‖
   bā-      je       re       bāṇ- su- rī-         yā

   2        o              1    2        o              1
   Pd mP |ᵐg  g  g | g  --  | R  S | R  --  -- | S  -- :)
   ma- dhu- ra ma-dhu- ra    su- ra bā-         je
```

Antara

```
   o              1    2    o              1         2
‖: P  --  -d |ᴾm  -- | --  -- | Pd  nd  Ṡ | Ṡ  -- | --  -- :‖
   mo-        re              nai-      na

   o              1    2    o                   1         2
   g̣  R  ᵍᴿ Ṡ ᴿṠ |n  -- | --  -- | Ṙ  Ṡ ᴿṠ nˢⁿ | d  -- | --  --
   ba- ra- sa-  na            lā-

   o              1    2    o              1
   Ṡ  n  d | P  -- | --  -- | R  g  -- | R  S
   ge              sa- khī      rī
```

Tarana in tintal M.208

Asthai

o 3 + 2
‖: R S -- S | R m P -- | -- -- ᴾd -- | ᴾm -- P -- :‖
ta nom ta de re na ta da re

o 3 + 2
P Ṡ -- Ṡ | Ṡ -- Ṡ' ˢṘ | -- ᴿn -- ⁿd | -- P -- P
ta da re da ni ta da re da ni

Antara

+ 2 o 3
‖: m m P -- | P' d d d | -- d' Ṡ Ṡ | -- Ṡ -- Ṡ
di ya na re, di ya na re, di ya na re

+ 2 o 3
Ṡ ġ -- Ṙ | -- ṠṠ Ṡ -- | -- nṠ - Ṙ - Ṡ | ⁿd -- P -- :‖
ta klan tom ki ta tak ga di ge na dha

+/3
‖: ṁ ġ -- ṘṘ - Ṡ - Ṡ' Ṙ n -- dd - P - P :‖
dha ga di ge na, dha ga di ge na

o 3 + 2
P d m P | dd Ṡ --' n - | dP - P m - - -' | g - gR - R S -'
ta klan tom ki ta tak ga di ge na dha ga di ge na dha

o
[R S -- S | R m P --] 3x
ta nom ta de re na

Two gats in tintal

Vilambit M.50, Masitkhani style

$$\begin{array}{l}
\overset{3}{} \qquad\qquad\qquad \overset{+}{} \\
\| : \underset{\wedge}{S\,S} \mid \underset{|}{R} \ \underset{\wedge}{m\,m} \ \underset{|}{P} \ S^{nR\dot{S}} \mid \overset{n}{d} \ \underset{|}{d} \ \underset{-}{P'} \\[2mm]
\overset{2}{} \qquad\qquad\qquad\qquad \overset{o}{} \\
\underset{\wedge}{P\,d} \mid \underset{|}{m} \ \underset{\wedge}{P\,n} \ \underset{|}{d} \ \underset{-}{(PdmP}\mid ^{m}g) \ \underset{|}{R^{SR}} \ \underset{-}{S} : \|
\end{array}$$

Madhya (medium tempo) M.144

$$\begin{array}{l}
\overset{3}{} \qquad\qquad \overset{+}{} \qquad\qquad \overset{2}{} \qquad\qquad\qquad \overset{o}{} \\
\| : \underset{|}{R} \ \underset{\wedge}{m\,m} \ \underset{|}{P} \ \underset{-}{\dot{S}} \mid \underset{|}{d} \ \underset{\wedge}{d\,d} \ \underset{|}{P} \ \underset{-}{d} \mid \underset{|}{m} \ \underset{\wedge}{m\,m} \ \underset{|}{Pd} \ \underset{-}{mP}\mid ^{m}g \ ^{m}g \ \underset{|}{R} \ \underset{-}{S} : \|
\end{array}$$

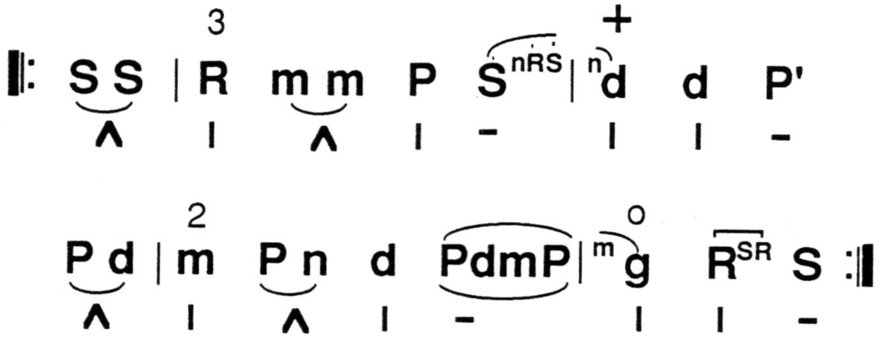

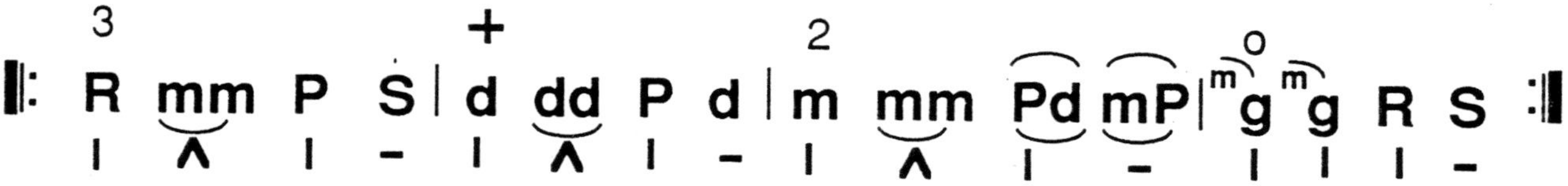

Alhaiya Bilawal

The Bilawal (*bilāval*) family of rags is another vast one, and includes mostly varieties based on the "natural" scale of modern North Indian music, Bilawal *ṭhāṭ*. Often komal **ni** is added, giving the feeling of Khammaj *ṭhāṭ*. Alhaiya (also *alahīyā*) Bilawal is the best known and most widely performed of this family. Also frequently heard are the morning rags Deshkar, Kukubh Bilawal, Devgiri Bilawal, and Shukla Bilawal. There are several important evening rags from Bilawal *ṭhāṭ*, such as rags Lom, Durga, Tilak Kamod, and Mand, but they are not of the morning Bilawal family, although they are in Bilawal *ṭhāṭ* —thus the vagueries of the *ṭhāṭ* classifications.

So many types of Bilawal are there—and also there are the Sakh family of rags, like Devsakh and Lachha Sakh. In old days, the dhrupad singers first recognized Shukla Bilawal. Now Alhaiya Bilawal is considered the most important rag of this family.

Rag Alhaiya Bilawal

That: **Bilawal**

Jati: **vakra sharav-vakra sampurn**

Vadi: **D**   Samvadi: **G**

Ang: **uttarang**

Time: **late morning (9 am-12 noon)**

Mood: **shringār, karuna**

Pakar: G R G P ^{N}D N Ṡ

Arohi-Avarohi: S R G P D N Ṡ   Ṡ N D n D P m G R S

NSGRGPDNṠ

Ṡ N D n D P D m G R   G m P m G R S

Chalan: S -- ^{S}N S --   G ^{m}G R --   G P ^{N}D N Ṡ

Ṡ G Ṙ G m G -R S --   Ṡ N D -- ^{D}n D P --

D m G ^{m}G R -- ^{m}G m P m G R S N --

^{N}Ḏ n Ḏ P -- ^{N}Ḏ ^{S}Ṇ S --

Sargam in tintal M.84

Asthai

```
     o             3              +                  2
||: G  m  R  -- | G  P  D  S^NRS | N  --  --  --^DN | S  --^NGRSNS  --  --  :||

    o              3              +              2
    S  N  D  n  | D  --  P  --  | D  m  G  R  | G  --  P  --

    o              3              +              2
    G  m  R  -- | G  m  P  m  | G  --  R  --  | S  --  --  --
```

Sargam in rupak tal M.168

Asthai

```
     o          1       2      o            1        2
‖: G  m  -- | G  -- | R  -- | G  P  -- | D  -- | n  --
   o            1       2       o          1        2
   D  --  -- | P  -- | P  -- | P  D  -- | m  -- | G  -- :‖
```

Antara

```
     o          1       2       o            1       2
‖: G  P  -- | D  -- | N  -- | Ṡ  --  -- | Ṡ  -- | Ṡ  --
   o            1       2      o           1         2
   Ṡ  Ġ  Ṙ | Ġ  -- | ṁ  -- | Ġ  Ṙ  -- | ṠN  DN | Ṡ  -- :‖
   o                                    o
   GP DN ṠṘ ṠN Dn DP Dm GR' Gm Pm GR S'N SG R
       o  (7th)
   [G PD NṠ] 3x
```

e ju kala ki - **dhamar**

ए जु काल की
ग्वालिन ए मेरो
मन ले गयो
ले गयो री

सांझ भई आज हूँ नहीं आयी
झुठे बचन दे गयी री

e ju kāla kī
gwālina e mero mana le gayo
le gayo rī

sāṇjha bhayī āja hū̃ nahī āyi
jhuṭhe bachana de gayī rī

Yesterday the milkmaid stole my heart.

Today, evening has come, and still she
has not come.
She had made false promises.

Dhamar M.76

Asthai

```
      3                    +                        o
‖: G P ND N | Ṡ -- N P -- | -- -- | Dn D P
    e-    ju   kā- la kī              gwā- li- na

      3                    +                        o
   D m G m | G -R S S -- | G R | SNRS NDN - --
    e          .me-    ro     ma- na le

      3                    +                  o
   S S -- -- | P -- -- -- -- | D n |ᴾ D P -- :‖
   ga- yo      le              ga- yo rī
```

Antara

```
      +              2        o          3
‖: G P -- ND | N -- | Ṡ -- -- | R -- Ṡ --
   sāṇ-   jha bha- yī     ā-  ja

      +              2        o          3
   S G R G -- | ṁ -- | G R -- | Ṡ -- -- -- :‖
   hū    na  hī  ā-   yī

      +                  2        o          3
   D n -- D -- | P -- | D N -- | Ṡ -- N --
   jhu-    ṭhe      ba- cha-  na

      +                  2        o
   D n -- D -- | P D | m Gm GR
   de    ga- yī      rī
```

ayo hai phagun - tilwara

आयो है फ़ागुना मास

चंचल पवन भयो याद पिया की आयो रे

āyo hai phāguna māsa

chanchala pavana bhayo yāda piyā kī āyo re

The month of phagun (spring) has arrived.

The restless breeze is stirring,
Thoughts of my beloved come with it.

Vilambit khyal in slow tintal M.40

Asthai

11th
G mGPmGm GRmGR GP NDN -
ā - yo hai phā- gu- na

\+
SNRSNS ND nDP D PmG m G mG R
mā - sa

G m G R GR G G P D n D n D PD P D
chan- cha- la pa- va - na

\+
PmG m G R G -R S N S GmGm G R G Pm G G P
bha- yo yā- da pi- yā

P SNSNDN SGRSNS RSNS N D nDP D PmG m G
kī ā- yo re

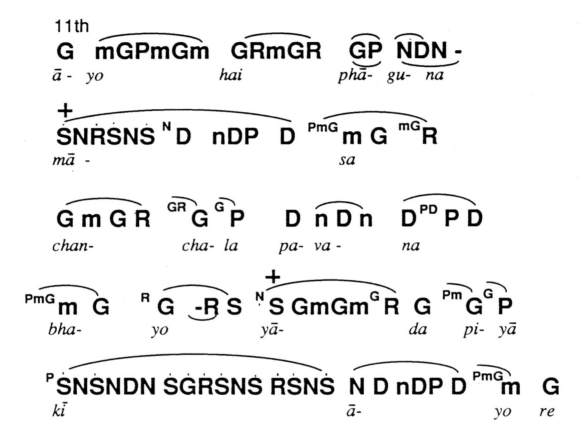

mana haruwa **- tintal**

मन हरुवा रे मैका
हरि हरि चुड़ियां देहो मंनगाय
रंग रंगीली और चटकीली तापर
धनकट के मन हरुवा

और गले को हार लुंगी
मोतियान थाल भरुंगी
खरक खरक मोरी चुड़ियां खरके
बंगरी मुरक गईली

mana haruvā re, maikā
hari hari chuṛiyā̃ deho maṅgāya
raṅga raṅgīlī aura chaṭakīlī
tāpara dhanakaṭa ke mana haruvā

aura gale ko hāra luṇgī
motiyana thāla bharuṅgī
kharaka kharaka morī chuṛiyā̃ kharake
baṅgarī muraka gayīlī

O beloved, bring me bangles of the
greenest green,
bangles colorful and dazzling
With beautiful designs on them

And necklaces to adorn my throat
With trays filled with pearls . . .
My bangles make a grating sound,
And my bracelets have gotten twisted.

Khyal in medium tintal M.80

Asthai

3 + 2 o
‖: G P ND N | Ṡ -- ṠN D | D n DP PD | PmG m -- Gm GR :‖
ma- na ha- ru - vā re ma- na ha- ru- vā re
2nd PmG m Gm RG R
vā re mai- kā

3 + 2 o
G P ND N | Ṡ N Dn DP | G m GmP- m | G R S --
ha- ri ha- ri chu- ri- yā de - ho maṅ-gā- ya

3 + 2
S G G G | Gm R G P | D n D PD | PmG m -- G G
raṅ- ga raṅ gī- lī au- ra cha- ṭa- kī- lī tā- pa- ra

3 o
G P ND N | ṠNṠĠ-Ṙ Ṡ Dn PD | GP mG RG Pm | RG - R S --
dha- na- ka- ṭa ke ma-na ha-ru- vā

Antara

3 + 2 o
‖: G P P P | N -D N -- | Ṡ -- Ṡ -- | ṠN Ṙ Ṡ --
au- ra ga - le ko hā- ra luṅ- gī

3 + 2 o
Ṡ ĠṘ Ġ ṁ | ĠṘĠ -Ṙ Ṡ Ṡ | Ṡ - - N Dn PD | G P m G :‖
mo- ti- ya- na thā - la bha- ruṅ- gī

3 + 2 o
G P P P | ND N Ṡ Ṡ | N Ṙ ĠṘṠN D | D n D P
kha- ra-ka kha- ra- ka mo- rī chu- ṛi - yā kha- ra- ke

3 + 2
PĠ Ġ Ġ ṁ | Ġ Ṙ Ṡ Ṡ | ṠN Dn PD GP | mG RGPm GR S -
baṅ- ga- rī mu- ra - ka ga- yī- lī

Tarana-laxsangit in tintal M.112

Asthai

```
   3                +                2                    o
‖: G  P  ND N | S  NRSNS --  N  -- | D  nDSn  D  P | G  m  G  R :‖
   ta na de re    dim   dim    ta  na      na na de re  na
```

Antara

```
   3                +                2                      o
‖: G  P  ND N | Ṡ  Ṡ  Ṡ  -- | ˢG  R  Ġ  ṁ | ᴿ G  Ṙ  Ṡ  Ṡ :‖
   rā-  gā  a- la- hai-yā     gā-   va- ta   sa-  ba  gu- ṇī

   3                +                2                    o
   Ṡ  N  D  n | ᴾD  P  --  -- | Ġ  m  G  R | G  P  ND  N
   vā-       dī         dhai- va- ta  sam- vā- dī

   3                +                 2
   ṠN  G-Ṙ  Ṡ  Ṡ | ᴺD  n  ᴾD  P | GP  DN  ṠG  ṘS
   gan-   dhā- ra  sa- ba- hī    mā-       na-

   o
   ṠNDn  DP'ṠN  DnDP  mGRS
   tā
```

Tarana in jhaptal M.120

Asthai

o 3 + 2
‖: G P | N D N | SN Dn | DP mG mR :‖
ta na de re na

+ 2 o 3
‖: G G | G m R | R G | P P P
ta na de re na ta na de re na

+ 2
G P | D ^Ṡ^n -- | - D PD | ^PmG^m -- G :‖
ta na de re na

+ (+)
[GP - N DN Ṡ] 3x
ta na de re na

Variation:

+ 2 o 3
‖: G - - P - P - P - D - n - D - ^D^P - m - G :‖
ta na de re ta da re ta da ni

+ 3/2 3/2 3/2 3/2 3/2
‖: G G G P P P D D D n n n D D P :‖
de re na, de re na, de re na, de re na, de re na

+ 3/2 3/2 3/2 3/2 3/2
‖: G GG P P' N DD N N' Ṡ Ṡ Ṡ Ṡ ṠN Ṙ Ṡ :‖
na deri da ni, tum deri da ni , ta da re ta da ni

+
[G GG P P' N DD N N' Ṡ Ṡ Ṡ Ṡ ṠN Ṙ Ṡ] 2x
na deri da ni, tum deri da ni , ta da re ta da ni

o o
ṠĠ - Ṙ Ṡ - Ṡ'D n - DP - P' GP - m G - | **first line**
ta da re da ni, ta da re da ni, ta da re ta

+
Sargam tan: ṠĠ ṘṠ ND nD Pm Gm RG mP mG RS

+ (+)
NS GR [GP DN Ṡ -] 3x
ta na de re na

Gats in tintal

Vilambit tintal M.48

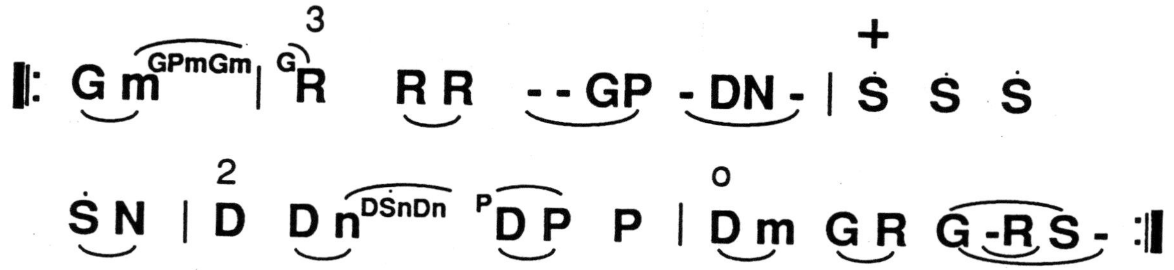

Drut (fast) tintal M.264; set at half speed, or M.132

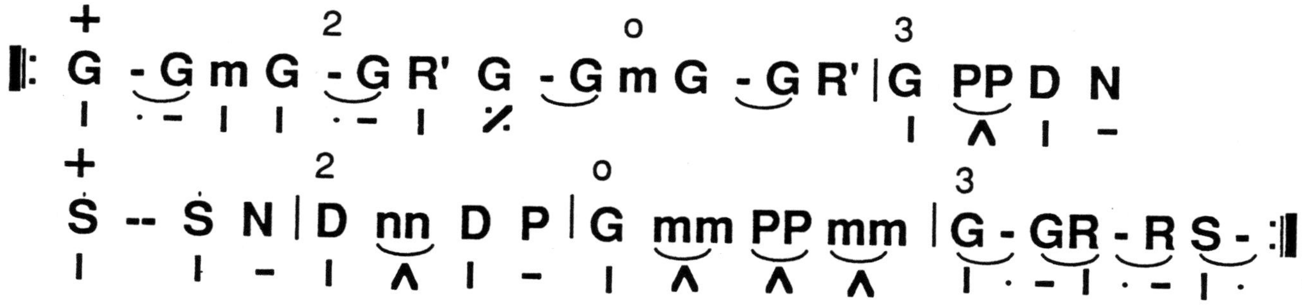

Allauddin Khansahib surrounded by students in Maihar in about 1930. From l. to r.: Jhurra Lal, who played nal tarang (tuned gun barrels) with the Maihar Band; young Ali Akbar Khan; Timur Baran Bhattacharya, sarodist and pioneering orcherstral composer; Baba Allauddin; Ram Ganguli, sitarist and later film music director; and Israel, an esraj player.

Todi

The Todi (*toḍī*) family of rags is tonally very broad, and includes rags classified in Todi, Kafi, Bhairavi, Bilawal, and Asawari *ṭhāṭs*. Rag Todi (also called Darbari Todi) and its close relatives Miyan ki Todi and Gujari Todi, have a unique and wholly non-Western modality. They are to be rendered in the late morning, and have great power, pathos, and dignity. In the old ragmala paintings, Todi is always depicted as a maiden in the forest surrounded with deer, and yet it is not clear which of the many Todis this iconography relates to. The afternoon rag, Multani, has the pitches of Todi but uses them in an entirely different manner; for this reason, its shadow must be avoided.

*Be careful of **pa** in Todi; too much makes it Multani, and then you spoil it. Keep **ga** as vadi note, even though it is a morning rag, or else (if you use **dha** as vadi) it sounds like Gujari Todi. It is filled with heroic mood and sadness.*

Rag Todi

That: Todi

Jati: sharav-vakra sampurn

Vadi: **g** Samvadi: **d**

Ang: **purvang**

Time: **late morning**

Mood: **bhakti, shṛingār, karuna**

Pakar: d N S r g -- M r g r S

Arohi-Avarohi: S r g M d N Ṡ Ṡ N d P M d M g r g r S

Chalan: S ---- d N S r g --- r g r --- S r g r S ---

N S NSrS ^Nd -- d g M r g -- r g r S --

S r g -- M r M g -- g M P M d -- d P -- P M d M r g --

M d N d P -- M r g r S --

Antara ^dM ^Nd N Ṡ -- d N Ṡ ṙ -- Ṡ ṙ g r S -- NSrS ^Nd

d g r Ṡ SNrSNS ^Nd P -- P M d -- M r g -- g M r g --

r g -- g r S --

Sargam in fast ektal M.264

Asthai

```
    +     o   2    o    3    4     +                o
|: S -- -- r -- -- |g -- -- r -- -- |S -- -- -- -- -- |-- -- -- -- -- -- :|
    +                   o              +              o
   S -- -- r -- -- |g -- -- d -- -- |r -- -- g -- -- |r -- -- S -- --
    +              o
|: S r g S -- r |g S -- r g S :|
    +              o                          +              o
|: M -- -- -- r g |M g r -- g M |g r -- g r -- |g r -- S -- -- :|
```

Antara

```
    +                o                   +                o
(: r -- g -- M -- |d -- N -- -- -- |-- -- -- -- -- -- |-- -- -- -- -- --
    +              o                   +              o
   d -- -- -- r -- |-- -- N -- -- -- |M -- -- -- N -- |-- -- d -- -- --
    +                o                   +                o
   S -- -- -- -- -- |-- -- -- -- -- -- |-- -- -- -- -- -- |-- -- -- -- -- --  :|
    +                o                 +              o
   d -- -- -- -- -- -- |-- -- g -- r -- |-- -- g -- S -- |-- -- r -- N --
    +                  o                 +              o
   -- -- S -- r -- |-- -- g -- -- -- |r -- -- -- S -- |-- -- -- -- -- -- --
    +                  o
   -- -- -- -- -- -- -- |-- -- -- -- -- -- -- :)
```

```
 +  ⌐3/2⌐  o         2         o         3            2
 Ṡ  r  g̣ |g̣ ṙ' g̣|g̣ ṙ' g̣|g̣ ṙ S'   |NṠṙ  ⁄    |dNṠ  ⁄
 +  ⌐3/2⌐     o         2         o      3      4        +
 M  d  N |Ṡ  ṙ  g̣|ṙ  Ṡ  N |Ṡ  ṙ  Ṡ|d  -- g̣|-- ṙ -- |Ṡ—one cycle—
 +  ⌐3/2⌐  o         2         o      3        4        +
 Ṡ  ṙ  g̣|ṙ  Ṡ  N'|d  N  Ṡ|N  d  P'|M  d  M |g  r  g
 +  ⌐3/2⌐     o         2         o      3      4          +
 r  Ṡ  Ṅ|Ṡ  r  g |M  d  N |Ṡ  ṙ  g̣|ṙ  -- -- |-- -- -- |Ṡ—one cycle——
 +  barabar (1/1)        o                 +                  o
 N  -- -- d -- -- |P -- -- M -- -- |d -- -- M -- -- |r -- -- |g -- --
 +                 o
 r -- -- S -- -- |S -- -- S -- --
```

adi anahata nad- chautal

आदि अनहत नाद
उपजो जगत में
ताको करुँ ध्यान
पाक मन घट में

खरज रिखब गन्धार सप्त सुर
अहत मिलायो निरगुण ब्रह्म व्यापक जगत में

ādi anahata nāda
upajo jagata mẽ
tāko karũ dhyāna
pāka mana ghaṭa mẽ

kharaja rikhaba gandhāra sapta sura
ahata milāyo niraguṇa brahma vyāpaka jagata mẽ

The original unstruck sound is generated in the universe. This I meditate upon in the pure region of my mind.

Kharaj, rishab, gandhar—the seven struck notes become one in the Supreme Being—above and beyond all attributes pervading the universe.

Dhrupad in chautal M.72

Asthai

```
+        o        2       o      3       4
[: S -- | -- S | ^g r  r | r  r | g  r | -- S :]
   ā-          di  a-  na- ha- ta      nā-    da
+       o       2       o      3       4
S  r | g  -- | -- ^g M | r  g | ^g r -- | S  -- :]
u- pa  jo             ja- ga-  ta  mē
+       o       2       o       3       4
P -- | P -- | P  PM | d -- | -- P | -- P
tā-     ko     ka- rū              dhyā-   na
+       o       2       o        3        4
M  d | N  d | P  P | PM d | Mg rg | r  S
pā-    ka  ma- na  gha- ṭa      mē
```

Antara

```
+ /3
|: M  M | d -- | N  M | d -- | Ṡ -- | -- --
   kha- ra- ja   ri- kha- ba    gan-
+/3
Ṡ -- | -- Ṡ | ṙ -- | ṙ  ṙ | -- ṙ | Ṡṙ g
dhā-      ra  sap-   ta  su-    ra  a-
+/3
ṙ -- | Ṡ -- | Ṡ  Ṡ | -- Ṡ | N  Ṡ | N  Ṡ
ha-    ta     mi- lā-    yo  ni- ra- gu- ṇa
+/3
NṠṙ ṠNṠ | ^N d -- | d -- | P  P :|
brahm-      a      vyā-   pa- ka
2        o         3        4
P  P | PM d | Mg rg | r  S
ja- ga- ta     mē
```

tuma samana - **chhadra**

तुमा समान न दूजो जग में मोरे राज
सकल गुण संपन्न तुम गरीब नवाज

भरण पोसण दुख दारिद्र भय हरण
खटा दरसन निवास तुम हो धरम राज

tuma samāna na dūjo jaga mẽ more rāja
sakala guṇa sampanna tuma garība navāja

bharana poṣhaṇa dukha dāridra bhaya haraṇa
khaṭā darasana nivāsa tuma ho dharama rāja

O my Lord, none is your equal.
Repository of all virtues,
Champion of the poor,

Supporter of all,
Remover of poverty, sorrow, and fear,
Upholder of truth.

Chhadra (jhaptal) M.69

Asthai

+ 2 o 3
𝄆 g r | S S -- | S Sr | -g -M PM
tu- ma sa- mā- na na dū- jo ja- ga

+ 2 o 3
d -- | -- M ^g^r | -r gMr | gr -- S 𝄇
mē mo- re rā- ja

+ 2 o 3
S S | d -- d | d d | P P P
sa- ka- la gu- ṇa sam- pan- na

+ 2 o 3
M d | N d M | ^g^r gM | rg r S
tu- ma ga- rī ba na- vā- ja

Antara

+ 2 o 3
𝄆 M M | d -- ^dP^M | d N | Ṡ -- Ṡ
bha- ra- na po- ṣha- ṇa du- kha

+ 2 o 3
d -- | N -- Ṡ | ṙ ġ | ṙ ṙ Ṡ 𝄇
dā- ri- dra bha- ya ha- ra- ṇa

+ 2 o 3
ṙ ġ | Ṁ ġ ṙ | ġ ṙ | Ṡ -- Ṡ
kha-ṭā da- ra- sa - na ni- vā- sa

+ 2 o 3
N Ṡ | NṠNṠ NṠṙṠ ^N^d | d d | P P
tu- ma ho dha- ra- ma

+ 2 o 3
PM | dM r- gr' Mg' PM' dM' Nd' NM' dg' Mr' gr -- S
rā- ja

"in loose rhythm--not like a tan"

neka chala **- tintal**

नेक चाल चलिये चतुर
प्रभु सो दरिये गरीब ना करिये
नहीं भरोसो या नर तन को

हररंग कहे उपदेश बजना अब
समझ समझ पग जग में धरिये
मनुष जनम नहीं बार बार
यहा करन हो सो करिये चतुर

neka chāla chaliye chatura
prabhu sō dariye garība nā kariye
nahī bharoso yā nara tana ko

hararaṅga kahe upadesha bajanā aba
samajha samajha paga jaga mẽ dhariye
manuṣha janama nahī bāra bāra
yahā karana ho so kariye chatura

Lead a virtuous life, O clever man!
Fear the all-knowing Lord.
Don't impoverish yourself;
There is little reliance on this human body.

Hararanga says, Listen to advice:
Watch your steps–
Human birth cannot be enjoyed again and again;
Watch your steps,
O clever man.

Khyal in medium tintal M.184

Asthai

```
  o           3           +           2
∥: S  r  g  r | S  S  S  r | g -- Mr  g | r  r  S -- :∥
   ne- ka chā- la cha-li- ye          cha-tu-ra

  o           3           +           2
   P  M  d -- | P  M  d -- | M  r  g rg̅M | g  r  S --
   pra-bhu sō    da- ri- ye   ga- rī-ba nā  ka- ri-ye

  o           3           +
   S  r  g  r | g -- M -- | d  M  d  N |
   na- hī bha- ro- so    yā    na- ra ta- na-

  2
   dN'Md'  gM'rg'  SrgM  grS-
   ko
```

Antara

```
   o           3           +           2
⦃: M  M  d  d | N  M  d  N | Ṡ -- Ṡ Ṡ | Ṡ  Ṡ  Ṡ  Ṡ :∥
   ha- ra- raṅ-ga ka- he u- pa- de- sha ba- ja- nā a- ba

   o           3           +              2
   Ṡ  ṙ  g̈  g̈ | ṙ  ṙ  Ṡ  Ṡ | N  N  Ṡ NṠr | N̊ d  d  d -- :⦄
   sa-ma- jha sa- ma-jha pa- ga ja- ga  mē̄    dha- ri- ye

   o           3           +              2
   d  g̈  g̈  ṙ | ṙ  ṙ  Ṡ  Ṡ | N -- Ṡ Ṡṙ | g̈  g̈  r  Ṡ
   ma- nu-ṣha ja- na-ma na- hī bā-    ra bā-    ra ya-hā

   o              3              +           2
   N  N  SNṙ SNṠ | N̊ d -- dPM  d | M  r  g rg̅M | g  r  S --
   ka- ra -na      ho so  ka- ri- ye   cha- tu- ra
```

Vistars for khyal, "neka chala"

Sing ākār: "ah"

```
    +          2          o           3
1)  S -- -- --|r -- -- --|g -- -- --|r -- -- --
    +          2
    S -- -- --|N -- S --
    +          2          o              3
2)  Nd -- -- --|P -- -- --|PM -- Md ---|dN -- NS --
    +          2
    Sr -- rg --|r -- S --
    +          2          o           3
3)  S r g --|-- -- Mr g|r -- -- --|Sg rg r S
    +          2
    Sr gM rM r-|Sr gM gr S-

    +          2          o           3
4)  M -- -- --|P -- -- PM|d -- -- --|d -- P --
    +          2
    P M d --|M r g r

    +          2          o           3
5)  M --d --|N -- d --|M d N d|M N d --
    +          2          o           3
    P -- M --|d -- M --|r g r S|Sr g rg M
    +          2
    gM r gM d|PM d Mg rS
    +          2          o           3
6)  M d N --|N --d --|M N d N|M d N --
    +          2          o           3
    r g M d|N -- Md N|Nd PM' dM gr|S'N dP Mg rS
    +          2
    Srgr g- - - rgMg M - - -|gMPM d - - - NdPM grS -
```

ja ja re - jhaptal

जा जा रे पथिकवा
जा जा रे मोरे पिया सों
कहीं देहो पतिया रे

पहले मुख सो कहियो
तुम्हारो खुदा हाफ़िज़क्
तुम बिना सदारंग
अब जली जाती छतियाँ रे

jā jā re pathikavā
jā jā re more piyā so
kahī deho patiyā re

pahale mukha so kahiyo
tumhārokhudā hāfiz
tuma binā sadāraṅga
aba jalī jātī chhatiyā re

Go... go, traveller,
Go to my beloved with my message.

God be with you—tell her face to face:
Without you, Sadarang is burning inside.

Khyal in jhaptal M.88

Asthai

o 3 + 2
|: d -- | grg r -- S | S r | g M r g -- :|
jā jā re pa- thi- ka- vā

o 3 + 2
d -- | r -- S | P P | P P M
jā jā re mo- re pi- yā

o 3 + 2
M d -- | M g r S -- | S r g | -- r gr S
sō ka-hi de-ho pa-ti- yā re

Antara

+ 2 o 3
|: M M | d d N | N Ṡ | Ṡ Ṡ --
pa- ha- le mu- kha so ka- hi- yo

+ 2 o 3
N N | Ṡ -- ṙ | ġ M | ṙ ġ ṙ Ṡ :|
tum- hā- ro khu- dā hā- fiz

+ 2 o 3
ġ ġ | ṙ ṙ Ṡ | N Ṡ ṙ Ṡ | N d -- d
tu- ma bi- nā sa- dā- raṅ- ga

+ 2 o 3
ṙ ṙ | ṙ ṙ Ṡ d | dNṠ ṙ -- | ġ ṙ -- Ṡ
a- ba ja- lī jā - tī

+ 2
S r | g M r g r S
chha-ti- yā re

Tarana in ektal M.240

Asthai

```
   +        o        2        o        3        4
‖: ᵈṠ  --  | N   d  | P   P  | M   d  | M   g  | M   d  :‖
   ta        na  de   re  ta        na  na   der tum der

   +        o        2        o        3        4
   S   S  | r   g  | g   g  | M   M  | M   d  | d   d
   na  der der, tum der der, na  der der, tum der der

   +        o        2        o        3        4
   Ṡ   Ṡ  | Ṡ   Ṡ  | Ṡ   Ṡ  | d   Ṡ  | --  M  | d   --
   der der der der der der dit lam      dit lam
```

Antara

```
   +        o        2        o        3        4
[: M   M  | M  ᴺd  | -- ᵈṠ  | --  Ṡ  | Ṡ   ṙ  | Ṡ   -- :‖
   na  der der tum     ta       na  de   re  na

   +        o        2        o        3        4
‖: ᴺd  d  | d   Ṡ  | Ṡ   Ṡ  | ṙ   g  | ṙ   -- | Ṡ   -- :]
   de  re   na  de   re  na   ta der da       ni

   +                           (12th)
[ Ṡ  --  N  MM    MM    dd    Ṡ  -- ] 3x
  ta     na tere  kita  taka  ta
```

Gats in tintal

Vilambit M.48

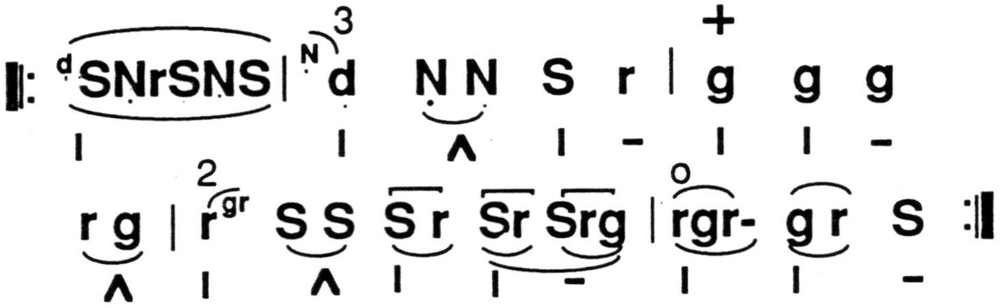

Fast tintal M.224

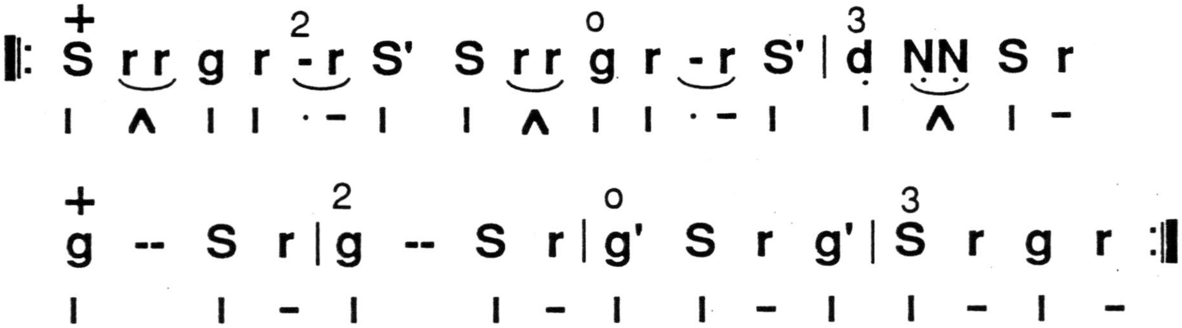

KAFI

Rag Kafi (*kāfī*) is one of the oldest rags, and its intervals are described as the ***sa** grama*, or basic scale, of the *Nāṭyashāstra*. Thus, in ancient times, it would seem that Kafi was considered the "natural" scale. The name "Kafi," however, does not appear until later in the Medieval period. As old and fundamental as it is, it naturally has a vast literature, and can be rendered in any of the three main styles: dhrupad, khyal, and thumri. In stricter styles, Kafi's movements are elegant and dignified, and the use of the natural **ga** very controlled in approach and quitting. In lighter music, where tunes in Kafi abound, the use of the two **ga**s, and sometimes two **nis**, is more casual. There are many songs for the Holi (Spring) season in Kafi, and the rag, which is normally rendered in the afternoon or evening, is sometimes considered to convey a mood of springtime.

*Kafi is an old, old rag from the time of Bharat muni. Sometimes in dhrupad way they sing in a very strict style; then they say it is Kafi Kanra. In our Kafi we keep komal **ni** strong, almost like a samvadi.*

Rag Kafi

That: **Kafi**

Jati: **sampurn-vakra sampurn**

Vadi: P Samvadi: S (or R)

Ang: **purvang**

Time: **late afternoon and evening, springtime**

Mood: **shringār, karuna**

Pakar: Rg SR m^G m P

Arohi-Avarohi: S R g m P D n Ṡ Ṡ n D P m G m g R S

S R g m P D n Ṡ
Ṡ n D P m G m P ^mgR g R S

Chalan: S -- R g m^G m P -- m P D n D P -- m P^mgR g R --

R n D n P D n Ṡ ------- Ṡ n D P m G -- m P^mgR g R --

g S R n S -- R^S R g R g^R g m^G m P ---

laxsangit/sargam - tintal

सरज रिशब गन्धार मध्यम पंचम
पा गा रे
पिया गा रे
पिया मोरा गा रे

saraja rishaba gandhāra
madhyama panchama
pā gā re
piyā gā re
piyā morā gā re

Saraj, rishab, gandhar,
madhyam, pancham,*
Pa, ga, re,
Sing, O my beloved.

*The full names of the notes

Sargam in medium fast rupak tal **M.288, set to M.144**

Asthai

o 1 2
‖: S S -- | R -- | -- -- | R R -- g -- -- -- | g g -- m -- -- --
sa- ra- ja ri- sha- ba gan-dhā- ra

m m -- P -- -- -- | P -- -- P -- P -- | m -- P g -- R -- :‖
ma- dhya- ma pan- cha- ma pā gā re

‖: R -- -- n -- -- -- | -- -- -- -- -- -- -- | D -- -- -- -- --

P -- -- m -- -- -- | P -- -- D -- -- -- | P -- -- -- -- -- -- :‖

m -- P g -- R -- ‖: -- m P g -- R -- :‖
pā gā re pi- yā gā re

Antara

o
‖: P D -- m -- -- -- | P D -- n -- -- -- | S -- -- -- -- -- -- | -- -- -- -- -- -- --

n -- -- g -- -- -- | R -- -- -- -- -- -- -- | -- -- -- -- -- -- -- | -- -- -- -- -- -- --

n -- -- g -- -- -- | R -- -- S -- -- -- | -- -- -- -- -- -- -- | n -- -- D -- P -- :‖

‖: P D -- m -- m -- | PDSnRS n -- -- -- | P D -- m -- m -- | D -- -- P -- -- -- :
pi-yā mo- rā gā re pi-yā mo- rā gā re

‖: -- n -- D n -- -- | -- D -- P D -- -- | -- P -- m P -- -- :‖
gā re gā gā re gā gā re gā

o (o)
S n -- D P m g R S [S R g m P D n S --] 3x

aye ri - chautal

आये री मेरे धाम श्याम
कुमर कृष्ण उन के
चरण नैनन सो परसों

बंसी बट तर कर
बंसी लिये राज नटवर
सँजरी ओढ़ पियारो पट धाय

āye rī mere dhāma shyāma
kumara kṛiṣhṇa una ke
charaṇa, una ke charaṇa
nainana so paraso

bansī baṭa tara kara
bansī liye sāja naṭawara
sājarī oṛha piyāro paṭa dhāya

I become ecstatic at the arrival of the
young Lord Krishna to my home.
I would touch his feet with my eyes.

Krishna, carrying his flute,
is dressed as a master of the dance.

Dhrupad in chautal M.69

Asthai

2 o 3 4 + o
‖: R g | R S | R g | - - m - - m - - | P -- | - m DP :‖
ā - ye rī me- re dhā- ma shyā- ma

2 o 3 4 + o
D D | D D | DS n | -- Dn | DP -- | Dm DP
ku-ma- ra kṛiṣh-ṇa u- na- ke

2 o 3 4 + o
g g | R -- | R n | D P | D m | D P
cha- ra-ṇa u- na - ke cha- ra- ṇa

2 o 3 4 + o
m mPDR | ᵐg R | ᵐR g Rg | R S | R Sn | R S
nai - na- na so pa-ra - so

Antara

+ o 2 o 3 4
‖: m -- | P D | n S | S S | n S | g --
ban- sī ba- ṭa ta- ra ka- ra ban-

R -- | S S | R n | D P | P D | n S :‖
sī li- ye sā- ja na- ṭa- wa- ra

+ o 2 o 3 4
D n | R -- | n S | nD n | DP m | G m
sā- ja - rī o- ṛha pi- yā- ro

+ o
m mP | mg R
pa- ṭa dhā - ya

Dhrupad in chautal, concluded

Bolbant

3 4 +
1) Rg RS Rg -m -m | P
ā - ye rī me-re dhā-ma shyām

2 o 3 4 +
2) Rg RS Rm -m P- P-Rg RS-R -mPm | P
ā-ye rī me- re dhā-ma shyā-ma, ā-ye rī me- re dhā-ma shyām

5th (+)
3) - - [Rg RSRm PmP- P] 3x
ā-ye rī me-re dhā-ma shyā-ma

+ o 2 o 3 4
4) DD DD -n -D nD PD mP gR mm P- Pm DP
kumara k.ṛiṣh-ṇa u-na ke cha-ra-na nai- na-na so pa-ra so

+
DDDD -n-D nDPD mPgR mmP- PmDP
kumara k.ṛiṣh-ṇa (etc., chaugun)

7th (+)
[-RRm -mP- P] 3x
mere dhā-ma shyā-ma

eri e mai - dhamar

एरी ए मैं कौन जतना
सों कोलौं मोरे
पिया के मन में परि गांठ

सब सखियां मिली बन बन
आयी मैं बैठी बिखरी

erī e maĩ kauna jatanā
sõ kolaũ more
piyā ke mana mẽ pari gānṭha

saba sakhiyā̃ milī bana bana
āyī maĩ baiṭhī bikharī

O, how shall I unravel the knots
in which my beloved
has left my heart entangled?

All my friends have come
and are ready;
I alone remain dishevelled.

Dhamar M.80

Asthai

+ 2 0 3
‖: R ᵐg -- ˢR -- | S -- | R n S | R g - - m- - P- -
e- rī e mai kau- na ja- ta -

+ 2 0 3
P -- -- D - P | m ᵐP | ᵐg ᵐR -- | gRmg Rg ˢR S
nā sō ko- lau mo- re

+ 2 0 3
R n S S -- | P D | n -- - -DP | ᵐg Rg ˢR S :‖
pi- yā ke ma- na mē pa- ri gāṇ- ṭha

Antara

+ 2 0 3
‖: P P -- P D | m -- | P D n | S S S S :‖
sa- ba sa- khi- yā mi - lī ba- na ba- na

+ 2 0 3
SRmg Rg-- -- R -- | S -- | S n -- | D -- P mP
ā- yī mai bai- ṭhī bi-kha-

0 +
ᵐᵍᴿg R S R g | R S | R n S | R g - - m- - m- - | P
rī, e- rī e mai kaun- na ja- ta nā

saba mile gawo - tintal
(laxsangit)

सब मिले गावो राग काफ़ि
अति सुन्दर राग कहावे
रस रंग रंग रस भर भर डालो

वादी पंचम सुर को सुहावे
सुर को सुहावे समवादी

saba mile gāvo rāga kāfi
ati sundara rāga kahāve
rasa raṅga, raṅga rasa bhara bhara ḍālo

vādī paṇchama sura ko suhāve
sūra ko suhāve samavādī

Let all sing together
the beautiful rag, Kafi.
Fill the air with sprayed colors...

Panchama* is vadi,
and charms with the samvadi note.

***pa**, the fifth note of the scale

Laxsangit (khyal style) in tintal M.92

Asthai

```
  2                o              3                       +
‖:R  n  D  P |mg  --  Rg SR |--  m  -  -m  -- |P  --  P  --:‖
  sa- ba mi- le  gā-      vo      rā-  ga      kā - fi
  2                o                   3
 P  D  n  S |Sn  RSnS  n  D |n  P   D  m |P  --  P  --
 a- ti  sun- da- ra   rā-     ga      ka- hā - ve
  2                    o                3                +
Sn  RSnS  n  D |nD  SnDn  D  P |PD  m- PD  nS |mg  --  Rg  SR
ra- sa   ran- ga ran- ga      ra- sa bha- ra bha- ra ḍā-      lo
```

Antara

```
  2                    o          3                 +
‖:PD  m- PD  nS |S  -- Ṡ  Ṡ |n  n  Ṡ  Ṙ |ṘṠ  nṠ  n-  DP :‖
  vā-    dī    paṇ- cha- ma su- ra ko su- hā-      ve,
  2                    o          3              +
 PD  m- PD  nṠ |Ṡ  -- Ṡ  Ṡ |n  n  gṘmg Ṙgg- |Ṙ  --  Ṡ  n
 vā-    dī    paṇ- cha- ma su- ra ko      su- hā-    ve
  2                      o            3               +
 -Pn  Ṙ  Ṙ  Ṙ |Ṙ  --  Ṡ  -- |Sn  RSnS  n  D |P  --  --  --
 su- ra  ko  su- hā-  ve    sa- ma-    vā- dī,
  2                    o                  3              +
 PD  m-  DP  nD |S  --nP  mg-- ˢṘ |--  m  -  -m  -- |P  --  P  --
 sa- ma- vā-        dī         rā-  ga      kā- fi
```

sundara surajanawa **- tintal**

सुन्दर सुरजनवा सांयि रे मन भाई रे

निसदिन तुमारो ध्यान धरत हूं
आन मिलो सब सांई रे

sundara surajanawā sā̃ī re mana bhāī re

nisadina tumāro dhyāna dharata hū̃
āna milo saba sā̃ī re

O, beautiful and noble Lord,
Bringer of pleasure to the mind,

I meditate on you day and night,
Come and unite with me.

Khyal in medium fast tintal M.240, set to M.120

Asthai

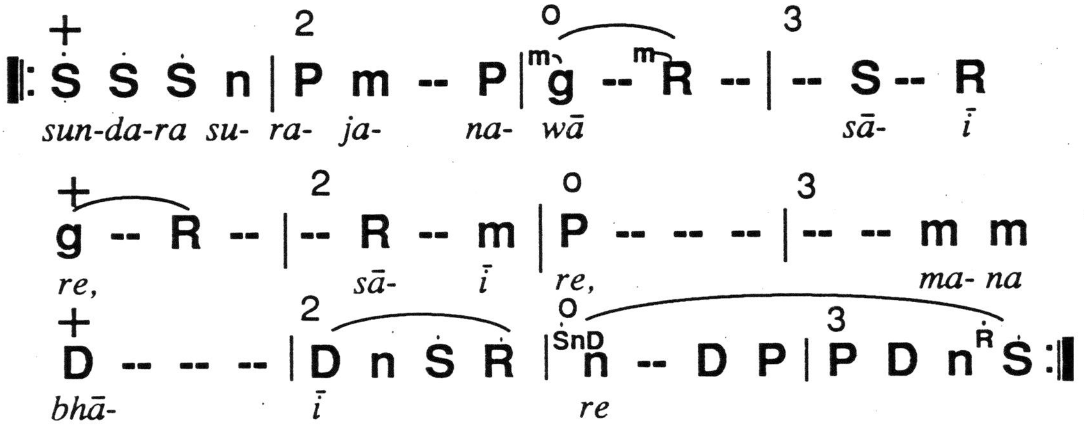

Antara

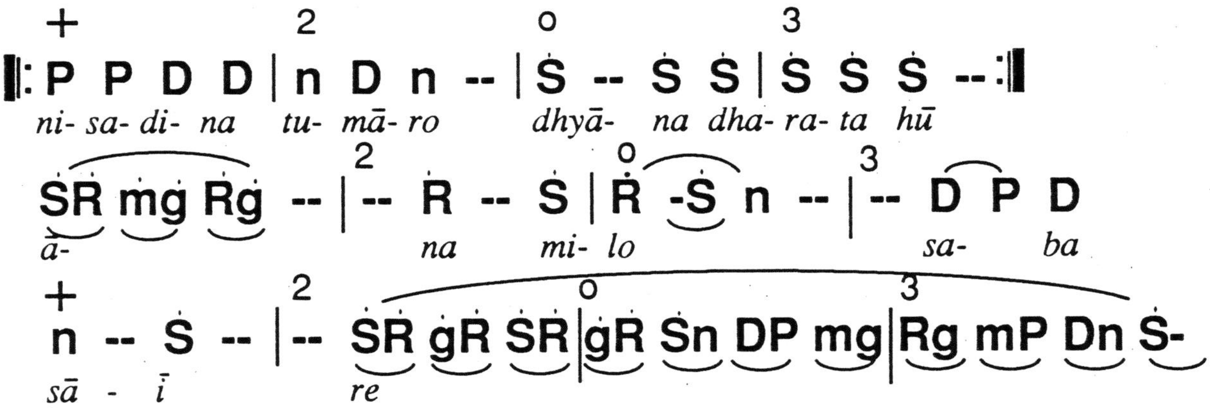

khyal, concluded

Tans

1) [Pm gR gm] 2x PD nD Pm gR gm PD nṠ nD PD nṠ

2) [Sn DP mg Rg mP Dn] 2x Ṡn DP' PD nṠ

3) SR gR Ṡn' nṠ RṠ nD' Dn Ṡn DP' PD nD Pm' mP DP mG'
    Gm Pm gR' Rg mg RṠ' ṠR g- Rg m- Gm P- -- mP D'P Dn'Dn

4) #3 to ∗ then [SRg'Rgm'GmP'mPD'PDn'DnṠ] 3x

             6th   (16th)

5) ‖: 1st line of antara, then

    1st: PDnD DnṠn nṠRṠ ṠRmgRṠnDPmgR SRgmPDnṠ :‖
          ni-   sa-   di-   na

    2nd: RgR ṠRṠ nṠn DnD P- P- PDnṠnDPmgRgmPDnṠ
          ni- sa- di- na tu- mā- ro

then sing whole antara in orginal format

Tarana in medium-fast tintal M.208

Asthai

o 3 2
‖: R gg S R | -- m P m | P -- -- -- | P D G --
na deri da ni dim ta nom

1st o 3 + 2
G -- G G | m -- P -- | mg -- g -- | R -- -- -- :‖
na de re da ni de re na

2nd o 3 + 2
-- G -- GG | m -- P -- | m G Pm Gm | g -- R --
na deri da ni de re na

o 3 + 2
-- -- R n | -- D n -- | D -- n -- | D P D --
ta na de re de re na

o 3 + 2
-- -- Sn RS | nS n D P | G -- Pm Gm | mg -- R --
ta na de re de re na

Antara

+ 2 o 3
‖: D D D n | -- n D D | D n - n | D -- P --
na de re da ni na de re da ni de re

+ 2 o 3
D -- -- -- | n -- R -- | n -- D -- | P -- -- -- :‖
na de re na

2nd P -- ‖: S --
na de

+ 2 o 3
S -- SR S | -- -- n -- | n -- nS n | -- -- D --
re na de re na de

+ 2 o 3
D -- Dn D | -- -- P -- | P -- PD P | -- -- :‖ -- --
re na de re na

tarana, continued

+ 2 o 3
R g R g | -- -- -- -- | -- -- g -- | R -- S --
na de re da o ni de na
R -- -- -- | -- -- -- -- | -- -- -- -- | -- -- -- --
na o
S R S R | -- -- -- -- | -- -- R -- | S -- n --
na de re da ni de na
+ o
S -- -- -- | -- -- -- -- | R S n S | R m g -- :
na 2nd -- -- -- -- -- -- -- --
+ 2 o 3
S S -- R | S -- n -- | n n -- S | n -- D --
de re na de re de re na de re
D D -- n | D -- P -- | mg -- g -- | R -- -- -- :
de re na de re de re na
+ 2 o 3 +
-- -- P P | P DP m m | m Pm g g | g mg R R | R -- :
de re na de re na de re na de re na
2 o 3 + 2
D D | D D D D | --' n n n | n n n --' | D D D D | D D --'
de re na de re na de re na de re na de re na de re na
o 3 + 2 o
P | P P P P | P -- -- -- | D -- -- -- | n -- R -- | S -- R --
de re na de re na
+ 2 o 3
n -- D -- | P -- -- -- | D -- n -- | S -- -- -- | -- -- -- --
de re na
+ 2 o 3
n -- -- S | S S S S | R -- -- S | S S S S :
dim ta na na na na tom ta na na na na
g -- -- g | g g g g | R -- -- R | R R R R
dim ta na na na na tom ta na na na na
+ o
n -- S n | S -- -- -- | -- -- S S | S S S S :
tom ta na na na na na
S -- R S | n -- -- -- | n -- S n | D -- -- --
dim ta na dim dim ta na dim
+
D -- n D | P -- -- -- | m g R R | R R' m --
dim ta na dim dim ta na na na, dim
+
m m m m' | P -- P P | P P' D -- | D D D D :
ta na na na, dim ta na na na, dim ta na na na

tarana, concluded

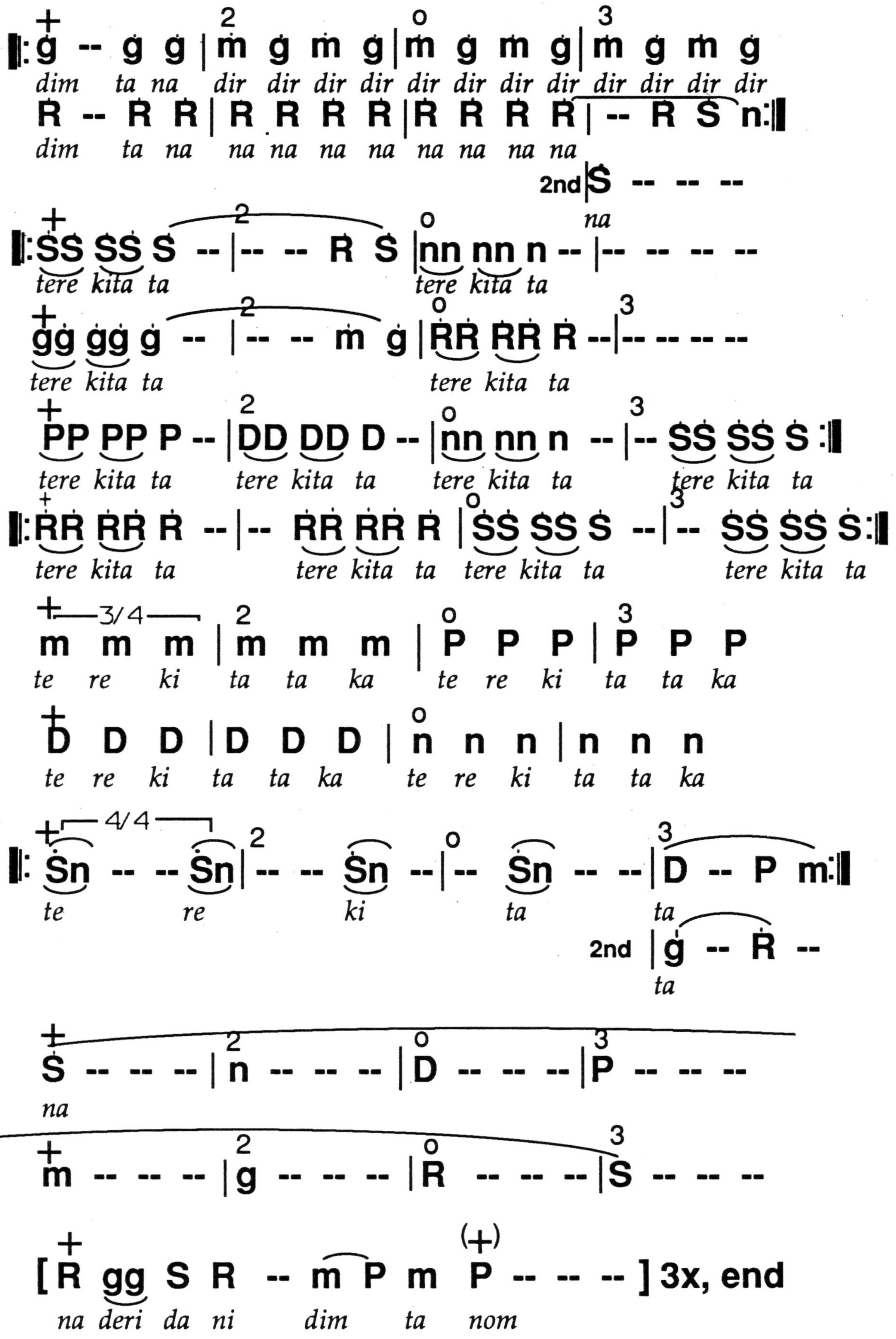
dim ta na dir dir dir dir dir dir dir dir dir dir dir dir
dim ta na na na na na na na na na
2nd
na
tere kita ta tere kita ta
tere kita ta tere kita ta
tere kita ta tere kita ta tere kita ta tere kita ta
tere kita ta tere kita ta tere kita ta tere kita ta
3/4
te re ki ta ta ka te re ki ta ta ka
te re ki ta ta ka te re ki ta ta ka
4/4
te re ki ta ta
2nd
ta
na
3x, end
na deri da ni dim ta nom

Tarana in medium ektal M.192

Asthai

+ o 2 o 3 4
‖: Ṡ -- | Ṡ n | D n | Ḋ P | D ^Pm^G | G m
dim ta de re na ta na de re na

+ o 2 o 3* 4
G m | G mG | nP ^mgR^g | -- R | mm mP | PP Dn :‖
na der da ni tom ta de re na, de re na, de re

3* (+)
3rd x [mm mP PP Dn Ṡ P] 3x
de re na, de re na, de re dim

3* 4 + o
4th x R g | R gR | mg R | -- S | S R | g -- | R g | m --
na der da ni tom ta de re na de re na

+ o +
g m | P -- | SR g | Rg m | gm P | SS SR | RR gg | gm mm
de re na dere na dere na dere na derena derena derena derena

2 o (+)
PP PD | DD [Dn Ṡ] 3x
derena derena dere dim

Tarana, medium ektal, concluded

Antara

‖: m̄ mm|mm P |PP PP|D- -n |- - D |n Ṡ
dha kita taka dhum kita taka dhin dhin   dha   kran

-̄- Ṡ |ṠṠ ṠṠ|ṠṠ ṠṠ |Ṡ - - Ṡ|- - Ṡ -|- Ṡ - -:‖
dha tete kata gadi gena dha dha   dha   dha

R̄ ġ|R̄ --|-- --|-- --|R̄ Ṡ ᴿˢ|n D
de re na

n̄ R̄|Ṡ --|-- --|-- --|Ṡ n ˢⁿ|DP m
de re na

Repeat whole antara from beginning, then

‖: [m̄ P g R m m P --] 2x
der der dim   der der dim

2
m n D n D P' P D P D P m' m P m P m' R m P :‖
ta na de re na   ta na de re na   ta na de re na   de re na

[mm mP PP DD Dn nn ṠṠ ṠD -n Ṡ- -'D -n Ṡ- -'D - n Ṡ--] 3x ⁽⁺⁾
de re na, de re na, de re na, de re na, de re na, gen ta dha, gen ta dha, gen ta dha

pathje amay - dadra
Bengali song

পথ যে আমায় বলে না গো
কোথায় যেতে চাই
মনের আমার অন্ত নাহি
পথের ও শেষ নাই

পথ যদি দেয় পথ দেখায়ে
ঘুমিয়ে থাকি পথ চেয়ে
জেগে উঠে নতুন করে
পথের সাথে যাই

মনের মত পথ মেলে না
পথের মত মন
তাই ত শুরু হয় না আমার
চলার আয়োজন

পথকে শুধায় কোথায় যাবো
পাওনা না হয় নাই বা পাবো
যা দেবে পথ মাথা পেতে
করবো গ্রহন তাই

I.

path jē āmāy bolē nāgo
kothāy jētē chāy
moner āmār anto nāhī
pather o shesh nāhī

II.

path jodī dēy path dekhāye
ghumiē thākī path chēyē
jegē uṭhē natun korē
pather sāthē jāī

III.

moner moto path mēlē nā
pather moto mon
tāi to shuru hoy nā āmār
cholār āyojon

IV.

pathkē shudāy kothāy jābo
pāonā nā hoy nāi bā pābo
jā dēbē path māthā pētē
korbo grohon tāi

The way informs me not
Where I intend to go;
My mind is limitless
And the path is without end.

The path itself shows me the way.
I can fall asleep by the wayside,
And waking up anew
I can follow the track,
Wherever it leads me.

I can neither get a path after my heart
Nor a heart that matches the path
No wonder my journey is not begun.

I ask the way where to go-
No matter whether I arrive or don't
Content with whatever
The path has to offer me.

Bengali and English lyric by B.P. Kriti

Light classical Bengali song in rag Misra Kafi in dadra M.126

Asthai

I.

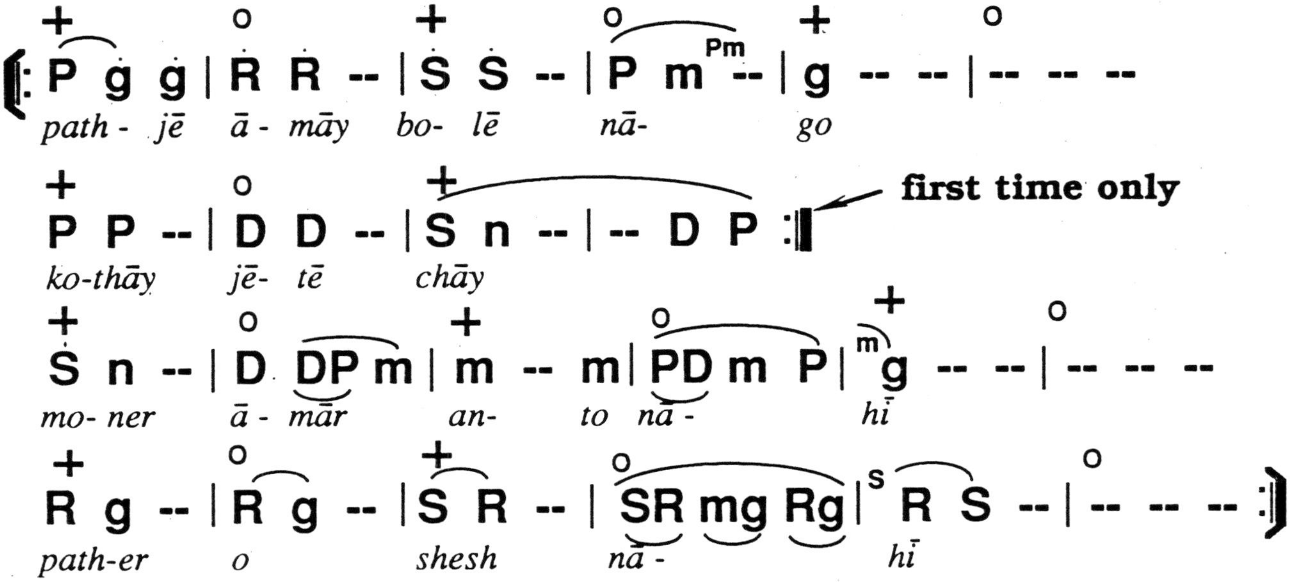
+ o + o + o
P g g | R R -- | S S -- | P m Pm -- | g -- -- | -- -- --
path - jē ā - māy bo- lē nā- go
+ o + first time only
P P -- | D D -- | S n -- | -- D P :||
ko-thāy jē- tē chāy
+ o + o + o
S n -- | D DP m | m -- m | PD m P | m g -- -- | -- -- --
mo- ner ā - mār an- to nā - hī
+ o + o
R g -- | R g -- | S R -- | SR mg Rg | S R S -- | -- -- --
path-er o shesh nā - hī

II.

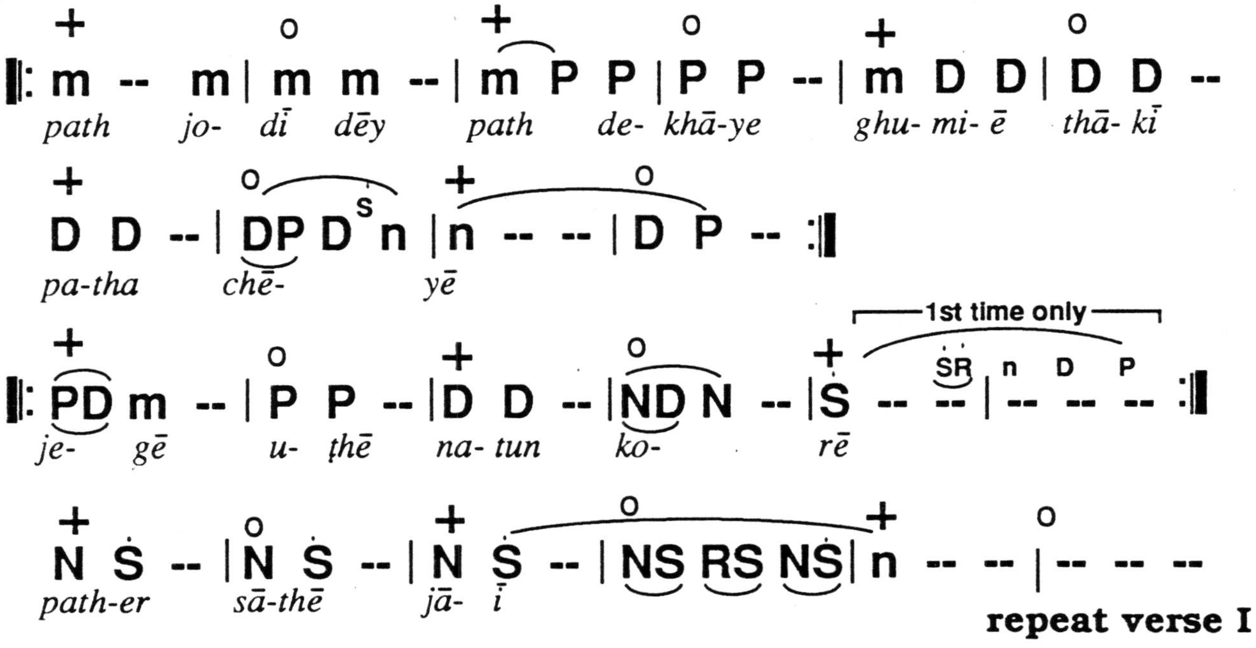
+ o + o + o
m -- m | m m -- | m P P | P P -- | m D D | D D --
path jo- dī dēy path de- khā-ye ghu- mi- ē thā- kī
+ o + o
D D -- | DP D S n | n -- -- | D P -- :||
pa-tha chē- yē
1st time only
+ o + o +
PD m -- | P P -- | D D -- | ND N -- | S -- SR -- | n D P | -- -- --
je- gē u- thē na- tun ko- rē
+ o + o + o
N S -- | N S -- | N S -- | NS RS NS | n -- -- | -- -- --
path-er sā-thē jā- ī
repeat verse I

Bengali song, concluded

III.

```
     +           o           +              o            +            o
 ‖: m  d  -- | d  d  -- | P  --  dm | m  Pd mP | m  G  -- | -- -- --
     mo- ner     mo- to      path       mē- lē      nā
```

```
     +           o           +              o
   G  G  -- | m  m  -- | P  --  -- | -- -- --  :‖
   path -er    mo- to      mon
```

```
     +           o           +              o            +            o
   n  --  n | n  n  -- | D  --  D | D  DP m | m  m  -- | PD  m  P
   tāi    to  shu- ru    hoy   nā  ā- mār     cho- lār   ā-  yo-
```

```
  m  +           o           +            o            +            o
   g  --  -- | --  --  -- | D  --  D | DP D  Ṡ | n  --  -- | -- -- --
   jon,                       cho-  lār ā-    yo- jon
```

proceed to verse IV

IV.

```
     +           o           +              o            +            o
 ‖:ⁿg  --  ġ | ġ  ġ  -- | Ṙ  g  -- | gṘ  SṘ mg | g  -- -- | -- -- --
   path - kē  shu-dāy    ko- thāy  jā -            bo
```

```
     +           o           +              o
   Ṙ  Ṙ  Ṙ | Ṙ  Ṙ  -- | ᴿĠ  --  Ṡ | Ṡ  Ṡ  -- | -- -- -- | n  --  --  :‖
   pā - o- nā   nā hoy     nāi      bā  pā - bo
```

```
     +                       +                          +
   P  Ṙ  Ṡ | Ṙ  --  n | n  n  SṘ | Ṡ  --  nD | D  --  D | D  P  DṠ
   jā dē- bē path     mā-thā pē - tē      kor-   bo  gro-    hoṇ
```

```
     +                       +              o            +            o
   n  --  -- | --  -DP | P  --  P | d  Pm P | ᵐg  --  -- | -- -- --
   tāi,               kor- bo  gro-hoṇ  tāi,
```

```
     +           o           +              o
   Ṙ  g  Ṙ | g  --  -- | Ṙ  g  Ṙ | g  --  --
   jā  dē bē path      mā- thā pē- tē
```

```
     +           o                         +            o
   Ṡ  --  Ṡ | SṘ  mg Ṙg | SṘ  Ṡ  -- | -- -- --
   kor-   bo  gro- hoṇ      tāi
```

repeat verse I, end

Gat in slow tintal M.44

3
‖: -n^nD^D P | mg^m R- R R RgSR --m--m-- | + P P P

PD ^P Dm | 2 P ^P D D ^D n nRS- | 0 nD ^nD P ^m G G ^RG m :‖

2) --RR -nn- | + S S S S ^nRSnS | 2 ^SnD n n n D ^P

mg R- | 0 R m P m P-

3) --Rg -SR- | + g g --Rg -SRg | 2 m m

--SR -mg | 0 R RPm- P P

3 mP mP mPmP mPDP | + ^m g^m R

Rm PD n | 2 DD DP ^m G G m

0 g R ^S n S

4) --Rg -Rn- | + R S S SR | 2 n n n D P

0 g R gmP-

Kafi gat, concluded

Antara

5) ‖: mm |D̈ DD PD n̂ᴰⁿ | Ṡ Ṡ Ṡ ṠR

  n nn g̈ᴿᵐᵍᴿᵍ R |ˢn̂ Dⁿᴰ P :‖

  PDnD |m mPDP g RgmS

  R SRgR S

6) ‖: g--g--g- g g R--R--R- R R | RgmP ᴾṠ :‖

  m--m--m- G G GmGm g g RgSg R R

  3rd
  ‖: R--m--m- m--P--P- RmPD mgR- :‖

  11th
  ‖: RnDn PDP- R-mP-DmP mgR- :‖

  3rd
  ‖: -nDn -DPD -PmP -mGm

  G-mG-mGm GmGm R-gR-gRg SgR- :‖

  3rd   **(11th)**
  [SRgRg--- Rgmgm--- GmPmP---] 3x

Rag Zila Kafi
Gat in medium tintal M. 132

1) |: -- D -- n | P D n^D n | S -- -- -- | SR nS Dn PD :|

2) |: -- R -- R | R g R S | R m m P | ^mgR g -- R -- :|

-- mP gm Rg | -- gm Rg SR | -- Rg SR nS | -- SR nS Dn

3) SR g- Rg m- | gm Rg SR nS

4) SR g'R gm' gm | Pm gR' gR S'R Sn

5) SR gm' Rg mP' | Pm gR' mg RS

6) SR gm P'R gm | PD' Pm gR Sn

7) SR gm PD' Rg | mP Dn' DP mg | RS

8) SR gm PD n'R | gm PD nS' S-

9) Sn D'n DP' DP | mg R'P mg RS | n-

10) PD P'n Dn' PD | P'S nS' PD Pn

11) SD' nP' Dm' Pg' | mR' gS' Rn' SD

12) SR' SR g'S Rg | m'S Rg mP' SR

13) SR' SR g'S Rg m'S Rg mP' SR gm PD' SR gm PD n'

S Rg mP Dn S'S D'n P'D m'P g'm R'g SR | nD

Zila Kafi, medium gat, concluded

```
      +                  2                     o                  3
14) ‖: S SS S SS | SR n -- -- | S SS S SS | SR nD -- -- :‖
       I  Λ I  Λ   I - I        I  Λ I  Λ   I - I -

    +
‖: Dn -n' DS -S' nR -R' nS -S :‖
   I I · -   ⁒

    +
‖: -D Dn' -D DS' -n nR' -n nS :‖
   ·I I I    ⁒

   +              2                o                  3
‖: SR -R SR -R | SR g -- -- | SR -R SR -R | SR n -- -- :‖
   I I · - I I · - I - I      ⁒

   +             2                o                 3
‖: SR Gm Gm -- | SR gm Rg -- | SR Sg R -- | nS nR S -- :‖
   I -

  +             2                                  +
[ Rm P-] 2x  [R- Rm -m P- P] 2x  P- Dn -n | S
              I · -
```

gat 2x

```
 +            (+)
[-D -n PD nn S- -- ] 3x, end
```

N.B. Rag Zila Kafi is a mixture of the rags Zila, whose primary movement is **D n P D n S**, and Kafi.

KHAMMAJ

The number of rags in the Khammaj (*khammāj, khambāj*) family is enormous—one of the largest groups of rags. Most of these rags are full shringar ras (here, romantic love), and so the rag is ideal for light classical music where this mood is primary. The main rag itself is sung in all three main styles. Often the light classical rags will use only the main features of rag Khammaj, and ignore its melodic subtleties: that is, these lighter interpretations will allow shuddh **re** in ascent, and omit **G m P G m R S,** the phrase which is used as a closing cadence in dhrupad-style Khammaj. Also, additional notes may be added, such as komal **ga**, and sometimes the two **n**is may be used adjacently, anomolous in most strictly classical rags. Khammaj is also sung from the note **ma** in light classical music. When combined with the rag Manj to form Manj Khammaj, this effect of **ma** as the tonic is very strong.

*Khammaj is a 'janpriya' (popular) rag—full of pathos and love and joy, and everyone likes that. In lighter styles you can end **G R S**, but in dhrupad style you must come **G m P G m R S**.*

Rag Khammāj

That: **Khammaj** **(both ni's)**

Jati: **sharav-sampurn**

Vadi: **G** Samvadi: **N**

Ang: **purvang**

Time: **evening (8 pm-midnight)**

Mood: **shṛingār, karuna**

Pakaṛ: G m P D G m G

Arohi-Avarohi: S G m P D N Ṡ Ṡ n D P m G R S

"More complete": Ṇ S G m P D N Ṡ
Ṡ n D P D G m G' G m P G m R S

Chalan: Ṇ S G m P D G m G -- G m n D P D N Ṡ

Ṡ -- n D P D G m G -- G m P G m R S

Sargam in tintal M.100

Asthai

```
  +          2                o                3
‖: G G S G | m P G m | n D — m | P D — m

  +          2                o                3
G — — — | D N S — | S n D P | m G R S :‖
```

Antara

```
                              o                3
                          ‖: G m D N | S' D N S
  +          2                o                3
D N S R | n N D — :‖ — G — m | G R S n
  +          2                o                3
D — m' G | — S' D N | S' G — m | G R S —
```

guru dayala - **chautal**

गुरू दयाल आयो
शरण भर भर परत दास
तुम्हारो शुभ कमल चरण

दजि स्वर ज्ञान पुर्ण
शुद्ध कर सुर कंठ भरण
तुम्हारो चतुर करूँ सुमिरण

gurū dayāla āyo
sharaṇa bhara bhara parata dāsa
tumhāro shubha kamala charaṇa

dije svāra gyāna purṇa
shuddha kara sura kaṇṭha bharaṇa
tumhāro chatura karū̃ sumiraṇa

My guru has arrived.
At his auspicious lotus feet
This servant takes shelter.

Endow me with the full knowledge of notes,
Fill my voice with pure melody.
I cherish thee in my mind, O Master.

Dhrupad in chautal M.69

Asthai

+ o 2 o 3 4
‖: G G | — mGm- | P — | P — | DP-n DP-D | m G :‖
gu- rū da- yā- la ā- yo

+ o 2 o 3 4
m m | m — | DP Ṡn | DPD- P | P--D--N- | --Ṡ--Ṡ--
sha-ra- ṇa bha- ra bha- ra pa- ra- ta dā- sa

+ o 2 o 3 4
N N | Ṡ — | N Ṡ | Ṙ Ṡn | DP PD | m G
tum- hā- ro shu-bha ka- ma- la cha- ra- ṇa

Antara

+ o 2 o 3 4
‖: G m | n D | n D | n D | P P | D P
di- je svā- ra gyā- na pur- ṇa

+ o 2 o 3 4
P D | N N | Ṡ N | Ṡ — | Ṡ Ṡ | Ṡ Ṡ :‖
shud-dha ka- ra su- ra kaṇ- ṭha bha- ra- ṇa

+ o 2 o 3 4 +
Ṡ ĠṘ | Ġ — | Ġ ṁ | ṁ — | Ġ Ṙ | Ġ N | ᴰN Ṡ
tum- hā- ro cha- tu- ra ka- rū su- mi-

o 2 o 3 4
Ṡ Ṡ | Ṡ--Ṙ n | D P | P--D GP | m G
ra- ṇa, su- mi- ra- ṇa, su- mi- ra- ṇa

khammaja raga **- tintal**

खम्माज राग सब मिले गावो
आरोही गन्धार मध्यम पंचम धैवत शुद्ध निशाद
अवरोही कोमल निशाद धैवत पंचम मध्यम गन्धार
गा मा पा गा मा रे सा

वादी गन्धार समवादी निशाद
करूण श्रंगार रस में भरी
गावो सब गावो

khammāja rāga saba mile gāvo
ārohī: gandhāra madhyama
panchama dhaivata shuddha nishāda
avarohī : komāla nishāda dhaivata
panchama madhyama gandhāra
gā mā pā gā mā re sā

vādī gandhāra samavādī nishāda
karuṇa shringāra rasa mẽ bharī
gāvo, saba gāvo, saba mile gāvo

Let everyone sing together rag Khammaj.
Arohi: gandhara, madhyama, panchama,
dhaivata, shuddha nishada;
Avarohi: komal nishada, dhaivata,
panchama, madhyama, gandhara;
ga ma pa ga ma re sa.

Vadi gandhara, samvadi nishada,
Full of pathos and feelings of love,
Everyone sing together.

Lakshangit in tintal M. 288

Asthai

\+ 2 o 3
𝄆 G — m — | P m — G | — m G R | — S S —
kham- mā- ja rā- ga sa- ba mi- le gā-

\+ 2 o 3
S — — G | — G m — | m P D G | P m — G 𝄇
vo, gā - vo, gā- vo, sa- ba mi- le gā - vo

\+ 2 o 3
G — m — | P — — D | m — — P | G — — —
ā- ro- hī

\+ 2 o 3
G — G — | G m — m | — m P — | P — P D
gan- dhā- ra ma- dhya- ma pan- cha- ma dhai-

\+ 2 o 3
— D — D | N — N N | N — Ṡ — | — — Ṡ Ṙ
va- ta shud- dha ni- shā- da a- va

\+ 2 o 3
n — D P | P — n — | n n n n | — n D —
ro- hī ko- mā- la ni- shā- da dhai-

\+ 2 o 3
D D — — | P — P P | — — m — | m m — —
va- ta pan- cha- ma ma- dhya- ma

\+ 2 o 3
G — G — | — — G — | G m P G | m R S —
gan- dhā- ra sargam

lakshangit, concluded

Antara

+ 2 o 3
‖: G m n — | D P D — | N — — — | Ṡ — Ṡ —
vā - *dī* *gan-* *dhā-* *ra*

+ 2 3
N — N — | Ṡ N Ṙ — | Ṡ N Ṙ Ṡ | n — D — :‖
sa- *ma-* *vā-* *dī* *ni-* *shā-* *da*

+ 2 3
Ġ — Ġ — | Ġ — ṁ — | Ġ -Ṙ Ṡ — | — — Ṡ —
ka- *ru-* *ṇa* *shṛin-* *gā-* *ra*

+ o 3
N — N — | Ṡ N Ṙ — | Ṡ N ṘṠ NṠ | nD Ṡn DP D-
ra- *sa* *mē* *bha-* *rī*

+ 2 o 3
Ḋ — Ṙ — | — — Ṙ Ġ | N — — — | Ṡ — — —
gā- *vo* *sa-* *ba* *gā-* *vo*

+ 2 3
N — N — | Ṡ N Ṙ — | Ṡ n D P | m G R S
sa- *ba* *mi-* *le* *gā-* *vo*

lagana lage - **tintal**

लगन लागे पिया तोरे दरसन को
मोरे जिया मानत नहीं नहीं नहीं
राह तक तक तेहारी रे पिया

चंद्र बदन मृग नयन मोरे पिया
वारी वारी जाऊँ मैतो
वारी वारी जाऊँ मैतो

lagana lāge piyā tore darasana ko
more jiyā manata nahī, nahī, nahī
rāha taka taka tehārī re piyā

chandra badana mṛiga nayana more piyā
vārī vārī jāū̃ maito, vārī vārī jāū̃ maito

O Love, my soul yearns to have a glimpse of you;
My heart knows no peace at all.
I spend my time watching for you.

Luminous as the moon,
Your eyes soft as a deer, my love;
I give myself to you.

Thumri (classical style) in tintal M.132

Asthai

o   3   +   2

‖: Gm n D P | — P P D | G m G R | G m P — :‖

la - ga- na lā-   ge pi- yā   to - re   da- ra- sa- na   ko

o   3   +   2

Gm n D n | P D N Ṡ | n DP — D | Pm — P mG :‖

mo- re ji- yā   ma- na- ta   na- hī,   na- hī,   na- hī,

o   3   +   2

D — D D | n D P D | Ṡ NRSNS — nD P | P D m G

ra-   ha ta- ka ta- ka te- hā-   rī   re   pi- yā

Antara

o   3   +   2

‖: N — N N | N N N D | N Ṡ — Ṡ | ṠṘ n D P

chan- dra ba- da- na mṛi- ga na- ya-   na mo- re pi- yā

o   3   +   2

N Ġ Ṙ Ġ | ṘṠ N N | ṠṘ n D | P D m G

vā- rī vā- rī jā- ū mai- to vā- rī vā- rī jā- ū mai- to

kauna sune - chachar

कौन सुने यह बात हमारे
समरथ और न देखो
तुम बिना और न देखो
कासो बिथा कहुँ तो बनवारी

kauna sune yaha bāta hamāre
samaratha aura na dekho
tuma binā aura na dekho
kāso bithā kahū to banavārī

Who will listen to these words of mine?
None but you (O Krishna) is capable.
Without you there is no one;
To whom else could I bare my sorrow?

Thumri in chachar M.108

Asthai

o 3 + 2
‖: G G m | P D N Ṡ | N — — | N — — N
kau- na su- ne ya- ha bā- ta ha-

o 3 + 2
Ṡ — — | Ṡ — Ṡ Ṙ | n DP D | m — G — :‖
mā- re, ya- ha bā- ta ha- mā- re

o 3 + 2
G G m | P — — — | Gm P D | m — G —
sa- ma- ra- tha au- ra na de- kho

o 3 + 2
D n D | nD n D P | P P D | m — G —
tu- ma bi- nā au- ra na de- kho

o 3 + 2
N N N | Ṡ — NS R | nD P D | m — G —
kā-so bi - thā kā - hū to ba- na -vā- rī

Tarana in slow tintal M.60

Asthai


```
        3                           +
‖: GG | m  PP  D  GmPD | N--D  N   S
   de re  na  de re na  ta di ya na re        ta

           2                      o
   SR | Sn  DP  Gm  PD | G ᴾ m   G  :‖
   da re  da  ni  da  ni   da        ni
        3/2                    +/o
‖: N N | S  S R n-DP PDNS | N ᴰ N   S:‖
   de re  na  de re na    ta di ya na da      ni
```

Antara

```
   +/o                      2/3
‖: G  mm  nnDD  P D | N  NN  ṠN  Ṡ:‖
   dim ta na deri deri  ta  na  dim ta na  de re  na

   +         ᴰ                  2
   P N N N  Ṡ N  Ṡ | N Ṡ N Ṡ ṠNRṠNṠ n D
   dim dim  de re na  ta di ya na re  ta      da re

   o
   D Ġ -Ġ mGRG N Ṡ | N Ṡ N Ṡ ṠNRṠNṠ n D
   ta dim dim ta     na na  de re na ta da re   da ni

   +              2
   P D  P Ṡ -n D P | Gm  PD Gm G-
   ta dim     ta na na  de re  na ta de re  na

   o
   NSGm PDNṠ  N Ṡ
   ta di ya na re ta da re da ni
```

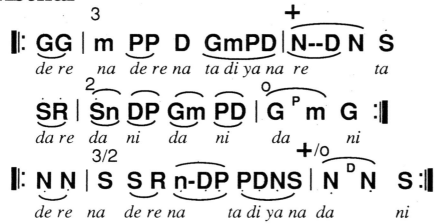

Tarana in tintal M.256, set to M.128

Asthai

+ 2 o 3
[: P N S NR | S n D P | n D P m | m G S R
o de na tom ta na na de re na de re na de re

+ 2 o 3
G — — G | — G — m | G R G — | mm mm P — :]
da ni de re da ni deri deri tom

+ 2 o 3
P n D n | P D N S | ND N S' SN | R — S n
dig klan ta da re da ni da ni dim ta na

+ 2 o 3
D P' PD n | — D P m | G' Gm P — | m G R S :]
na na dim ta na na na dim ta na na na

asthai, pt. 2

+ 2 o 3
||: G m G m | G m G m | GR -G R- G- | m m P —
na der da ni na der da ni dim dim ta de re na

+ 2 o 3
— n — D | — P' D — | P — m' P | — m — G :||
ta da re ta da re ta da re

+ 2 o 3
P n D n | D n D n | P — D — | N — S' P
dig klan ta da re da ni da re da ni da

+ 2 o 3
D N — S' | P — D N | — S' P — | D N — S
re da ni da re da ni da re da ni

first line of asthai, then antara

Tarana, antara, concluded

+ 2 o 3
‖: D — n D | — n P D | N -D N — | Ṡ — — —
dim ta dim ta da re da ni

+ 2 o 3
N N N — | — N N N | — N Ṡ NṠ | Ṙ n — D :‖
ya la loom ya la loom ya la le

+ 2 o 3
Ġ ĠĠ ĠĠ' Ġ | ĠĠ ĠĠ' ĠĠ ĠĠ | ṁ- -ṁ - - ṁ- | — — — —
dha kita taka dhum kita taka ga di ge na dha dha dha

+ 2 o 3
Ġ ĠĠ ĠĠ' Ġ | ĠĠ ĠĠ' NN ṘṘ | Ṡ — — Ṡ | — — Ṡ —
dha kita taka dhum kita taka ga di ge na dha dha dha

+
[ṠN ṠR ṠṠ nn D D P' nn DD PP mm m m m'
tete kata gadi gena dha dha dha, ٪

(+)
DD PP mm GG G G G —] 3x sam of tihai is second sam of asthai
٪ *(da)*

Gat in chachar tal M.120

```
    +          2               o           3
1) |: G G — | G — m m | G R — | G — m m
    +          2               o           3
      P — — | P — P D | G P — | m — G — :|

    +          2               o           3
2) |: D D — | D — D — | n D — | P — P —
    +          2               o           3
      G m — | P D N Ṡ | P D — | m — G — :|
```

Play these first and second lines with the repeat scheme **aabb aabb a**, then the antara (next), then each successive numbered line with the 1st line (two cyles of tal—called the "gat") after each new line. Occasionally, play both first and second lines together as a unit.

Antara

```
    +          2               o           3
3) |: G m — | n — D — | P D — | N — Ṡ —
    +          2               o           3
      N — — | N — N — | Ṡ N — | Ṡ — Ṡ — :|
    +          2               o           3
      P P — | Ṡ N ṘṠ NṠ | n D — | P — P —
    +          2               o           3
      G m — | P — D G | G Pm Pm | G — S —
```

chachar gat, continued

```
          +          2              o          3
4)     ‖: S  n  D | P  m  G  — | G  m  P | D  N  S  —
          +
          N  S  G | m  —  P  — | G  m  P | D  m  G  — :‖

          +          2              o          3
       ‖: G  m  P | P  —  —  — | m  P  D | D  —  —  —
          +
          P  D  n | m  P  D  — | G  m  P | D  —  G  — :‖

          +          2              o          3
          G  m  P | D  N  S  — | S  n  D | P  m  G  —
          +              (+)
        [ N  S'  N  S  — ] 3x, gat

          +          2              o          3
5)     ‖: P  P  — | P  —  D  — | G  m  — | P  —  P  —
          +
          S  G  m | P  —  P  — | S  n  D | P  —  P  — :‖

          +          2              o          3
       ‖: P  G  — | G  —  G  — | G  m  R | G  m  P  —
          +
          m  D  P | G  P  m  — | G  P  m | S  m  G  —
          +
          n  D'  n | P'  D  m'  P | G'  m  R' | S  G  m  P :‖

          +          2              o          3
       ‖: P  S  n | D  D  D  — | m  n  D | P  P  P  —
          +
          G  D  P | m  m  m  — | P  m  R | P  m  G  — :‖

          +            (14th)
          —  — [ S  G  m  P ] 3x, gat
```

chachar gat, continued

6) +
|: G G G | mm mm mm mm | n n n | DD DD DD DD
I I I ^ ^ ^ ^ %
P P P | DD DD NN NN | S S S | NN NN SS SS :|

+
|: m m m | GG GG GG GG | P P P | mm mm mm mm
m D P | GG PP mm mm | P D n | GG mm GG GG :|

+
|: G m P | DD DD DD DD | m P D | nn nn nn nn
G m P | DD NN SS SS | N N N | nn nn DD DD :|

+
S G m | P D N S | NN NN NN | n D P —
I I I I I I I ^ ^ ^ I I I

[G m P D n] 2x Gm P D N (14th) **gat**
I I I I I I – I I I

7) Short tans, taken from the second sam of the gat

a. + NN SS G m P D N S n D P m GR S- | + **gat**
^ ^ % I – I

b. + SS GG m P D N S Sn D- nD P- DP mG RS RS | + **gat**
^ ^ % I – I I – I I – I – I –

c. + |: SG SG m-' SG mP SG mP'
I –
Gm Gm P-' Gm PD Gm PD :|

+ (+)
[Gm PD G G G] 3x, **gat**
I – I – I I I

chachar gat, concluded

```
    +/o
7) |: D D — | D n D — | P P — | P D P —
    o/+
      m m — | P m G — :|

     +          2                 o           3
   |: N N N | N n D — | n n n | n D P —

      D D D | D P m — | P P — | P m G — :|

     +        2                    o           3
   |: S G m | P — — — | G m P | D — — —

      Ṡ n D | P — — — | n D P | m G — — :|

     +
   [ S G m P — — m G — — ] 2x
        o                  +
      S | G m P | — — — m | G
```

gat, end; or continue on and play fast gat in tinta

Gat in medium fast tintal M.196

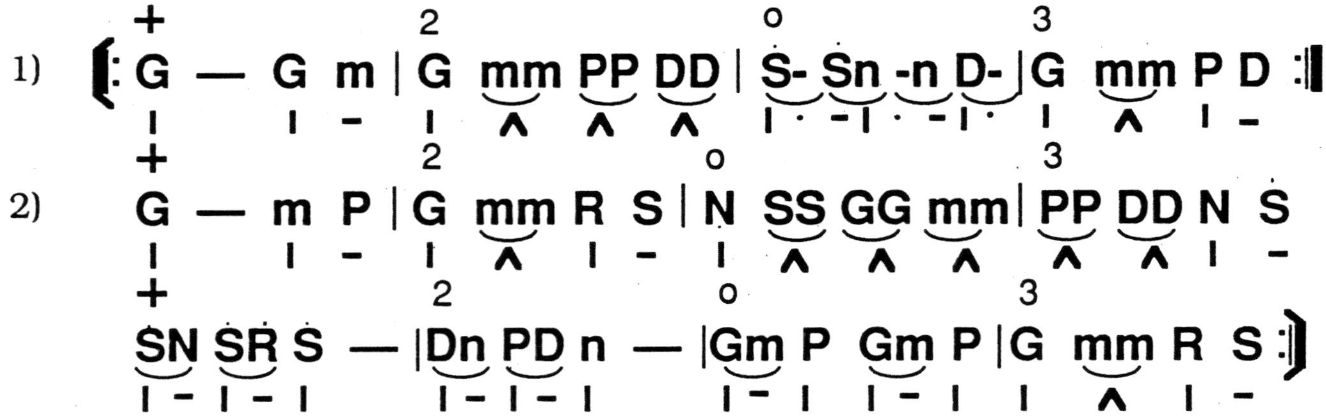

These first two lines comprise the gat proper, and the following variations, shaped by bols, are tora or tora tans. When returning to the gat, the first line may be played alone, with occasional repetitions of both lines together.

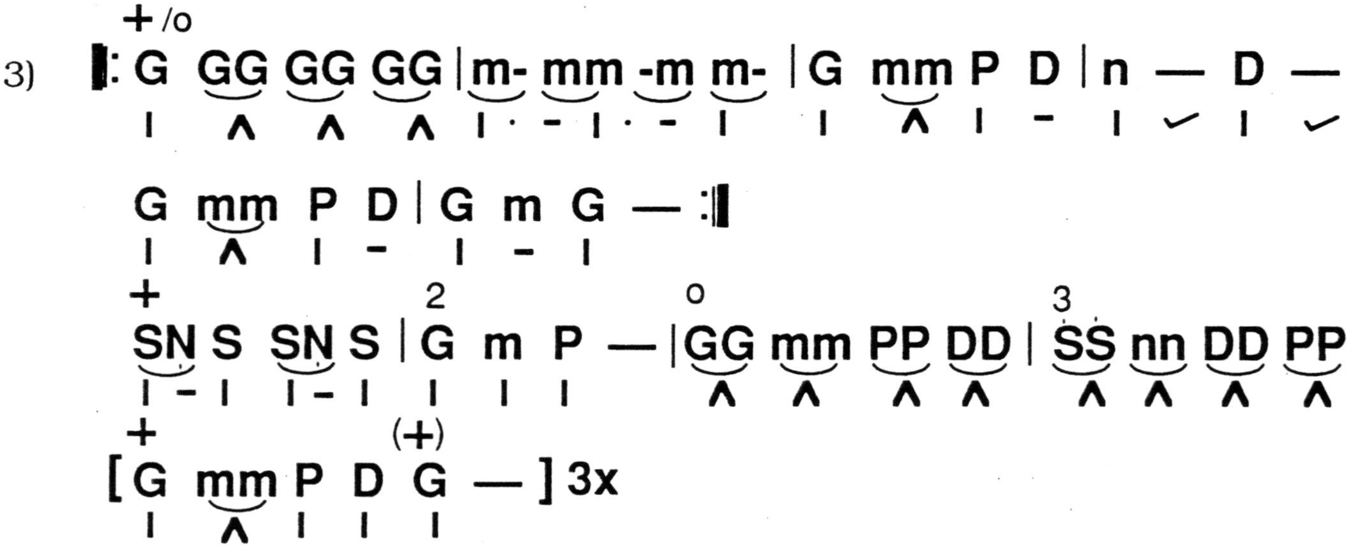

gat in tintal, continued

‖: [P- PP -P P-] 2x n- nD -D P- Pm -m GG GG :‖

‖: G- Gm -m G- GP -P m- mD -D P- Pn -n| DD PP mm G- :‖

[Gm Gm PD Gm G S] 3x, gat

‖: S nn D n| P D P —| G — m —| P D N S

P GG GG GG| m — G —| N — n —| D — P — :‖

‖: P m G —| G P m —| m D P —| G P m G

GG GG GG GG| n nn n —| D nn P D| N S N S :‖

[NS -S Gm -m G —] 3x, gat

‖: GG G'G GG' GG| m ⁒ | PP P'D DD' DD | mG ⁒ :‖

‖: DD D'D DD' DD | P ⁒ | D ⁒ | m ⁒ | Pm ⁒ | G ⁒ :‖

‖: mm mD DD PP | GPm ⁒ | RmG ⁒ | S G m P :‖

‖: Dn D Dn D | PDP ⁒ | mPm ⁒ | GG Gm mm GG :‖

‖: NN N'N NN' NN | S ⁒ | PP PD DD mm mP PP mm GG :‖

[SS SG GG mm mP PP GG mm G — — —] 3x, gat

gat in tintal, continued

Play gat four times, accelerating to jhala speed

Jhala (all I ✓✓✓)

7)
```
    +
‖: G ✓✓✓| G ✓✓✓| m ✓✓✓| P ✓✓✓
   G ✓ m ✓| P ✓✓✓| G ✓ m ✓| G ✓✓✓ :‖

   +       2        o        3
‖: Ṇ ✓✓✓| Ṇ ✓✓✓| S ✓✓✓| S ✓✓✓
   S ✓ ṇ ✓| Ḍ ✓ P̣ ✓| Ḍ ✓ Ṇ ✓| S ✓✓✓ :‖

   +
‖: S ✓✓✓| G ✓✓✓| m ✓✓✓| P ✓✓✓
   G ✓✓✓| m ✓✓✓| P ✓✓✓| D ✓✓✓
   n ✓✓✓| n ✓✓✓| D ✓✓✓| D ✓✓✓
   G ✓✓✓| m ✓✓✓| P ✓✓✓| D ✓✓✓
   G ✓✓✓| m ✓✓✓| G ✓✓✓| G ✓✓✓ :‖

   +                                 +          +
‖: G ✓✓✓| m ✓✓✓| P ✓✓✓| P ✓✓✓| mPD ⁒ | PDn ⁒
   D ✓✓✓| m ✓✓✓| P ✓✓✓| G ✓✓✓ :‖

   +
‖: N ✓✓✓| Ṡ ✓✓✓| N ✓✓✓| Ṡ ✓✓✓
   Ṡ ✓✓✓| Ṡ ✓✓✓| n ✓✓✓| D ✓✓✓
   G ✓✓✓| m ✓✓✓| P ✓✓✓| Ṡ ✓✓✓
   n ✓✓✓| D ✓✓✓| m ✓✓✓| G ✓✓✓ :‖
```

gat in tintal, concluded

```
  +          2         o           3
‖: m ✓✓✓ |D✓ P✓ |G ✓✓✓ |P✓ m✓

   R ✓✓✓ | P✓ m✓ |G ✓✓✓ |G ✓✓✓ :‖
   +
   G✓G✓ |m✓ D✓ |P ✓✓✓ |P ✓✓✓

   G✓G✓ |m✓ P✓ |m ✓✓✓ |m ✓✓✓

   R✓R✓ |G✓m✓ |G ✓✓✓ |G ✓✓✓   no repeat
   +
   G G G G | m✓D✓ |P ✓✓✓ |P ✓✓✓
   I I I I
    +              +
   GmPm ⁒        |RGmG ⁒          no repeat
   +
‖: Ṡ ✓✓✓ | n ✓✓✓ | D ✓✓✓ |P ✓✓✓

   G✓ m✓ |P✓ D✓ G✓ m✓ |G ✓✓✓ :‖
   +
‖: Ġ ✓✓✓ | Ṙ ✓✓✓ |n ✓✓✓ |D ✓✓✓

   G✓m✓ |P✓ D✓ |G✓m✓ |G✓✓✓ :‖
   +                 o       +
‖: G m G m|P ✓✓✓ |mPD ⁒ | PDn ⁒
   I I I I
   o                   2
   D✓✓ P✓✓m✓✓G✓✓Ṡ✓✓G✓✓ m✓✓P✓✓ :‖
   +                  3          o           2
‖: N✓✓ Ṡ✓✓n ✓✓ D✓✓'|PDGm ⁒ | GmPD ⁒ |NṠNṠ ⁒ :‖
   +
‖: Ṡ✓✓n✓✓D ✓' | nDP ⁒ | DPm ⁒ | PmG ⁒ :‖
   +/3
‖: Ṡ✓✓ n✓D✓'    nDP ⁒   DPm ⁒ PmG ⁒ :‖
   o
‖: ✓Ṡ✓✓ n✓D✓' | nDP ⁒ |DPm ⁒|PmG ⁒ :‖
   o              +
[ Ṡ Ġ ṁ Ṗ ] 2x ‖: N Ṡ N Ṡ  D n D n  P D P D m P m P :‖
  I I I I          I I I I  etc.
   +                                                            (+)
[ Ṡ Ġ — m P D — N Ṡ✓✓Ṡ Ṡ Ṡ Ṡ✓✓Ṡ Ṡ Ṡ Ṡ✓✓Ṡ Ṡ Ṡ Ṡ] 3x
  I I   etc.                                                    end
```

Two of the great masters of the early twentieth century: Benares tabla master Pandit Kanthe Maharaj and Baba Allauddin Khansahib.

Iman Kalyan

Iman Kalyan (or *Yaman Kalyān*) is a rag of the Kalyan *prakār* (type, family), a large and centrally important group of evening rags. It is very close to the rag *Yaman*, but differs in that it introduces a very slight shuddh **ma** in closing phrases, and generally avoids the ascending progression **sa-re-ga** (using **ni-re-ga** instead). Iman Kalyan is a serious rag full of pathos and devotion. Its notes are all very strong and make important combinations in **ga-ni, ma-ni, pa-sa,** and **dha-re**. It is filled with the blossom of evening, and its practice should be restricted to this time.

From 75,000 ragas, think of Iman Kalyan as the number one rag of the evening. Kalyan means "blessing." Yaman rag is like Kalyan ṭhāṭ–the notes are there in a straight line. But in Iman Kalyan you just touch the shuddh ***ma*** *from* ***ga*** *when you are closing. Then it is different from Yaman, you see.*

Rag Iman Kalyan

That: **Kalyan**

Jati: **sampurn**

Vadi: **G** Samvadi: **N**

Ang: **purvang**

Time: **evening (8 pm to midnight)**

Mood: **bhakti, shanti, shriṇgār, karuna**

Pakaṛ: **Ṇ R G — G M P — P M G R G -m G R S**

Arohi-Avarohi: **Ṇ R G M P D N Ṡ Ṡ N D P M G R S**

Ṇ R G M P D N Ṡ

Ṡ N D P M G -- G -m G R S

Chalan: **S -- Ṇ Ḍ P̣ ---- Ṃ Ḍ Ṇ R S --- Ṇ Ḍ Ṇ Ṙ G R --**

R G Ṇ R G -- M G M P -- P M G R -- G -m G R --

Ṇ Ḍ Ṇ R S --

Antara **M D N Ṙ Ṡ --- N Ṙ Ġ Ṙ Ṡ --- N D N Ṡ -- N D P --**

M N D N M D P -- M R G -- Ṇ R G M P M G R --

G -m G R ' Ṇ R S ---

Sargam in slow tintal M.50

Asthai

3 + 2 o

‖: N D N R | S (NRSNS) -- -- -- | N D N R | N D P (MDPMP) -- :‖

3 + 2 o

N D N R | G -- -- -- | R -- M -- | R -- G --

3 + 2 o

G M P D | N D P M | G -m G R | N R S --

Antara

2 o 3 +

‖: M -- G -- | P M D -- | M D N R (GR) | S -- -- -- :‖

2 o 3 +

N D N S | (D)N D P -- | M N D P | M R G --

2 o 3 +

G -- R -- | S (NRSNS) -- N D | N M G R | S N D P

2 o

M (G)R G -m | G R S --

dhyana daru - **chautal**

ध्यान दरूँ तेरो प्रभु
मेरे मौला गरीब नवाज़
दीन बन्धु रहिम करिम

तुही दाता तुही बिदाता
परवर दिगार तेरो
सेवक पर कृपा दृष्टि कीजिये

dhyāna darū tero prabhu
mere maulā garība navāza
dīna bandhu rahima karima

tuhī dātā tuhī bidātā
paravara digāra tero
sebaka para kripā dṛiṣti kījiye

I meditate on thee, Lord.
My Master, protector of the poor,
Dina Bandhu, Rahim Karim
(Compassionate Lord).

You provide and take away;
Nurturer of the distressed,
Cast a glance of grace
At this servant of yours.

Dhrupad in chautal M.63

Asthai

+ o 2 o 3 4
‖: S -- | N D | SN R | -- -- | G R | GR S :‖
dhyā- na da- rū te- ro,

+ o 2 o 3 4
P -- | M ᴳR | G^RG -- | -- ^RSN -- | ˢN ᴳR | GR S
dhyā - na da- rū te- ro,

+/2
‖: S -- | N D | ND P | -- -- | M ᴺD | ˢN ᴿD | ᴰS -- | -- -- :‖
dhyā -na da- rū te- ro,

3 4
R -- | GR S **repeat from beginning, then first line 1x, then**
pra- bhu

+/2
‖: P MG | M G | ᴹP -- | P -- | ᴰM ᴺD | N D | N-D P | P -- :‖
me - re mau- lā ga- rī- ba na- vā- za

3 4 + o 2 o 3 4
P -- | ᴹᴾM ᴳR | G -- | Gᵐ GR | ᴳN N | R R | G-R S | S --
dī- na ban- dhu ra- hi- ma ka- rī- ma

Antara

+/2
‖: ᴰM D | N D | N S | S -- | ᴿN R | G R | SN DN | ᴰᴾᴹP ᴹG :‖
tu - hī dā- ta tu- hī bi- dā- ta

3 4 + o 2 o 3 4
G ᴳG | R S | N ᴰN-D | P P | ᴰᴾM -- | Gm GR | N R | G M
pa- ra- va- ra di- gā- ra te- ro se- ba- ka

+ o 2 o 3 4
D N | R G | GRSN S - | NDPM P - | ᴿG R | SN S
pa- ra kṛi- pā dṛiś- ti kī- ji - ye

guru bina - **tintal**

गुरू बिन कैसे गुण गावे
गुरू ना माने तो गुण नहीं आवे
गुणियन में बेगुणी कहावे

माने तो रिझावे सब को
चरन गहे सादी कान के जब
आवे अचपल ताल सुर

gurū bina kaise guṇa gāve
gurū nā māne to guṇa nahī āve
guṇiyana mẽ beguṇi kahāve

māne to rijhāve saba ko
charana gahe sādi kāna ke jaba
āve achapala tāla sura

None can sing His praise without the help of the guru.
None can become adept without accepting the guru,
Or else among the wise would be called foolish.

One who submits to the guru pleases everyone,
And when one perserveres steadfastly
At the feet of the the guru,
There comes to the ear
Sureness in rag and tal.

Khyal in slow medium tintal M.96

Asthai

0 3 + 2

‖: MP P ᴹN D | PM D P -- | M ᴳR M ᴳM | P -- -- -- :‖

gu- rū bi- na kai- se gu- ṇa gā- ve

0 3 + 2

‖: MP PN D MP | -- M ᴿG R | G R GMP- ᴳR | SN R ᴳᴿ S :‖

gu- rū nā mā- ne to gu- ṇa na- hī ā- ve

0 3 + 2

SN S R R | G -- G M | P -- D N | ᴰᴾM Dᴺᴰ P -

gu- ṇi- ya- na mē be- gu- ṇi ka- hā- ve

Antara

0 3 + 2

[: P P M G | M ᴺD N -- | M D N R ᴳᴿ | S -- -- -- :‖

mā- ne to ri- jhā- ve sa- ba ko

0 3 + 2

S N G R | SN R S -- | N D N S | N D P P :]

cha- ra- na ga- he sā- dī kā- na ke ja- ba

0 3 + 2

PM G GM P | G R S S | NR GM PD NS | ND PM GR SS

ā - ve a- cha- pa-la tā- la su-ra

***mero mana bandha* - tintal**

मेरो मन बान्ध लिनो रे हारे
इन जोगिया के साथ रे

सदारंग करम करो
क्यूँ न इन प्राणनाथ के हाथ

mero mana bāndha lino re hāre

ina jogiyā ke sātha re

sadāranga karama karo

kyū̃ na ina prānanātha ke hātha

My heart has been captured;
It has been vanquished by the ascetic yogi.

Sadaranga says,
"Why not place yourself
In the hands of your Lord?"

Khyal in tintal M.72

Asthai

o + 2
‖: N D P M | GR SS --N- -R-- | G -- -- -- | M ᴳR M G :‖
me- ro ma- na bān- dha li- no re hā- re

o +
G M P P | P MN DN P MDPMP | GMD N -- S NRS | N ᴰP ᴹG --
i- na jo- gi- yā ke sā- tha re

Antara

o +
‖: M D N MDN | S -- S -- | N R R R | NG-R S-ND N--D P--- :‖
sa- dā- raṅ- ga ka- ra- ma ka- ro

+
G -- R N | GR S -- S | N DN-- D P | P-MG R ᴳM G
kyū na i- na prā- na- nā- tha ke hā- tha

Vistar (sing akar, "ah")

‖: S -- NRSNS -- | N -- -- -- | ᴰN D P -- | M D N R :‖

‖: S -- -- -- | R -- -- -- | G -- -- -- | G R S -- :‖

‖: M -- -- -- | G -- -- -- | P -- -- -- | M ᴳR G -- :‖

‖: D -- P -- | D -- M -- | P M G R | M - G -- :‖

‖: M -- D -- | N -- -- -- | NDPM GRG- M-D- N- | ᴰN D P -- :‖

+
NSN- DND- PDP- MPM-' | DND- MPM- RGR- S- - -

lagana lage — **tintal**

लगन लागी तोरी साजनवा
पाये परूँ तोरे मानजा

निठुर बलमा
कहा नहीं माने
मैतो गयी बिनति कर करत
मान जा

lagana lāgī torī sājanavā
pāye parū tore māna jā

niṭhura balamā kahā nahī māne
maito hāra gayī binati kara karata
māna jā

My love,
I am so attached to you.

But my unfeeling beloved
Does not listen to my words.
My repeated pleas have gone in vain.

Khyal in medium fast tintal M.160

Asthai

o 3 + 2
|: N R GR S | -- S N D | S -- S S | -- -- N D :|
la- ga- na lā- gī to- rī sā- ja- na- vā

o 3 + 2
N N N R | -- R G R | G -- G R | G -- -- --
la- ga- na lā- gī to- rī sā- ja- na - vā

o 3 + 2
N N M M | G G R G | ^RS^N -- R R | G -- -- --
la- ga- na lā - gī to- rī sā- ja- na - vā

o 3 + 2
|: P ^MDPMP^-- -- -- | M -- G -- | P -- M D | P -- -- -- :|
pāy pa- rū to- re

o 3 + 2
^D^N -- D P | --' ^M^D -- P | M -- --' P | M R G --
mā- na jā, mā- na jā, mā- na jā

Asthai

+ 2 o 3
|: M D N DN | S S S -- | N R G R | SN DN ^DPM^P -- :|
ni -ṭhu- ra ba- la- mā ka- ha na- hī mā- ne

+ 2 o 3
G R S NR | S S N N | N D N S | ND ND P P :|
mai- to hā- ra ga- yī bi- na- ti ka- ra ka- ra- ta

+ 2
S - ND -' N - D M -' G - RS - -
mā- na jā, mā- na jā, mā- na jā

Tarana in tintal M.176

Asthai

o 3 + 2
|: S- -N DP MG | RS N - - R - - | G -- -- M | --ᴳR G -- :|
dim ta na na na na na na na de re na de re na

o 2
[PM DPM P- M -- G] 2x | PM D P --
ta da re da ni

o 3 + 2
M D N -D | PM D P -- | ND PM GM PD | N -D P --
de re na de re na dim tom

o 3 + 2
SN S --' ND N --' DP D --' PM P --' | P ᴹᴰᴾᴹᴾ-- ᴿG R :|
de re na de re na de re na de re na de re

+ 2 o 3
|: P- -M -G M- GM -G MG M- | N- -D PP PP | P - MG MM G- :|
ta dim dim dim dim dim ta na na na na ta de re na

+
[P- MG MG' D- PM PM' N- DP DP' S- ND PM] 2x
ta de re na ⁒ ⁒ ⁒

o 3 + 6/4 2 6/4
NR GM DN RG ᴿˢᴺS -- -- -- | N S N S' D N | D P' M P M P
ta na dere, tana dere dim na der da ni, tum der da ni, na der da ni

o 6/4 6/4 + 2
R G R S' G - | - R - R S - | NR GM PD NS | RG RS ND PM
tum der da ni, ta de re na dim

o 3 + 2
GM G -- -- | SN DN S -- | -- PM GM P | -- SN DN S
tom ta na de re na ta na de re na ta na de re na

tarana, concluded

Antara

o 3 + 2
[|: P -- P P | -- M G M | D -- D D | PDN Ṡ Ṡ Ṡ :|
dim ta dim ta na na dim ta na dim ta na
o 3 + 2
Ṡ N D D | N Ṙ Ṙ -- | Ġ Ṙ ṠND NṘṠ | ND N DPM P :|]
u da ni ta da ni de re na de re na

o/+
|: P G R G | ṘṠNṠ -- -- -- | N D N Ṡ | N -D P --
ta di ya na re ta di ya na re
DPMP -- GR G | -- G G G :|
ta re da re da ni

o 3 + 2
|: NN NN R -- | GG RR G -- | P- P DP -P M - | M- M GR -R G -:|
te re ki ta tak te re ki ta tak te re ki ta tak te re ki ta tak
o 3 + 2
NR G - RG M - | GM D - MD N - | DN Ṙ - Ġ - - Ṙ | Ṡ -
de re na de re na de re na de re na de re na de re

6th
[NR GM PD NṠ' Ġ - ṘṠ - N Ṡ - -' N - DP - M P - -'
dhadhatete dhadhatuna te re ki ta tak te re ki ta tak

(8th)
G - RS - N Ṡ -] 3x
te re ki ta tak

***darasa bina tarase* - tintal**
(Meera Bhajan)

दरस बिन तरसे सखि नैन	श्यामला तम्हारो पन्थ निहारो
जबसे छोड़ गयो मोरे प्रभुजी	भायो छिन नासी रैन
कब हूँ ना पायो चैन	बिरहा बिथा कासो कहुं सजनी
सबद सुनत नित छतियाँ कांपे	बहा गयी आँसुअन नैन
मिठे लागे तोरे बैन	मीरा के प्रभु आवो प्राण
	दुख मेटन सुख देन

asthai	antara
darasa bina tarase sakhi naina	*shyāmalā tumhāro pantha nihāro*
jabase chhoṛa gayo more prabhujī	*bhāyo chhin nāsī raina*
kaba hū̃ nā pāyo chaina	*birahā bithā kāso kahū̃ sajanī*
sabada sunata nita chhaṭiyā̃ kāṇpe	*bahā gayī ansuana naina*
miṭhe lāge tore baina	*Mīra ke prabhu āvo prāne*
	dukha meṭana sukha denā

My eyes grow restless without catching a glimpse of him.
Since the day my Lord (Krishna) departed, I have had no peace of mind.
My heart quivers at every sound.
Even just your message sounds sweet.

O Shyamala, I ever watch for you.
My nights are completely shattered.
My friend, with whom can I share the pangs of separation?
Meera prays for her Lord to come and trade her sorrow for joy.

Bhajan (classical style) in tintal M.120

Asthai

o 3 + 2
G R S N | ᴺD -- S N | R -- PM DPMP | ᴳR -- S --
da- ra- sa bi- na ta- ra- se sa- khi nai- na

o 3 + 2
N R G G | -- R G G | N D P M | G R S --
ja- ba- se chho- ṛa ga- yo mo- re pra- bhu-jī

o 3 + 2
N R G M | P ᴺD N S | N D P M | G R S --
ka- ba hū nā pā- yo chai- na

o 3 + 2
M M G G | M M P M | P M D -- | NDPM GMN- -D P
sa- ba- da su- na- ta ni- ta chha-ṭi- yā kāṇ- pi

o 3 + 2
N -- S -- | N ᴰN ᴰP P | PMGR -- RGMP -- | ᴳR ᴳᴿ-- S --
mi- ṭhe lā- ge to- re bai- na

sing first line of asthai, then antara

Antara

o 3 + 2
M M G -- | P M D -- | MDNS -- S S | SN R S --
shyā-ma- lā tu- mā -ro pan- tha ni hā- ro

o 3 + 2
N N -- N | N -D N -- | MDNS -- -- ND | ᴾN-D P P --
bhā-yo chhin nā- sī rai- na

o 3 + 2
G G G R | G -- R G | ᴿˢN N -- D | N ᴳᴿR S --
bi- ra- hā bi- thā kā- so ka- hū sa- ja- nī

o 3 + 2
N N N N | N N N N | MDNS -- -- ND | N-D P P --
bā- ha ga- yī ān- su- a- na nai- na

o 3 + 2
M -- M -- | M D M G | N -- R - | PM GM G G
mī- rā ke pra- bhu ā- vo prā- ne

o 3 + 2
G m G R | G R N D | N -- Rᴳᴿ-- | S -- -- --
du- kha me - ṭa- na su- kha de- nā

Gat in medium tintal M.100

```
        +        2        o        3
‖: S N D | S SS S S | S' S N D | R RR R R | R'
   I I I I ^ I - I2 ⁄.     o        3
 NR -G R- | G GG G G | G' NR -G MP | R -- S -- | -- :‖
```

In the lines below, the five beat patterns which are below annotated with rests, may be played with bols as they are in the gat itself:

```
            +              2              o              3
2) ‖: NR -G R- | G -- -- -- | --' GM -P M- | P -- -- -- | --'
            +              2              o              3
      PM -G R- | M -- -- -- | --' MG -R S- | G -- -- -- | -- :‖

            +              2              o              3
3) ‖: S N D | P -- -- -- | --' M D S | N -- -- -- | --'
            +              2              o              3
      D N R^GR | S -- -- -- | --' SN -S N- | R -- -- -- | --'
            +              2              o              3
      NR -G R- | G -- -- -- | --' NR -G MP | R -- S -- | --' :‖

            + /o           2            N o              3
4) ‖: GM -P M- | P -- -- -- | --' PD -P D- | M -- -- -- | --'
            +                                  +             2
      MP -M P- | G^MG -- -- -- | -- :‖ ND -P M- | --' DP -M G- | --'
               o              3              +
      PM -G R- | --' Gm -G R- | --' DN -R S- | --'
               2              o              3
      NR -G R- | G -- -G MP | R -- S -- | --
```

medium gat, concluded

5)   NR -G MD | N^{+} -- -- -- | --'   ND -M D-ND | P^{o} -- -- -- | --'^{3}

     DN -M R- | M^{+} -- -- -- | --'^{2} MR -N M- | R^{o} N -- -- | --'^{3}

     GR -N R- | G^{+} -- -- -- | --'^{2} NR -G MP | R^{o} -- S -- | --'^{3}

Antara

6) ‖: MD -N S- | N^{+} -- -- -- | --'^{2} MD -N R-^{GR} | S^{o} -- -- -- | -- :‖^{3}

     NR -G R- | --'$^{+}$ DN -R S- | --'^{2} MD -S N- | --'^{o} GM -D P- | --'^{3}

     PM -G R- | G^{+} -- -- -- | --'^{2} Gm -G R- | N D^{o} -- -- -- | --'^{3}

     NR -G MP | R^{+} -- S -- | --'^{2} GM -G MP | R^{o} -- S -- | --^{3}

Gat in medium fast tintal M.160

```
    3              +            2            o
‖: N |-N R G M|P -- -- R|G R S --|G R S :‖
   |  .- |  |  - |      |  |  - |  |  - |

    +            2            o            3
2) ‖: D NN D S|N RR N S|N RR GG MM|G- GR -R S- :‖
    |  ^ |  - |  ^ |  - |  ^  ^  ^ |  .- | .- |.

    +            2            o
   PM GR G --|GR SN S --|GR SN S  gat

    +            2            o            3
3) ‖: P PP P P|M DD P P|PM GR G --|M -- G -- :‖
    |  ^ |  - |  ^ |  - | - | - |   |      |

    +            2            o
   ND N DP D|PM P MG M|GR G RS  gat
   | - |

    +              2              o              3
4) ‖: G- GG -G G-|N R G --|MM -G -R' MM -G -R' M G :‖
    | .- | .- |.  |  |  |  |  |  |  - |  |  |  - |  |  |

    +              2              o            3
‖: GM PM P --|MP DP D --|ND PM P --|M R G -- :‖

    +              2            o
   Ṡ ND N DP|D PM P MG|M GR S gat
```

Antara

```
    +              2            o            3    ⌢GṘ
5) ‖: M MM G G|M DD N D|Ṡ -- Ṡ Ṡ|N Ṙ Ṡ -- :‖
    |  ^ |  - |  ^ |  - |

    +            2            o            3  ⌢ND
   N R G Ṙ|Ṡ N D N|D N S NDP|M D  P --
```

repeat from beginning of antara, then go on to next page

medium fast gat, continued

```
+                  2                 o           3
PM GR G -- |GR SN S -- |NR G -- RG|M -- GM P

+
||: S- ND -P M- GR -S' SR GM PD NS :||
    I · - I · -

2                   o
SR G'R GM' GM P'M PD NS   gat
I - I             I - I - I
```

Tans **(da ra)**

```
      +                 2                  o
6)    RG RG RG RG |RG RG RS NS |G  R  S
      +                 2                  o
7)    MP MP MP MP |GM GM GM GM |RG RG RS
       +                    o
8)   [ND PM GR S- ] 2x  |G  R  S
      +                 2                   o
9)    SR GM PD NS' |SN DP MG RS |G  R  S
      +                 2                    o
10)   SR -R' RG -G'|GM -M' MP -P |G  R  S
      I I · -
      +                  2                      o
11)   PM P- -' P MP - -' PM P- - -' |G  R  S
      +                 2                      o
12)   SN S'P MP' SN S'P MP' S- P- |G  R  S
      I - I                  I  I
         +               2                o                 3
13) ||: PM GM P -- |PM GM D -- |PM GM N -- |MD PM P -- :||

      +                    2                      o
      NS NS' DN DN' |PD PD' MP MP |G  R  S
```

medium fast gat, continued

Accelerate slightly and play all da strokes

+ 2 o 3
14) ‖: D N D S | N R N S | G R N S | R S N S :‖

+ 2 o 3
‖: M M M M | M G R R | G G G G | G R S S :‖

+ 2 o 3
‖: G M P M | G M P M | G M P' G | M P' G M :‖

+ 2 o 3
‖: M D P -- | P D M -- | M P G -- | G M R -- :‖

+ 2 o 3
‖: N N N N | N D P M' | D D D D | D P M G'

+ 2 o 3
P P P P | P M G R' | M -- G' M | -- G' M G :‖

+ 2 o 3
N R G M | D N R G | M P M G | R S N D

+ 2 o 3 +
P M G R | S' NR GM P-' | NR GM P-' N | -- R G M | P gat

+ o 3
15) ‖: [N S S S] 2x | D S S S | N R S S :‖

+ + 2
‖: [N R R R] 4x N R G R [N R S S] 3x :‖

+ 2 o 3
‖: D S S S | N R R R | N G G G | N R R R :‖

+ 2 o 3
‖: N R' N G' | N M' N G' | N R' N S' | D S' N S :‖

+ o 3
‖: [N M N M] 2x N M G R | N R S S :‖

+ 2 o 3
‖: P P P P | P M G R | M M M M | M G R S :‖

+ 2 o 3
‖: PM P -- PM | P M G R | MP M -- MP | M G R S :‖

+ 2 o 3
‖: MP M -- PD | P -- DN D | -- PD P -- | M G R S :‖

+ 2 o 3
‖: PM PM P -- | DP DP D -- | ND ND N -- | PM GR S -- :‖

+ (11th)
[P- S- ND PM GR S- NR GM P-] 3x

medium fast gat, concluded

Jhala

16) ‖: [N ✓✓✓] 4x S ⁒ :‖: D ✓✓✓ N ✓✓✓ R ✓✓✓ S ✓✓✓ :‖

‖: N ✓R ✓G ✓R ✓G ✓✓✓G ✓✓✓ | NRGRSS ⁒ :‖

‖: [M ✓✓] 4x M ✓✓✓ | M ✓G ✓R ✓✓✓G ✓✓✓G ✓✓✓ :‖

‖: [P ✓P ✓] 4x G ✓✓✓M ✓✓✓P ✓✓✓P ✓✓✓ :‖

‖: D ✓D ✓D ✓D ✓P ✓✓✓P ✓✓✓' | DM ⁒ | PG ⁒ :‖

‖: M ✓D ✓N ✓D ✓M ✓D ✓P ✓✓✓

P ✓M ✓G ✓R ✓M ✓✓✓ G ✓✓✓ :‖

‖: [M M M M] 4x [P ✓✓✓] 4x :‖: DP ⁒ DM ⁒ PG ⁒ :‖

^ ^ ^ ^

‖: M ✓✓✓D ✓✓✓N ✓D ✓N ✓✓✓ [S ✓✓✓] 4x :‖

‖: N R G M P D N S [S ✓✓✓] 4x :‖

‖: N R G R S N D P M G R S' M D N N [S ✓✓✓] 4x :‖

‖: PM P -- P| ✓✓✓✓ | DPD ⁒ | PMP ⁒ | GRG ⁒ :‖

‖: N R G M P D N S N D P M G R S -- :‖

[M D N S -- M D N S -- -- --] 3x

(11th)

3rd x S -- -- [M D N S -- --] 7x

7th N |-- R G M | P

12th

Gat 2x, then [N -- R G M P -- --] 3x, end

Puriya Dhanashri

Puriya Dhanashri (*pūriyā dhanāshrī*) is the main rag of the Purvi family of rags, which are played at twilight, "at the first lighting of the lamps." These rags usually feature komal **re**, shuddh **ga**, and shuddh **ni**, along with tivra **ma**, the note which typically distinguishes the evening from the morning rags of *sandhyāprakāsh*, "the meeting of the light"— that is, dawn and sunset. Puriya Dhanashri may have long ago been a combination of the separate rags Puriya and Dhanashri, but even though the shadow of rag Puriya can be felt strongly in the lower tetrachord, most modern versions of Dhanashri are in Kafi and Bilawal *thāṭ*s, and do not appear to be directly related.

My father taught Puriya Dhanashri in this way, which is different from the khyal style of this rag. The feature ***M d r N d P*** *is very strong in my father's picture of the rag, but not so in other versions. Puriya Dhanashri is a serious rag, filled with devotion and pathos.*

Rag Puriya Dhanashri

That: **Purvi**

Jati: **vakra sampurn**

Vadi: **P** Samvadi: **S**

Ang: **purvang**

Time: **after sunset (7- 10 pm)**

Mood: **bhakti, shṛingār, karuna**

Pakaṛ: **M d ṙ N d P M G M r G**

Arohi-Avarohi: **Ṇ r G M P d N Ṡ Ṡ N d P M G r G r S**

Ṇ r G M P d P' M d N Ṡ
Ṡ N d P M G M r G ' G r S

Chalan: **S -- Ṇ r G -- M r G -- M P -- Ṇ r G M P --**

P d P -- d M d N -- Ṡ ------ Ṡ N d P --

M d ṙ N d P --- M G M r G -- r G M d M G --

^{r}G ---- ^{G}r ---- S ----

Sargam in rupak M.72

Asthai

```
    2      o        1        2         o          1       2
‖: M  d | ṙ  N  d | P  MG | -M r - | G -- -- | GM d | M  G
   o         1       2        o           1           2
   r  G  r | S  -- | -- -- | N - - r - - | G - - M | - -' r -
   o                 1
   G  M  P | -- -- :‖
```

Antara

```
    o         1        2       o       1      2
‖: M  --  d | N -- | M  d | N  Ṡ -- | -- -- | -- --
   o            1         2      o        1       2        o          1       2
   N  ṙ  G  | Ġ  ṙ | S  -- | N  d  N | ṙ  N | d  P | M  G  M | r  G | -- -- :‖
   o            1        2         o
   Ṁ  Ġ  ṙ  | N  d | P'  Md | ṙ      (asthai from first sam)
```

Rama japo re - dhamar

राम जपो रे बाँवरे

rāma japo re bāṇvare

O wanderer, take the name of Ram.

Dhamar M.72

Asthai

```
     o              3                    +                         2
𝄆: M d r̄ | N d    - - P - - P - - | P  - -  - -  MG Mr | G  - - :𝄇
   rā-      ma       ja-   po    re
                                        +                         2
                         2nd x  P  - -  - -  - -  M | GM  r
                                re             bāṇ-      va-

     o              3              +                    2
   G  - -  - - | r G M d | M G  - -ʳM G | r S
   re            rā-       ma      ja- po re
```

Vistars

```
      o              3                    +                         2
1)  rGM P  - - | P  - -  - -  PMd- | P  - -  - -  dP - d | M  - -
    rā-          ma           ja- po re,

      o              3                  +                         2
    M  - -  - - | M  - -  M  Pᴹᴾ| ᴳM  G  - -  rGM- GMd- | M d P
    rā-           ma          ja- po    re,      bāṇ-           va-  re

      o                3                    +                      2
2)  r S  - -  - - | r M G r  S  - - | S  - -  - -  - -  - - | Ṇ d
    rā-                          ma                          ja- po

      o              3                   +                        2
    N  - -  - - | - -  - -  d N r N | - -ᵈN ḍ  P  - -  - - | M ḍ Ṅ S
    re,                     rā-                 ma              ja- po re
```

nita hari **- tintal**

नित हरि नाम ले तू मन मेरो
जासो बड़े तेरे ज्ञान

जा कारण रची सब रचना
सोच समझ नादान

nita hari nāma le tū mana mero
jāso baṛe tere gyāna

jā kāraṇa rachī saba rachanā
socha samajha nādāna

O my mind, constantly dwell on Hari,
The Lord whose name
Enriches your knowledge,
Whose works create all manifestation—
Seek to realize your foolishness.

Khyal in tintal M.84

Asthai

o 3 + 2
‖: M PMdP M G | M d r N | ᵈN d P P -- | M ᴳr M G :‖
ni- ta ha- ri nā- ma le- tū ma- na me- ro

o 3 + 2
ʳG r S -- | N r G G | M d r N | d -- P --
jā so ba- ṛe te- ro gyā- na

Antara

o 3 + 2
‖:ᵈᴾM d N S | S S S S | N r G r | S -- -- -- :‖ (NrNd ← 1st x only)
jā ka- ra- na ra- chi sa- ba ka- ra- na

o 3 + 2
P -- P' P | M d M G | M d r N | N r N d N d P -
so- cha sa- ma- jhā nā- dā- na

Vistars

1) + 2 o 3 +
S -- -- -- | N -- -- -- | r G r -- | S -- -- -- | N r N d
2 o 3 + 2
P -- -- -- | M d N -- | S -- -- -- | N r G M | P -- M G

2) + 2 o 3
P -- -- M | d -- -- -- | M -- G -- | r M G --
+ 2
rG M P -- | GM Pd PM G -

3) + 2 o 3
d -- -- -- | P -- -- -- | Md N -- -- | dN d P --
+ 2
MP MP GM rG | Nr GM Pd PM

4) + 2 o 3
N -- -- -- | dPMG M d N -- | Nd P dP M | PM G Md P
+ 2
Pd - P d - MP | - M P - GM rG

tere darasa ki - tintal

तेरे दरस की लालसा करत सब
देव गन्धर्व गण किन्नर नर मुणि

आराधना तेरे नाम की जो करे
पावत सकल सिद्धि
हररंग कहत गुणी

tere darasa kī lālasā karata saba
deva gandharva gaṇa kinnara nara muṇi

ārādhanā tere nāma kī jo kare
pāvata sakala siddhi
Hararaṅga kahata guṇī

Everyone thirsts to catch a vision of you:
Men, gods, heavenly singers, and sages.

Whoever offers his prayers unto you
Attains all perfection, says Hararanga.

Khyal in slow tintal M.69

Asthai

o 3 + 2

‖: d P d^P M | P ^MG - - M - r - M - | ^MG -- -- G | M PM ^dPd P :‖

te- re da- ra- sa kī lā- la - sā ka- ra- ta sa- ba

o 3 + 2

d P d P | -- PMdP - M G | M ^Nd N d | ṙ N d P GMP -

de- va gan-dhar- va ga- ṇa kin- na -ra na- ra mu- ṇi

Antara

2/o

‖: M ^Nd N N | Ṡ -- Ṡ -- | N ṙ G ṙ | Ṡ -- Ṡ -- | N ^dN - ṙ Nd P - :‖

ā- rā- dha- nā te- re nā- ma kī jo ka- re

3 + 2

PMdP MP - - M G | M r - M G -- | GMP d P --

pā- va- ta sa- ka- la sid- dhi

o 3 +

M d N ṙ N | d N d P -- | M - PM dPMP M G

ha- ra- raṅ- ga ka- ha- ta, ha- ra- raṅ- ga

2

G r - S NrGM P -

ka- ha- ta gu- ṇī

Tarana in slow-medium jhaptal M.72

Asthai

o 3 + 2

‖: dPMP -M | G M d N - r | N d -- | P PMdPMP M G

ta nom ta na de re na ta nom

o 3 + 2

-M rG | -M G r S S | S - S P | - P P d M P :‖

de re na ta da re da ni da re da re ta da re ta

Antara

\+ 2 o 3

‖: M M - d | d - S S S S | - S' M-dN | S'M-d NS'M- dNS- :‖

der tum der tum ta da re da ni, ta de re na, ta de re na, ta da re na

\+ 2 o 3

N r G - | r' S S S - S' | N r N - | d'P - P - P

di ya na re, di ya na re, di ya na re, ta da re

\+

‖: PMGM G - - - | G - - M - P - d PMP - :‖

ta na de re na ta na de re na

\+

‖: MN - d P -' Md - PM -' MP - M G - - [G M - rG - -] 3x :‖

na dre re na, na de re na na de re na na de re na

\+ 2

N NN N - r rr r - G--G--M- P - P -

dha kita tak dum kita tak dhin dhin dha kran dha

5th (o)

[dPMP GGMM P] 3x [^{dP}M - dS - -] 3x

te te ka ta ga di de na dha gen ta dha

Gat in vilambit tintal M.46

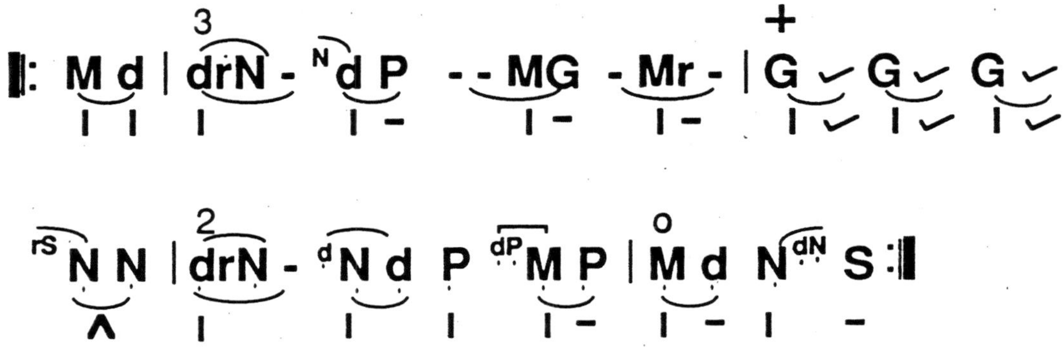

Gat in medium tintal M.160

```
      o               3                +            2
1) ‖: S  PP  P  P | P  P  M  G |ᴳM  G -- M | G  r  S -- :‖
      I  ^   I  -   I  I  I  -   I  -      I  I  -  I

      3                       +
2)    S PP  PP MP MG | M  G
      I  ^  I- I- I-   I  -

      o                 3                 +
3)    S PP  PP MP MG |- M G - MG -M |G
      %                  I -  I -  I   -

      o                 3               +
4)    S PP  PP MP MG |MG - M G - - M |G

      +
5)    Nr GM dN ᵈrN -ᵈr N -ᵈrN - d PM Gr S
   [S PP P PM G - MG rS NS] 3x S PP PP | M  G

      +            2                           +
6)    Md Nr Gr SN dP MG rS [S PP PP MG] 3x |M  G

      +              2               o
7)    Nr GM PM GM |PM GM Gr SN |

      +            2                o
8)    Nr GM Pd Nd |PM GM Gr SN |

      +                2                o
9)    GM P'G MP' GM P'G MP' MG rS |

      +                 2                o
10)   MM G'M MG' MM G'M MG' MG rS|

      +            2              o
11)   Nr dN Pd MP GM rG Sr NS |

      +            2              o
12)   Nr Gr SN dP MG PM Gr SN |

      +                 2                 o
13)   Nr N'd Nd' Pd P'M PM' GM G'r Gr' Sr S -
      12th                            +
   [S PP  P  P  M - GM - G] 3x | M  G
```

Marwa

The mood of rag Marwa (*Māruvā*) is very strong and instantly recognizable. There is no use of the note **pa** at all, and **sa**, the tonic, is avoided until it comes almost as a surprise (*chamatkar*) at the very end of multiples of phrases. The notes komal **re** and shuddh **dha** are very important, and may sometimes sound like the tonic note. It is said that if one can sing Marwa in tune, one can then sing any rag in tune. It is a difficult rag, and unique in its tonal color. The **pa** drone of the tanpura should be raised to **dha**.

Marwa is sometimes classified as a *shandhyāprakāsh* rag (sunset), but it is usually rendered after rags in that time group. It should be completed before the feeling of late night begins.

Marwa and Puriya are very close together. You must be very careful when you use ***ga*** *and* ***ni****, or else you will make the sound of Puriya. In Marwa the* ***dha*** *and* ***re*** *are more important. All the notes are very bold, but* ***sa*** *is only a shadow until the very end. You must take great care to get these notes in proper tune.*

Rag Mārwā

That: **Marwa**

Jati: **vakra sharav**

Vadi: **r** Samvadi: **D**

Ang: **purvang**

Time: **evening (8-11 pm)**

Mood: **karuna, vir, bhakti**

Pakaṛ: **Ṇ Ḍ r S**

Arohi-Avarohi: **Ṇ r G M D N D Ṡ Ṡ N D M G r S**

Ṇ r G M D N D ṙ Ṡ

N ṙ N D M G r Ṇ Ḍ r S

Chalan: **Ṇ Ḍ r ----- Ṇ Ḍ Ṃ Ṇ Ḍ S ---**

r G M D ------ M N D M G r ---

Ṇ Ḍ r ----- S -----

Sargam in dhamar tal M.72

Asthai

3 + 2 o

‖: - - D M - - D - - | D r -- -- Gr -- -- | N SN D | S -- -- :‖

3 + 2 o

-- -- r N | D ND -- -- -- -- | M G | r Gr -- --

3 + 2 o

-- -- G r | G r -- -- -- | N D | r S --

Antara

+ 2 o 3

‖: M D -- D -- | D -- | MD M DN | D DN MD --

+ 2 o 3

r - - N - D' N - - D - M' D - - M Gr ND r - r - S - - - :‖

+

[ND S - - - ND r - ND S -] 2x

+ 2 o

rN - D - M' ND - M - G' DM - G - r - S

Sargam in fast tintal M.288

Asthai

```
    o           3           +           2
‖: N  D -- N | D  M  G  r | N  D  r -- | -- -- S -- :‖

 o      3       +       2       o       3
 r -- r N -- N D -- D M -- M G -- G r -- r N -- N D -- D

 +          2
 r -- -- -- | r -- -- --
```

Antara

```
    +             2             o             3
‖: M -- -- -- | D -- -- -- | N -- -- -- | r -- -- --

 +          2             o                 3
 N -- D -- | r -- -- -- | -- -- -- -- | -- -- -- --

 +                                    o           3
[S -- -- S | -- S -- S ] 3x | N -- D -- | r -- S -- :‖

 +         2          o          3          +          2
 N r N' D N D' M D M' G M G' r G r' N r N' D N D --

 7th                      (o)
[r -- r -- N D M G r S -- -- ] 3x
```

avaguna bakasa - tintal

अवगुण बकस करम कर मेरे
ए करतार शरण द्वार तेरे

इतनो ही वर माङ्गत अब मैं
दिन दिन बड़ो ज्ञान सर सर्वत
तान राग ताल सुर मेरे करतार

avaguṇa bakasa karama kara mere
e karatāra sharaṇa dvāra tere

itano hī vara māngata aba mai
dina dina baṛho gyāna sarva sarvata
tāna rāga tāla sura mere karatāra

O Lord, forgive my faults;
I seek refuge in you.

I seek only this boon from you:
Let my wisdom increase day by day,
And my musical skills (tan, rag, tal, and sur)
Develop more and more.

Khyal in slow tintal M.66

Asthai

o 3 + 2
‖: ᴹᴺD D M G | r S - N DN | r r ʳG r | D M Gr S :‖
a- va- gu- ṇa ba- ka- sa ka- ra- ma ka- ra me- re

o 3 + 2
G -- M M | D -- D -- | MD M -- DM | ṙ -- NDMD N D
e ka- ra - tā- ra sha- ra- ṇa dvā-ra te- re

Antara

o 3 + 2
[: G G M G | M D D D | MDN ṙ ṙ ṙ | ṙNDM DNṙ - -- Ṡ :‖
i- ta- no hī va- ra mān- ga- ta a- ba mai

o 3 + 2
N ṙ Gṙ ṙ | N ṙ ᴺD D | ᴺM M MDN ṙ | --ᴳṙ Ṡ Ṡ :]
di-na di- na ba- ṛho gyā- na sar- va sār- va- ta

o 3 + 2
N ṙ N D | M ᴹṙ N D | D M Gr -- | ND MG ʳGr S -
tā- na rā- ga tā- la su- ra me- re ka- ra- tā- ra

Vistars

\+ 2
1) S -- -- -- | N D -- ᴰD

\+ 2
2) ṙ -- -- -- | ND r S --

\+ 2
3) G -- -- -- | MG r - ND r -

\+ 2
4) M -- D M | MD MG rG - -

\+ 2
5) MD - - MN D - | ND MG r'D - -

\+ 2
6) MD N -- NDMD | ND - - - - NDr - D

piya more - **tintal**

पिया मोरे अनत देस
गईलवा ना जानुँ कब घर
आवेंगे करतार

उन के दरस देखावे को
आंखियां तरस रही
उन बिना मोहे कछु ना भावे

piyā more anata desa
gaīlavā nā jānū̃ kaba ghara
aveṅge karatāra

una ke darasa dekhāve ko
āṇkhiyā̃ tarasa rahī
una binā mohe kachhu nā bhāve

My love has gone to a distant land.
O, Lord, when will he return home?

My eyes thirst to catch a glimpse of him;
Without him, nothing is pleasing to me.

Khyal in medium fast tintal M.176

Asthai

```
        +              2              o          3
‖: N D N | r -- -- -- | r N D -- | r r S -- | S :‖
   pi- yā  mo- re        a-          na- ta de-   sa
        +              2              o          3
‖: r G M | D -- --ᴰM | -- D -- D | N N D D | -- :‖
   ga- ī- la- vā       nā     jā-     nu ka- ba gha- ra
        +              2                   o             3
   M -- D | -- D N N | D D Nʳᴺ Dᴺᴰ | Mᴰᴹ Gᴹᴳ rᴳʳ S | --
   nā   jā-    nu ka- ba  gha- ra ā-       ven-          ge
```

Tans **(in sargam or ākar: "ah")**

```
    +                 2                 o                3
1)  Nr GM DN rN DM Gr' r - ND MG r'r ND MG rS
    +                 2                                  3
2)  DN rN D'N rN D'r ND' ND' rN D'D ND r - - S - -
    +                 2             o                3
3)  DN rG rN' DN rG - -' rN DN r - - -' rN Dr S -
    +                 2                 o                3
4)  rG MD - -' MG rN D - -'D - - MG rN Dr S - - -
    +                 2                 o                3
5)  rG MD ND MG rN D'N rG MD - M Gr ND rS - -
    +                 2                 o                3
6)  Nr GM DN rG - r ND MG rN D -' Nr GM DN r - -
               +                2                o                3
    N DM Gr ND M - -'D Nr GM DN rG rN DM Gr ND r - S -
```

Khyal in medium fast tintal, concluded

Antara

+ 2 o 3

‖: M M D | r -- r r | r r -- r | G r S -- | -- :‖

u - na ke da- ra- sa de- khā- ve ko (2nd time)

3 + 2 o

N D N D | M D ᴺr N | DM D M G | r G r S

āṇ- ki - yā ta- ra- sa ra- hī

3 + 2 o 3

N r G M | D M D -- | M D ᴺr N | D M G r | S

u - na bi- nā mo- he ka- chhu nā bhā - ve

Tarana in tintal M.152

Asthai

```
   o             3                       +              2
‖: N  DN r --  | ND  M'G  rS'  DN  | r  --  --  S | --  S  N  S :‖
   dim de re na  de r e na de re na de re  na        dim      ta na  na

   o           3              +             2
   D  N  r  G | r  --  N  D | r  --  --  S | --  S  N  S
   ta na de re  na     ta na  dim        dim     ta na na

   o                     3                        +                        2
   DM  - D  MG  r'N  D -  ND  MG'  rN  - r  ND  M'G  r-  Gr  ND'  MG  rS
   ta na  ta  de re  na  %            %                %          ta de re na
```

Tans

```
       +            2              o            3
1) ‖: r  --  D  -- | --  --  M  -- | r  G  r  -- | --  --  S  -- :‖

      +                                      +               2
   [  D  --  --  r | --  S  --  --] 2x      r  M  --  -- | --  G  r  --

      o              3                +               2
      r  D  --  -- | --  M  G  -- | M  r  --  -- | --  N  D  --

      o              3                +                        2
      M  r  --  -- | --  S  --  -- | Nr  ND  MG  rN | D  --  D  --

      o              3                +                  2
      r  --  --  G | r  --  S  -- | M  r  --  ND | MG  rS  ND  r -

      +                2                o               3
2)    S  --  --  -- | --  --  N  D | N  r  --  N | D  --  --  --

      +                2                 o               3
      N  G  --  r | N  D  --'  N | M  --  G  r | N  D  --'  N

      +                2                 o               3
      D  --  M  G | r  N  D  --' | N  N  --  D | M  G  r  N

      +                2                 o               3
      D  --'  N  S | --  N  D  M | G  r  N  D | --'  N  r  --

      +                2
      N  D  M  G | r  --  S  --
```

3) **Sing the previous tan 2x at double speed (dugun)**

Gats in tintal

vilambit M.46

```
                3                               +
‖: DMMD | D M  GrrG  G r  N D | r  r  S
   I   -   I     I  -  I    I -   I  I  -
             2                  o
   DSNrSNS - | DN   DD  M  G | M  r  S :‖
   I   -       I    ^   I  -   I  I  -
```

Drut M.232

```
   o                           +               2
‖: r  N  - D  D | N  r r  G  M | D  M  D  -- | M  G  r  S :‖
   I  I  · -  I   I  ^    I  -   I  I  I       I  I  I  -
                          3rd X  D  M  D  -- | --  r  N  r
                                 (all da)
 o              3                +                2
 --  --  D  M | D  --  --  M | G  r  --  -- | G  M  D  -- | --
 10th      (8th)
 [M  G  r  S  -- ] 3x
```

Two of Allauddin Khansahib's most illustrious students: Ravi Shankar, sitarist, and Ali Akbar Khan, sarodist.

Exercises

Exercises are repeating rhythm and pitch patterns abstracted from the music. The practice of these exercises, or *palṭās* (turning), develops many facets of musicianship: accuracy, evenness of tone, suppleness of voice (or hands), agility, speed, stamina, and power. All these can be improved through a regular practice of exercises. There are traditional sets of basic exercises, and hundreds more derived ones which emphasize specific problems of fingering, stroking, and note combinations. They have various groupings, such as "scales," "intervals," "murchhanas," "alankars," and "bol patterns." They have in common their design to develop rigorous technical control of rhythm and pitch in contrast, perhaps, to the emotive, compositional, or imaginative aspects of music.

Below are given some age-old exercises. They are grouped into eight categories, the first four of which are suited to both voice and instruments, and the last four are mainly for plucked instruments, although they may be adapted for wind and bowed instruments as well. They should initially be practiced in each of the ten *ṭhāṭ*s not in rag; practicing most of them in rag introduces configurations of melody which are not found in the rag, and the mental working out of these rag patterns takes valuable time away from concentrating on technique, which is, after all, the main point in doing the exercises at all.

For the first two years in one's progress in the music, a large part of one's practice time will be involved with exercises, but their practice is lifelong. At the age of ninety, the distinguished cellist, Pablo Casals, remarked, "I am still practicing the exercises I learned when I was eight years old."

These exercises can be effectively practiced with a metronome. At a slow-medium speed, for instance 60-80 beats per minute, the patterns can be practiced at single, double, triple and quadruple speed without changing the tempo setting.

In a normal sitting, a musician may focus on only one from each group, or spend his entire time on one exercise alone. A thorough instrumental practice sitting will normally include at least one from each of the eight categories. A two hour session might be divided into 15 minutes spent on one of each section; or perhaps, a heavier concentration on alankars on one day, murchhanas, the next, bols the following day, etc. It is recommended that the student stay in one *ṭhāṭ* for a week or more at a time. The exercises are given in Bilawal *ṭhāṭ*. The patterns below are written in one octave only, but after learning, should be practiced in the full range of the instrument or voice.

I. Scales and *sapāṭ*

A. **S R G m P D N Ṡ Ṡ N D P m G R S**

B. **P̣ Ḍ Ṇ S R G m P D N Ṡ Ṙ Ġ Ṙ Ṡ N D P m G R S Ṇ Ḍ**

or, from the lowest note to the highest note of one's voice or instrument—this is known as sapat (flat, straight), or "full sweep."

C. **with gamak from above**

G m P D N Ṡ Ṙ   Ṙ Ṡ N D P m G
S R G m P D N S   Ṡ N D P m G R S

D. **one note higher (or lower) each time**

SRS, SRGRS, SRGmGRS,etc. to **SRGmPDNṠNDPmGRS**

ṠNṠ, ṠNDNṠ, ṠNDPDNṠ, etc. to **ṠNDPmGRSRGmPDNṠ**

II. *Murchhana* (taking a fixed scale, and starting a new scale on each note, keeping the tones of the original scale).

A. **S R G m P D N Ṡ Ṡ N D P m G R S**
R G m P D N Ṡ Ṙ Ṙ Ṡ N D P m G R
G m P D N Ṡ Ṙ Ġ Ġ Ṙ Ṡ N D P m G
m P D ⟶ ṁ ṁ ⟶ m,etc.

B. **ascending only**

S R G m P D N Ṡ
R G m P D N Ṡ Ṙ
G m P D N Ṡ Ṙ Ġ etc.

C. **descending only**

ṠNDPmGRS
NDPmGRSṆ
DPmGRSṆḌ **etc.**

D. **with octave leap**

S -- Ṡ -- ṠNDPmGRS
R -- Ṙ -- ṘṠNDPmGR
G -- Ġ -- ĠṘṠNDPmG

III. Intervals

A. **3rds**
SG Rm GP mD PN DṠ
ṠD NP Dm PG mR GS

B. **4ths**
Sm RP GD mN PṠ
ṠP Nm DG PR mS

C. **5ths**
SP RD GN mṠ
Ṡm NG DR PS

D. **6ths**
SD RN GṠ
ṠG NR DS

E. **7ths**
SN RṠ
ṠR NS

F. **8ves**
SṠ RṘ GĠ **etc.**
ṠS NN DD **etc.**

IV. Alankars and paltas

Alankars (ornaments) and *paltas* (turns) can vary from simple to complex. In the general theory of alankar, they are classed according to how many notes are in the pattern (from one to seven), and the number of beats (commonly from 2 to 24). For instance, a 2 note alankar with 2 beats could be either SR or RS. A 2 note, 3 beat alankar could be SSR, RSS, SRR, RRS, SRS, or RSR. For a 4 note, 6 beat alankar, the possibilities are enormous, but a few of them might be: SRGmRS, SGRmGR, SmRGSR, etc.

In working out mathematical possibilities, literally millions of variations can be generated by the four classical methods of permutating a melodic figure. For example, the alankar SGRmGRS in its four permutations is:

1. **Original** (prime)	**S G R m G R S**
2. **Upside-down** (inversion)	**Ṡ D N P D N Ṡ**
3. **Backwards** (retrograde)	**S R G m R G S**
4. **Upside-down and backwards** (retrograde inversion)	**Ṡ N D P N D Ṡ**

When played as exercises, each alankar is repeated on each degree of the scale:

S G R m G R S
R m G P m G R
G P m D P m G etc.

and, when descending, it is common to invert it and play it upside-down in descent:

Ṡ D N P D N Ṡ
N P D m P D N
D m P G m P D etc.

There are so many possible alankars that only a few can be notated here. Those notated below are some of the most common in the musical literature, and are selected for their utility in developing musical skills.

A. Straight alankars

3-note SRG, RGm, GmP...
SND, NDP, DPm...

4-note SRGm, RGmP, GmPD...
SNDP, NDPm, DPmG...

5-note SRGmP, RGmPD, GmPDN...
SNDPm, NDPmG, DPmGR...

6-note SRGmPD, RGmPDN, GmPDNṠ
SNDPmG, NDPmGR, DPmGRS

7-note SRGmPDN, RGmPDNṠ
SNDPmGR, NDPmGRS

B. Ornamental alankars

These are effectively practiced *ākār* ("ah") with the voice,
or with one stroke (*miṇḍ*, "glide") on an instrument.
They are not usually inverted in descending patterns.

1. S͡RS R͡GR G͡mG...
2. S͡NS R͡SR G͡RG...
3. S͡NRS R͡SGR G͡RmG...
4. S͡NRSNS R͡SGRSR G͡RmGRG...
5. S͡NRSRSNS R͡SGRGRSR G͡RmGmGRG

C. Some important additional alankars

1. SRG'GRS, RGm'mGR, GmP'PmG...

2. SRS'GRG'RS, RGRmGmGR, GmGPmPmG
     | - | | - | | -

3. SGRGmGRS, RmGmPmGR, GPmPDPmG...

4. SG-G'RGRS, Rm-mGmGR, GP-PmPmG...
     | | · - | - | -

V. Gamak

Gamak (ornament) is a typical way of embellishing a note with its neighbor note from above or below. If there are two or more notes played with gamak in succession, it is notated with a wavy line above the notes:

GGG R S is played ^R^G ^R^G ^R^G R S or RG RG RG R S

Occasionally, gamak comes from above, and is then so stated adjacent to the notated pattern, and played thus:

^m^G ^P^m ^D^P ^R^S ^S^N ^N^D P (see exercise IC)

Gamak exercises are not inverted in descent.

1. **SRGGRS RGmmGR GmPPmG...**
   played S R RG RG R S...
2. **SR GGR GGR GGRS, RG mmG mmG mmGR...**
3. **GGGGRS, RRRRSN, SSSSND ... descending only**

VI. Lari for plucked instruments

Lari (string, chain) means stringing the notes in a continuous series with diri-diri strokes of the right hand.

From low **sa** to high **sa** and back again, play each note eight beats with diri-diri; then repeat the pattern with seven beats of diri-diris, then six beats, five, four, three, two, and one.

VII. Bols

Play each pattern from low **sa** to high **sa** and back, as in lari patterns above.

I = da **∧ = diri** **- = ra**

1. S SS S S, R RR R R, G GG G G...
   I ∧ I - I ∧ I - I ∧ I - **(da diri da ra)**

2. [SS S'S SS' SS] 2x R ⁒ G ⁒ ...
   I - I I -I I - **(darada darada dara)**

3. [S - SS - S SS] 2x R ⁒ G ⁒ ...
   I · - I · - ∧ **(da- rada -ra diri)**

4. [S - SS - S S - SS - S SS SS] 2x R ⁒ G ⁒ ...
   I · - I · - I · - I · - ∧ ∧

5. **Combine patterns 1 & 2, 1 & 3, 1 & 3 & 4, etc.**

6. I ∧ ∧ ∧ I ∧ I - I - ∧ ∧ I · - I · - I ·

7. S RR G m P DD N Ṡ **etc., sapat or murchhana**
   I ∧ I - I ∧ I -

8. S RR GG mm G -GR -R S-, R ⁒ G ⁒ **etc.**
   I ∧ ∧ ∧ I · - I · - I · **(da diri diri diri da-rada-rada-)**

VIII. Jhālā

Jhālā (sparkling) patterns involve fast repeated down-strokes with chikari strings. Work on cleanliness and stamina.

1. ***Sīdhā*** **jhala (straight, perfect)**

a. S ✓✓✓ S ✓✓✓ S ✓✓✓ S ✓✓✓ R %
   | | | |

b. S ✓✓✓ S ✓✓✓ S ✓✓✓ S ✓✓✓ R %
   –   –   –   –

c. S ✓✓ S ✓✓ S ✓ S ✓✓ S ✓✓ S ✓ R %

d. S ✓✓ S ✓✓ S ✓✓ S ✓✓ S ✓ S ✓ R %
(play c and d patterns all da, then all ra)

2. ***Ṭhok*** **jhala (strike, beat)**

✓ | | | ✓ | | | ✓ | | | ✓ | | |

3. ***Laṛī*** **jhala (with diri-diris)**

✓ ʌ ʌ ʌ ✓ ʌ ʌ ʌ ✓ ʌ ʌ ʌ ✓ ʌ ʌ ʌ

4. **Sarod and other style jhala-s**

a. | – ✓✓ | – ✓✓ | – ✓✓ | – ✓✓

b. | – ✓ –

c. | – ✓ | – ✓ | –

d. | – ✓ | – ✓ | – ✓ | – ✓ | – | –

Rhythm and Tal

The rhythmic element of Indian classical music is preeminent and becomes highly elaborated during a performance. Ideally, a melodic soloist should display as much command of the rhythm as the drum accompanist. Moreover, the drummer does much more than accent the pulse; s/he plays a fundamental role in the intricate counterpoint of the rag's performance.

The major framework of the broad rhythmic conception is known as *tāla* (Hindi: *tāl*), a word which is usually used to refer to a rhythmic cycle. However, *tāli* also means the "clap of the hands" which delineates these cycles, for all the cycles are shown with claps and waves of the hands. This gesturing is known as the *kriyā* (action) for the tals, and is more elaborate and important in the dhrupad style than in khyal or thumri. In a dhrupad performance, there is sometimes a separate accompanist who simply has the job of keeping track of the tal with hand gestures.

Tals are made up of sections (*vibhāgs*, divisions) which are stressed and shown by a clap of the hands (hence, they are known as *tālī*), or unstressed (called *khālī*, empty), shown by a wave of the hands. In theory, tals are from 3 to 108 beats long and 360 in number, although there are only about thirty in common use today. Of these, those of 6, 7, 8, 10, 12, 14, and 16 beats long are most often heard. However, there are many less common tals for the odd-numbered beats such as 5, 9, 11, 15,

17, etc., and even tals which use half-beats in their structures, such as 5-1/2, 8-1/2, and so on, played by more advanced musicians.

Different groupings of beats in the subdivisions of a tal distinguish different tals having the same number of beats. For instance, there are several tals with fourteen beats in their cycles (*avarta*s, *avartan*s) which are divided in several different ways: 5+2+3+4 (dhamar tal), or 3+4+3+4 (chachar tal), or 2+2+2+2+2+2+2 (ada chautal), etc. The first and most important beat of any tal is called *sam* (rhymes with English "from" and means "equal"). In written notation it is marked with a plus sign: + (sometimes an x). The other tali (vibhags) are marked with consecutive numbers except for the khali divisions, which are all marked with a zero: o.

Tintal (literally "3 claps"), the most common of the tals, is thus marked and clapped as follows:

	sam	tali	khali	tali
Tal markings —	+	2	o	3
Beats ——	1 2 3 4	5 6 7 8	9 10 11 12	13 14 15 16
	└ vibhag ┘			
	└——— avarta ———┘			

Since tal nearly always implies drum accompaniment, the pattern for any given tal is thought of and memorized in drum syllables (*bol*s). These patterns are memorized by all musicians, and are known as the *ṭhekā*s (support, rhythm; pronounced like English "take-ah"). The thekas for a few of the common tals are given below:

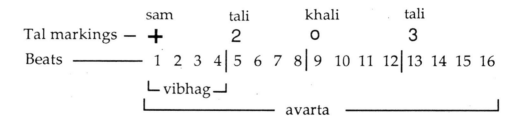

TINTĀL 16 beats (4 + 4 + 4 + 4)

+ 2

dha dhin dhin dha | dha dhin dhin dha |

o 3

dha tin tin ta | ta dhin dhin dha

DĀDRĀ 6 beats (3 + 3)

+ o

dhi dhi na | dha tun na

KAHARWĀ 8 beats (4 + 4)

+ o

dha ge na ti | na ka dhin na

RUPAK 7 beats (3 + 2 + 2)

o 1 2

tin tin na | dhin na | dhin na

JHAPTĀL 10 beats (2 + 3 + 2 + 3)

+ 2 o 3

dhi na | dhi dhi na | ti na | dhi dhi na

CHAUTĀL 12 beats (2 + 2 + 2 + 2 + 2+ 2)

+ o 2
dha dha | dhin ta | kat dhage
o 3 4
dhin ta | tete kata | gadi gena

EKTĀL 12 beats (2+ 2 + 2 + 2 + 2 + 2
or 3 + 3 + 3 + 3)
+ o 2
dhin dhin | dhage terekita | tun na |
o 3 4
kat ta | dhage terekita | dhin dhage

or, if counted in three's:
+ 2
dhin dhin dha | tete tun na |
o 3
tet ta dhage | tete dhin na

DHAMĀR 14 beats (5 + 2 + 3 + 4)
+ 2 o 3
kat dhe te dhe te | dha - | ge te te | te te ta -

DHAMĀRĪ 11-1/2 beats (5 + 2 + 3 + 1-1/2)
+ 2 o 3
kat dhe te dhe te | dha - | ge te te | te te ta/2

CHACHAR 14 beats (3 + 4 + 3 + 4)

```
+               2
dha dhin - | dha dha dhin -
                        o        3
                        ta tin - | dha dha dhin -
```

SITĀRKHĀNĪ 16 beats (4 + 4 + 4+ 4)

```
+                        2
dha- gedhin -ge dha- | dha- gedhin -ge dha-
       o                 3
       dha- ketin -ke ta- | ta- gedhin -ge dha-
```

Patterns of Performance

In the khyal style, and in most instrumental styles as well, the drummer always maintains the theka clearly while the melodic soloist improvises. In contemporary performance practice, the drummer may ornament the theka more so than in previous eras, although this varies considerably with the nature of the rag and its development, and, naturally, the personalities of the performers. Drum solos can occur when the melodic soloist returns to the first line of the composition, which is repeated as many times as is necessary for the drummer to complete his presentation of a solo section. The melodic soloist retakes the lead, and then alternates with the tabla player in presenting variations. One of the two is always keeping track of the tal with either the fixed melody (*gat* or *chiz*) or the theka.

Chhand

The fabric of rhythm is made up of the interplay of *chhand* and *laya*. In some sense, they can be talked about separately, but since they happen simultaneously, like strands in a braided rope, it sometimes seems difficult to separate their concepts.

The *chhand* (meter, measure) is the grouping of a regular pulse. It can be regular, as with continuing 2s, 3s, 4s, etc., when it is similar to Western regular meter. It can also be irregular, as with a grouping of 2 followed by 3, then 7, then 2, then 4, etc. (like Western multimetrics). Most frequently it is found in small, irregular groups repeated as larger rhythmic units. The most common patterns in 8 and 16 beats, are:

a. 3 + 3+ 2
b. 3 + 2 + 3
c. 2 + 3 + 3
d. 3 + 3 + 3 + 3 + 4

These groups and resulting accent patterns are common, for instance, in Latin dance rhythms, and are usually thought of as "syncopated" in the West.

Lay

The *laya* (Hindi, *lay*: rhythm, tempo—pronounced somewhat like a short, Southern American English, "lie") is the tempo or the relative speed of a pulse. In the general sense of the word "speed," there are three standard tempos:

slow	***vilambit*** or ***dhīma***
medium	***madhya***
fast	***drut*** or ***duni***

Sometimes specific ratios are assigned to them: medium (*madhyalay*, middle speed) being twice as fast as vilambit, and drut being four times as fast. In normal practice, though, these terms are used to give a general sense of tempo. For extremely slow and fast speeds, the adverb *ati* (very much) is used: *ati vilambit, ati drut,* or even, *ati ati drut* ("very very fast").

Lay can also refer to relative speed in a more specific mathematical sense. A chart of the common relative speeds is given below which gives an idea of the way these speeds are related in tintal, the most common tal of sixteen beats. Not all musicians use the names for these speeds, but the idea about *lay* as "relative speed" can be easily grasped. The names of the most commonly used lays are written in capital letters.

The Layers (*darja*) of Relative Speeds

Name	Simple fraction	Beats in the time of 16
Pāv (pāo)	1/4	4
Ardha	1/2	8
Paun	3/4	12
BARĀBAR	1/1	16
SAWĀĪ	5/4	20
Deṛh ("DERI")	3/2, 6/4	24
Paune do	7/4	28
DUGUN (DUNI)	2/1	32
Sawāī do	9/4	36
Aṛhaiyā	5/2	40
Paune tīn	11/4	44
TĪGUN	3/1	48
Sawāī tīn	13/4	52
Saṛhe tīn	7/2	56
Paune chau	15/4	60
CHAUGUN	4/1	64
etc.		
PANCHGUN	5/1	80
CHHEGUN	6/1	96
SĀTGUN	7/1	112
ĀTGUN	8/1	128
NAUGUN	9/1	144

Again, not all musicians use these terms, partly because of their verbal complexity. Many prefer a simpler, and condensed vocabulary. In such cases, all rhythms which have the basic duple quality of 2, 4, 8, etc. are referred to as *barābar* (equal, even). Those which have triple feeling, i.e., 1-1/2, 3, 6, or 9, are called *āṛī* (oblique). 5s (1-1/4, 2-1/2) are just termed *kuārī,* and 7s (1-3/4, 3-1/2) are called *viārī (or julnā).*

The word *laykārī* (*laya* + *karnā*, to do) is used to describe a section of composition which involves working or playing with the rhythm.

Time Division

On both the practical and philosophical level in India, the perception of temporal division has been taken to a high refinement, and in ancient times was scientifically contextualized as an aspect of musical yoga. Establishing the duration of the pulse or beat (*mātrā*) in music was derived from this spiritual science, and was based on the smallest unit, the *kshaṇ* (instant). A kshan is sometimes fancifully defined as the time it takes for a sharp needle to pass through one of a hundred lotus petals (one matra=one hundred lotus petals). The matra has also been defined as the time it takes to say the first consonant from each of the first five groups in the Devanagari alphabet: "*ka cha ṭa ta pa* ." Sometimes the matra is described as a "normal heartbeat." In the following chart, derived from old treatises describing tal, it is the *anudrut:*

8 kshaṇ	=	*1 lāv (lāo)*
8 lāv	=	*1 kashta*
8 kashta	=	*1 nimish* ("blink of an eye")
8 nimish	=	*1 kalā*
4 kalā	=	*1 anudrut* (1 *mātrā;* heartbeat)
2 anudrut	=	*1 drut*
2 drut	=	*1 lāghu* (1 *vibhāg* in tintal)
2 lāghu	=	*1 gurū*
3 lāghu	=	*1 pluta*
4 lāghu	=	*1 kakapad* (1 cycle of tintal)

In this theoretical meditation on the division of time, each heartbeat is divided into more than 16,000 parts. And, while these extremely small ratios can be conceived of only in atomic standards, they indicate the subtlety of perceptions which the ancients recognized as an ideal. It is a vision of the finely critical levels upon which this musical science of rhythm is based, and one to which the practicing musician continually aspires to further realize.

Rhythm is like your skeleton, you see, and the notes are like your flesh. If your music is all rhythm and no notes, it will be too hard; and if it is just the notes, it will be too flabby. It is a matter of balance, and playing in rhythm is a matter of balance, too. When you go out of rhythm it is like you are drunk, reeling out of control. All the time you must concentrate on just the one beat and keep that steady. Only then you can think of tal and mathematics and all these things.

Tabla

The history of *tablā* can be traced with accuracy only back to eighteenth-century Delhi. Perhaps this important era, which also witnessed the emergence of the sitar, sarod, and khyal style, also gave birth to the tabla, the most common drum heard in modern North Indian classical music. Oral tradition dates it from the sixteenth century, and it is sometimes maintained that the tabla was another of the many legacies of the fourteenth century's Amir Khusrau, which may indicate that it has an even older undocumented tradition. What is clear is that its traditional style of playing did not begin as recently as the eighteenth century, for it had already inherited a huge repertoire of techniques and compositions from the playing of older drummers, primarily ones who had mastered the double-ended, barrel-shaped drum associated with the dhrupad tradition, the *pakāwaj* (*pakhāwaj*), or the *ḍhol* (*ḍholak*) from folk music.

Drums figure prominently in all Indian classical, light classical, and popular music. Even "folk" drumming, which might otherwise be supposed to be primitive, is often highly complex both technically and rhythmically. There are literally hundreds of drum types, played with hands or sticks, and used for every reason, from ceremonial and processional, to accompany dance and music, to solo playing. The classical drums, the *mṛidaṅgam* of the South, and the *pakāwaj* and *tablā* of the North, are supremely refined in style, technique, and literature.

The vast oral literature of drumming has two main formal categories: fixed compositions and theme and variations. Of the former, the most important has become the *thekā*, the fixed composition which is the identifying signature line of a tal. Although the theka has been around since very ancient times, the coming of the tabla, with its ability to strongly contrast the open sounds (*khulā bāj*) with the closed sounds (*bandh bāj*), was a major step in the development of North Indian classical music, for it made it possible to articulate the framework of the tal without the necessity of someone's having to show the tal structure through hand gestures. It thus relaxed the grip of meter (*nibaddh*) on the melodic soloist, who could now compose variations with a looser sense of the confinements of tal, since the tabla could be assigned the responsibility of maintaining the theka and delineating the rhythm cycle. This concept of showing the structure clearly on a secondary musical level is manifest in the gestures of the tal (*kriyā*) in dhrupad, and an ancient one in the music.

The other fixed compositions played on the tabla are *gats*, *tukrās*, *paṛhans*, and *chalans*, which are a staple of the repertoire of the tabla player and used for solo interludes in a performance of a rag with a melodic soloist. Theme and variation types include the *kāydā*, *relā*, *peshkār*, and the light classical *laggī*. These can be played in short forms in a performance of rag, but are most effectively demonstrated in tabla solos where the player is more free to elaborate without the restraints of the rag's melodic development. Theme and variation forms can be elaborated on for long intervals by an expert drummer, and stories abound of duels (*daṅgal*) in former times where players sometimes competed for days in matching and outwitting each other in invention, stamina, and repertory. In a tabla solo, a fixed melodic line, known as the *laharā* (or *nāgmā*) is played over and over again in a simple form to delineate and maintain the structure of the tal.

One time someone challanged my teacher, Pandit Anokelal, to a contest. He agreed, but exercised his prerogative in choosing the first composition. "Okay, I will play," he replied, "but we must start with the kayda, ***dha te te,"*** *a famous beginner's composition with only a few strokes in its theme. He began to play the kayda. He played and played, using only 'dha te te' strokes. Everything he composed in the khulī (open left-hand drum section) was matched exactly in the mūṇdī (closed section). Two hours later he was still playing this simple composition and showed no sign of relenting in his outpouring of energy or invention. Hearing this incredible display of mastery, the challenger decided not to try to answer at all, and packed up his drums.*

Mahapurush Misra

The tabla players travelled from their place of origin in eighteenth-century Delhi north and eastward. Courts and individuals developed the art and literature of drumming into distinctive styles *(bāj)* which today are generally recognized as the six main tabla *gharanās* (houses, or schools of playing): Delhi, Lucknow, Benaras, Ajrada, Farukhabad, and Punjab. These are identified by their differences of technique, literature, and style, but as modern players continually hear each other in concerts and recordings, the differences in the regional playing styles, as in other aspects of modern music, grow less distinct.

Baba Allauddin Khansahib

ALLAUDDIN KHANSAHIB

Do you know what true music is? To a musician, music should be the Supreme Deity who will be worshipped with the eagerness of an undivided mind, and tears shall be his ritual ingredients.

Allauddin Khansahib

The life story of Allauddin Khan is so filled with single-minded intention and devotion that it reads like a heroic saga from long ago, one filled with resolute accomplishment, inspiration, and improbability. His contribution to music is inestimable, for he both reached far back into the past for the widest mastery of the oral literature and practice, then melded North Indian styles so that a whole new presentation of instrumental music was born. And this he did over a long life which spanned a century, and taught his legacy to many students, so that today, when modern audiences hear classical Hindustani instrumental music, they are likely to hear music touched by—and often even largely shaped by—Ustad Allauddin Khan.

Allauddin Khansahib was probably the first artist to deviate from the tradition of specialization—where one instrument or gharana played this style and another that one—and set up a new tradition consisting inter alia of finer blends and worthy assimilation of various materials of different famous gharanas which, in effect, created a scope for development in string instrumental music immensely wider and more prolific, and which was at the same time well advanced in point of time and culture. It was something like removing blockages and permitting fresh air and new life to rejuvenate the traditional art.

Ravi Shankar

All citations in this chapter are from Dhar Chowdhury, 1982.

The history of Allauddin Khan's ancestors can be traced back to eighteenth-century Bengal. In the "Northeast Territories," as the recently arrived British called the Tripura district of what is now Bangladesh, there was political strife among the semisavage tribal people, the local farmers, the landowning zamindars, and the British army. One Hindu man of this district, Dina Nath Deb Sharman, set up a temple to the goddess Kali, which was a spiritual refuge to many of the rival factions. His son, known as *Sirāju*, became involved with the political resistance against the zamindar-British alliance, and had to flee from his village. He was taken in by a Moslem family, and eventually married into that family and converted to Islam, taking the name Samash Fakir. With others in his party, he was like a Robin Hood who stood for the poor against the rich, and by the time stability returned to the area was in a powerful position both politically and financially. He settled in the village of Shivpur and was scion of the family that, several generations later, was still prestigious when Allauddin was born to Sadhu Khan and his wife Harasundari (Khatun) in October, 1862, on the eighth day of the Durga Festival.

Of the seven children born to Sadhu Khan, five were sons, and four of them were capable musicians. Ayat Ali Khan was a surbahar player, and later a famous maker of instruments, most notably the maker of Ali Akbar Khan's famous sarod. Elder brother Fakir Aftabuddin was adept at many instruments, especially tabla, and was a devotee of the goddess Kali. He took young Allauddin, who was known as "Alam" as a child, under his tutorial wing. For his part, the child Alam was a prodigy, and played on nearly every instrument he came across. He had early training on his elder brothers' classical instruments, notably the sitar, tabla, and pakawaj, and played a number of the folk instruments of that region, including bamboo flute, dotar, and Bangla dhol. But music as a profession was in bad repute in those days, and Alam's family tried to discourage him, despite his obvious gifts. Alam began staying out of school to learn and play, which frequently took him to the nearby Shiva temple to accompany the devotional songs, and occasional trips into the city of Dacca, where he picked up rudimentary knowledge of the shahnai, trumpet, clarinet, and saxophone. Whenever he returned home, he was punished for missing school. This discord was too much for him, and at the age of eight he ran away to Calcutta to learn music.

During the second half of the nineteenth century, Calcutta was the "Queen City of the Orient," and had a thriving musical life of both Western and Indian classical and popular styles. After a time of penniless struggle, little Alam was lucky to find a teacher who took him under his wing, the dhrupadiya Gopal Chandra Bhattacharya, or "Nulo Gopal" as he was known. A respected dhrupad singer (who had also studied khyal), Nulo Gopal believed in an old style of training, where a student masters exercises first, and only then receives the literature. For six years, Alam lived and worked in the household of his guru, cleaning and cooking, and practicing some three hundred sixty-five vocal exercises—playing a baya (drum) with his left hand, and a tanpura with his right. In this way, he developed extraordinary skill in pitch and tal.

When he was fourteen, his brother Aftabuddin traced him down in Calcutta and demanded that he come home for the marriage which had been arranged by his parents some years before. Despite the reluctance of his guru to let him go, or, for that matter, Allauddin's own wishes, he went to Raipur (Dacca district), near his ancestral home of Shivpur, to be married to the eight-year-old Madina Khatun (Madan Manjari). Immediately after the ceremony, he made his way back to Calcutta, but in the short weeks of his absence, Nulo Gopal had died suddenly of cholera. The death was so unexpected that there was no will, and his guru's estate passed into the hands of the government. Alam was homeless and bereft again.

He was determined to pursue instrumental music, and was fortunate to meet and be accepted as a disciple by the violinist Amritlal "Habu" Dutta, a cousin of Swami Vivekananda, and a man skilled in both Indian and Western music. As a kind of overseer to Allauddin's education, Habu Dutta helped arrange for tutors in several instruments: violin and Western classical music with the European conductor Asher Lobo and his wife, as well as a number of other teachers for Indian-style violin, mridangam, tabla, dhol, and clarinet and shahnai. Habu Dutta also helped him get employment at Calcutta's popular Minerva Theater. Thus, by the time he reached his late teens, he was accomplished in a number of musical idioms.

Allauddin Khansahib, who was left-handed, playing the sarod.

Then he heard about a festival at the estate (now in Bangladesh) of a big landowner, "Maharaja" Raja Jagat Kishore, and there presented himself proudly and announced that he was ready to play any of his many instruments. He was told to come back in the morning, and when he returned, the sarod master Ustad Ahmad Ali Khan was tuning, preparing to play. The rag was *Darbārī Toḍī*. When Alam heard the master tune to this rag and begin to play, he was struck dumb in awe and humility. It came to him that actually he knew nothing at all. Tears came to his eyes, and he realized that from that moment he would have to learn this majestic and moving instrument.

But in those days, one could not just "hire a guru," and it was only by pleading with the generous host, Raja Kishore, that he was able both to be accepted as a student and acquire a sarod of his own. Ustad Ahmad Ali was descended from musicians of the Moghul court at Delhi, and was a frequent performer at the prestigious court of Rampur, the greatest seat of classical music at the time. But, as Nulo Gopal before him, this ustad did not introduce Alam to the repertoire right away, instead confining him entirely to exercises. Furthermore, he required household chores from the boy, although he would take him along to play tabla or solo violin with him in concerts. He even took Alam with him when he visited musicians in the courtesans' quarters in Calcutta, where they heard some of the great thumri singers of the day. Alam listened to his master teach, perform, and practice, and then practiced in secret on his own. One day, Ahmad Ali heard the boy playing *Darbārī Toḍī* behind a locked door. He became enraged, and accused the lad of stealing his music, saying that he was not ready for that level of playing. From that day, the boy's training became even more sparse.

The ustad decided to go to Rampur and take the boy with him, thinking that he would perhaps be able to leave him there. They played programs along the way. During his few years under the ustad, Allauddin had been earning some money playing violin in public, and kept a strict account of it. He had also saved money in managing the household accounts. When they reached Rampur, he gave it all to his guru, along with the account book, so that there would be no ill feelings about money.

When Ahmad Ali returned to Calcutta, he left Allauddin alone in Rampur, living in a very small room. Allauddin resolved to meet the Rampur court musician Ustad Wazir Khan, son of the renowned Ustad Amir Khan, two of the greatest names in North Indian vina playing, and direct descendents of Miyan Tansen. For six months he went daily to the palace in order to arrange an audience, but the master would not hear or see him. Desperate, he bought a suicidal dose of opium. Fortunately, a Moslem priest persuaded him not to act rashly and drafted a letter to the Nawab of Rampur explaining the boy's plight and why the Nawab should hear him. By dashing in front of Nawab Hamid Ali's carriage, he got his message into the hands of the ruler. The Nawab, a respected musician himself, agreed to hear him perform, which he did shortly thereafter. Alam sang, and played on the sarod and violin, all much to the delight and amazement of the ruler who, upon hearing Alam's sad story, arranged for his discipleship to his own guru, Mohammad Wazir Khan. Allauddin was to learn the traditions of the Seni Gharana in vocal music, sarod, sursringar, and rabab with this esteemed teacher for more than forty years.

Wazir Khansahib imparted khas talım (special training)*to Allauddin Khansahib meticulously in every respect. Thus, in Allauddin Khansahib a unique and unprecedented assemblage of invaluable materials and styles belonging to different renowned gharanas was realized, and by dint of his extreme perseverance, practice, and wholehearted devotion he became the most excellent and versatile musician of his day.*

Ravi Shankar

Although Allauddin did not learn vina from Wazir Khansahib, for it was the ustad's principle to give this special training only to blood family members, he was so impressed with his disciple's ability and dedication that he showed him all the techniques of the Seni Beenkars (vina players) on sarod. In later life, Wazir Khansahib even offered to teach Allauddin vina, but the latter declined in deference to the family tradition. In Rampur, there were at times five hundred musicians at the court. Alam (Allauddin's nickname and later pen name) was well respected, and many renowned court musicians who resided there were happy to share their knowledge with this eager, humble, and dedicated young man. He set up his rooms at a corner near the main gate of the town, and hosted many visiting artists, involving them in conversations about music, and learning their compositions. Among his many guru brothers were the ustad's three sons, the Nawab himself and his son, and the preeminent sarodiya Hafiz Ali Khan. Later, the influential musicologist Vishnu Narayan Bhatkhande also became Ustad Wazir Khan's disciple.

Shortly after World War I, Allauddin followed the suggestion and financial sponsorship of his guru and made a concert tour of North India to learn, listen, and play with many of the famous musicians of the day. He began in Calcutta where a wealthy zemindar was hosting an all-night program in his palatial home.

At first there was no place assigned for my father to play in that program, but when there was a break for tea in the early hours of the morning, the host thought that my father could play at that time, and he could be free of his social obligation. My father began to play at four a.m. When they heard his music the guests and other musicians all came back into the room. There was a stunned attention: cigarettes went out in their hands and tea became cold in the cups. My father played for four more hours; no one had ever heard a concert like that before.

Ali Akbar Khan

The host of the party was a friend of the Maharaja of the small state of Maihar, Madhya Pradesh, who had asked him to be on the lookout for a suitable person who could play many instruments, to serve as chief court musician. Allauddin was invited to audition for the position, and so went to Maihar. The Maharaja had many instruments spread out all over a large room, and asked each to be played, interrupting every one or two minutes. "Why does he keep stopping me?" Allauddin thought to himself. Finally the Maharaja stopped the testing and said that Allauddin's music was the most powerful he had ever heard. The position was offered, but at first Allauddin deferred, saying that he was not ready, and further, that permission must be had from Wazir Khansahib. This was secured by a dispatch sent to Rampur.

Can anyone adore the Almighty without a music?
Allauddin Khansahib

For more than fifty years, Allauddin, or "Baba" (father) as he came to be known, was the musician-saint of Maihar. This village has a famous temple to Sharada-ma, which is a place of pilgrimmage to thousands of devout Hindus. Baba himself made a daily walk up the small mountain to the temple. In time, pilgrims also came to see Baba and to get his *darshan,* or the spiritual benefits of beholding a saint or god. It was in Maihar that his home became a musical *āshram* (hermitage), where hundreds of students were trained, and hundreds more came for guidance and inspiration.

Oh, my mind!
You think you understand so much!
When your own faults and shortcomings have no limits,
You go on looking for blemishes in others!
A favorite song of Allauddin Khansahib

In his own life and practice, Allauddin pursued music with single-minded zeal, practicing up to sixteen and twenty-three hours a day. On occasion, he is said to have tied his hair to the ceiling so that if he fell asleep, his head would be jerked back and he would awaken and continue to practice. He would have his food liquified so that he could drink it with one hand while practicing with the other. His daily ritual included a bath, *namāz* (prayers), respectful acknowledging to his instruments, and ritual offering of flowers and incense to pictures of Saraswati (or Sharada) and all the great saints and musicians of antiquity, including Beethoven. He was a vegetarian and never touched alcohol. He was a personal friend of Rabindranath Tagore. His teachings and his self-composed song lyrics were filled with devotional aphorisms, and he paid equal homage to Moslem and Hindu precepts.

He made no distinction between people on the basis of religion, language, race, etc. He was an angel of Hindu-Muslim unity and national integration of all sections of Indians, be they Christian, Sikh, Buddhist, Parsee, Muslim, or Hindu.

Anjana Debnath Roy

Baba Allauddin's character was saintly, loving, and pious, and at the same time austere and stern. The tales of his bursting into tears of devotion and joy while playing and teaching are many—as many as the ones about his legendary temper which would flare into a rage if he sensed the least bit of arrogance or lack of attention to the music. He would listen behind closed doors while a student practiced, and then burst into the room if the student began wavering in pitch, rhythm, or concentration. He would teach at all hours of the day, from before dawn to late into the evening, and hurriedly call students to his room to learn a composition that came fresh to his mind. He taught in all styles and demanded that every student practice vocal music as well as that student's chosen instrument. The knowledge and technique he imparted is a derivation founded on a bedrock understanding of vocal and instrumental traditions refashioned into a comprehensive new stylistic fusion: the Baba Allauddin Gharana of Hindustani classical music.

He had a strong antipathy toward anything narrow in the sphere of teaching. He was a teacher incarnate with the purest vibration. Any student, if really deserving, had from him the shower of his blessings, and by the sheer touch of his genius felt quite transformed.

Nikhil Banerjee

From his home in Maihar, Baba would often tour and play concerts all over India. His concerts were awesome for their depth and fecundity, speed and stamina. On more than one occasion the tabla player had to be replaced in mid-recital having been worn out by Baba. His command of the old rags and rhythmical varieties, rare rags, and newly composed rags and tals was astounding, and the extent of his compositions and command of their development became legendary.

I had the proud privilege of accompanying him on tabla on numerous occasions and each time I played I was thunderstruck with his inimitable and masterly display. He created an atmosphere surcharged with sur, tal, and laya (tone, meter, and rhythm) *of unique nature. On some occasions while playing he was found in a trance with tears in his eyes as if holding communion with the Almighty.*

Hirendra Kumar Ganguly

In the 1930s, he made several trips to Europe as Music Director for the Uday Shankar Dance Company. His early experiences in stage music made him ideal for this position, but his heart was not in it and he begged leave to return to India to concentrate on classical music and teaching. During these tours, he started teaching the young dancer and sitarist Ravi Shankar, a brother of Uday Shankar, and the youth was so impressed with the master, that he, too, left the dance a year later to concentrate on sitar in Maihar.

Whenever you are giving a performance, meditate on your guru first and then you will see that he takes you over and carries you through. Whenever you play a rag, begin with worshipping and welcoming it. Imagine it to be a deity. Bow down and pray that it should have mercy on you, and it should become alive through your medium. Never approach a rag with a feeling of pride or vanity in your heart. Music grows out of the purest feelings of your soul, and hence the mind of the musician, if only purified, can produce the vibration.

Allauddin Khansahib

Today, the sarod and the sitar are the two most popular instruments played in North Indian classical music, and Baba redesigned them both to accommodate his expanded ideas about their music. He enlarged the sarod, adding additional sympathetic strings, and to the sitar he added two bass strings which made it a kind of crossbreed between the treble sitar and the bass surbahar. Each instrument was better designed, therefore, to present the full alap-jor-jhala of the Seni Beenkar dhrupad style. He also designed several new instruments, among them the sitar-banjo, the nul-tarang, and a bowed combination of the sarinda and the sarod, which he called the chandrasarang.

Of historic significance was the new trail Allauddin Khan blazed in the field—the veena-based fusion of gayaki, layakari, and tantrakari (vocal, rhythmic, and instrumental techniques) *and its adoption of the playing of instruments like the sarod, sitar, and several others. And he himself showed how this approach made it possible for our ragas and raginis to emerge in their true form, dignity, grandeur, colour, and sparkle.*

Illustrated Weekly of India

In Maihar after World War I were a number of homeless orphans. Baba Allauddin assembled them, made arrangements for their provision, and taught them to play Indian classical instruments in an orchestra which he called the Maihar Band. It was a pioneering effort in this type of ensemble, for although there is evidence that such combinations may have been common in ancient and medieval India, they had not been heard for centuries. The Maihar Band learned compositions by heart and toured all over India, playing a repertoire which included classical traditional compositions and newer, light classical and harmonically innovative ones as well. He was also the director of the Maharaja's brass band and a bagpipe band, and was responsible for ensemble music for many court occasions.

You will be surprised to know that Baba's orchestral compositions were roughly five hundred in number, composed mostly in the middle period of his long life. The more surprising to me was that he never wrote anywhere, even in his personal notebooks, anything of those huge number of compositions. But he could easily detect the slightest fault in the application of any note or ornament on any of those compositions even thirty years after their creation. What an uncommonly sharp memory he was master of!

Robin Ghosh

For his lifelong creative and musical contributions to the culture of India, Baba received numerous degrees and awards. He was in great demand to sit on examining boards at a number of schools, including the Maris College of Lucknow. He was a governing fellow in the Sangit Natak Akademi (National

Academy of the Performing Arts), and held doctorates from Shantiniketan and Rabindra Bharati Universities. He was accorded the Indian government's highest honors, *Padmabhusan* ("Lotus Adorned Master") and *Padmavibhusan*, in 1958 and 1971. Today there are several music festivals and scholarships honoring his name. Amid these honors, many of which came ironically late in his life, he remained humbly indifferent to worldly acclaim, and did not change his manner of simple dress or life-style in rural Maihar. He passed away in 1972.

One of the great instrumentalists, Ustad Allauddin was a greater teacher, and perhaps the greatest among musicians who cared for devotion and discipline as the way towards music. His humility and unassuming character, his belief in music as a way of life rather than a profession, earned for him a place in the music world rarely equaled by his contemporaries. His entire life had been filled with a richness of melody and the incomparable beauty he created during the depiction of a raga that transcended the material.

What was his contribution to Hindustani music? His fundamental contribution was to music and not to Hindustani music alone. Music, in its essence, was what he practiced through ragas.

Arun Bhattacharya

Ali Akbar Khansahib

Ustad Ali Akbar Khan's life is also a manifold epic: it is the story of a brilliantly gifted musician and his fecund creative life; the story of the achievements of one reared in the life-style of an ancient princely court musician who, through both circumstances and inclination, adapted his life and music to the demands of the worldwide concert stage; and it is the chronicle of a teacher who has brought his classical traditions to the West and taught them for years and to thousands of students the world over.

Shorty before Khansahib was born on April 14, 1922, in Shivpur, East Bengal, his father, Baba Allauddin Khan, had established himself as chief court musician of Maihar in Madhya Pradesh. It was here that Ali Akbar grew up; but Baba Allauddin always maintained close ties with Bengal, and these two homes have been focal throughout both their lives. In the spacious home built in Maihar, which is called the "Madina Bhavan" after Ali Akbar's mother, Khansahib received his long training from his father.

After initiating his son to music with singing, Allauddin Khansahib put a great variety of instruments in front of him, and for a few weeks, he would be asked to play on one or another of them. But he took to the sarod from a very early age, and the father decided to teach his son all the instrumental styles on one instrument. Thenceforth, Ali Akbar concentrated on vocal music, sarod, and tabla. Ali Akbar's uncle Aftabuddin gave him training in tabla when the family visited East Bengal where they lived for a short while in the ancestral home in Shivpur in the Tripura District. The rigors with which young Ali Akbar was trained, and the restrictions that his father made followed his father's ascetic principles: he was frequently made to get up before dawn and practice for four hours before a light breakfast, then take a lesson and practice again before lunch. After a short nap, more practice, another lesson until late at night. Then a light supper, and short sleep. And this stern regimen went on until Khansahib was in his twenties, frequently up to eighteen hours a day. If he deviated in his practice or forgot a passage, his father was quick to become upset, and if there was any playing out of tune or rhythm, his father's temper would rise so quickly that the whole house trembled in silent fear. Baba Allauddin showered him with all his own rich background in rag, tal, and composition, and the whole atmosphere of the house was filled with devotional music and the mood of spiritual practice, or *sādhanā*.

He was joined in his studies by his sister Annapurna, who sang and played sitar and surbahar. Many other students lived there from time to time, including Timir Baran and Pannalal Ghosh, and many famous musical visitors whose recitals Ali Akbar was continually called to accompany with tabla or pakawaj. When Ali Akbar was fourteen, Ravi Shankar joined the household to learn sitar. Everyone was usually taught separately, but on some occasions, Ali Akbar, Annapurna, and Ravi Shankar would learn together at the feet of Baba Allauddin.

While receiving lessons from the Acharya (venerated teacher), *Ustad Ali Akbar Khansahib, Smt. Annapurna Devi and I used to sit before him in a semicircle. Baba would give us two tans, then shed tears out of profound devotion and feeling and we would join him. During our lessons from Baba and on many other occasions we felt considerably the love of music and spiritual realizations.*

Ravi Shankar

Annapurnadevi and Ravi Shankari were eventually married and, when Ali Akbar and he later played duets together, the music emerged as if out of one mind from the years they had spent learning from the same guru.

In 1944, Khansahib began his professional career as a music director for All India Radio in Lucknow. Shortly thereafter, the Maharajah of Jodhpur in Rajesthan asked his father to become court musician there. Allauddin Khansahib declined, saying that he was like a father to his own Maharaja, and instead sent his own son. Ali Akbar's function there was to play concerts for the court, provide music for official functions, compose for and direct the orchestra, and teach music. The Maharajah was a forward-thinking ruler, and he and Khansahib planned a large university for the arts in Jodhpur, with schools of music, dance, drama, film, and the visual arts. They formed a radio station in Jodhpur, the first in Rajasthan. But the Maharaja died in an airplane accident in 1948, and many of those dreams vanished in the new waves of enthusiasm for Indian Independence.

Khansahib moved to Bombay, where he had been persuaded to compose for some films. Despite succuss in the film industry, this life was not satisfying to him and he moved in the late 1950s to Calcutta. From his base there, he began his regimen of practice, teaching, recording, and playing concerts. Since 1968, he has devoted increasingly more time to teaching, and until his father's death in 1972 Khansahib would continue to receive lessons during visits to his family home in Maihar.

In 1955, he visited the United States at the invitation of his lifelong friend Yehudi Menuhin, who was one of the first people in the West to recognize his genius.

I have been transported beyond dreams and enveloped within the magic weave he spins of sound and time...[he is possibly] the greatest musician in the world.

Yehudi Menuhin

On arriving in New York, Khansahib appeared on the *Omnibus* television show and recorded the first Western long-playing record of Indian classical music. This was the beginning of many concert trips to the West and around the world. He performs regularly in European countries, the United States and Canada, Japan, Australia, and, still frequently, in India.

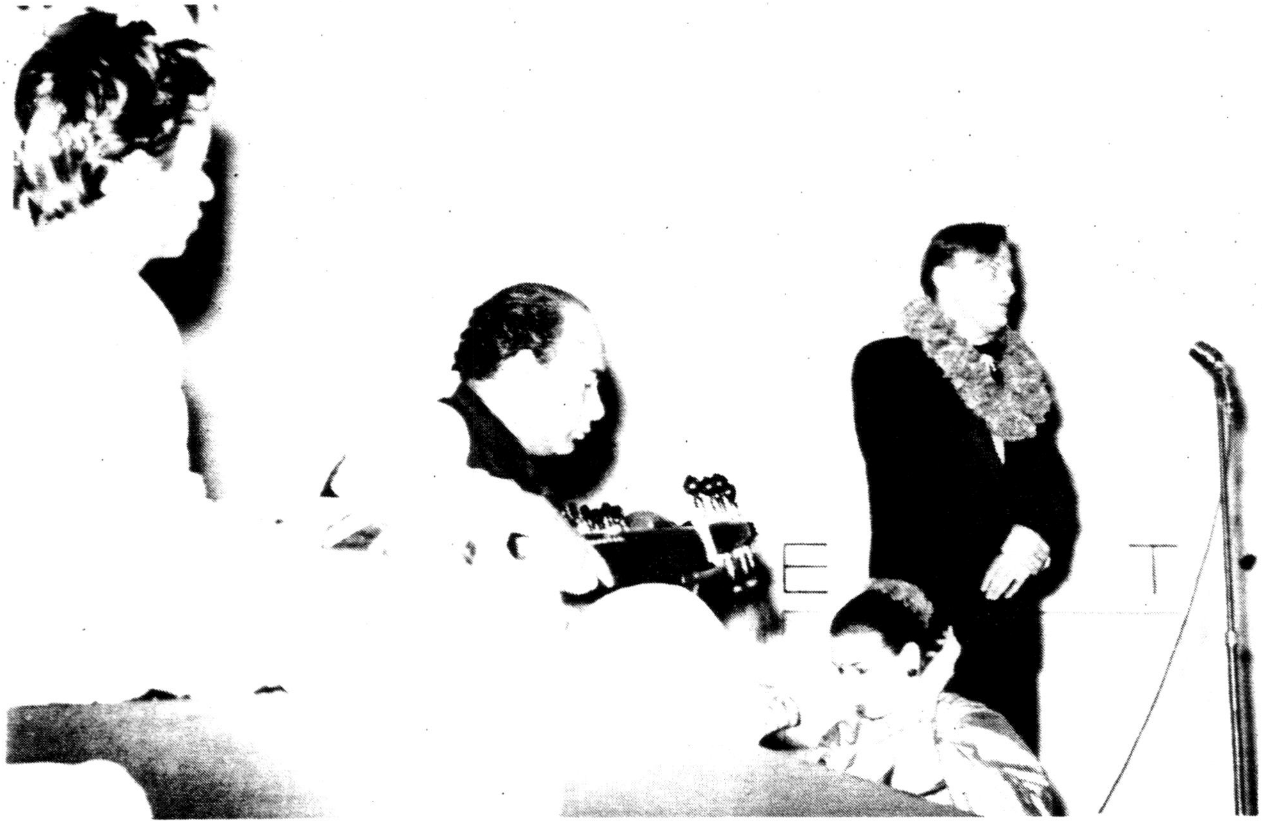

In the autumn of 1955, Yehudi Menuhin introduces Khansahib and tabla player Chatur Lal to Western audiences in a New York concert. Prof. Diana Brown, now of the University of Hawaii, arranges flowers on the stage.

In 1965, he was invited by Mr. and Mrs. Samuel Scripps to teach at a summer school in Berkeley, California, organized by the American Society for Eastern Arts. That summer there were five students. He went on concert tour that fall, and returned the next year to find forty students eager to learn. The following summer there were eighty, and the older students were clamoring for regularly continuing instruction. In the fall of 1967, plans were made at the home of Alan Watts to establish a full-time school devoted to the Baba Allauddin Gharana traditions of North Indian classical music, and in 1968 the Ali Akbar College of Music opened on Warring Street, Berkeley, for the summer session. It has been in full-time operation ever since, moving to its present location in San Rafael in 1977. Khansahib has been in residence at the school continually for more than twenty years, and spends at least nine months of the year teaching students of all backgrounds who come from all over the world. It is a unique situation—students can sit with one of the great masters in the traditional setting, learning music by rote in the time-honored oral fashion at the feet of the guru.

In his attitude toward the literature of rag, Khansahib is at the same time narrowly conservative and widely imaginative. He will teach and play hundreds of compositions from the standard rags in the general repertoire, and often teaches the same composition a number of times over the course of the years. Before teaching a composition, he will look over his father's notes and those he made himself while a student. He also checks in the published literature for versions of certain rags, but it is rare that he is satisfied with them. For example, it is common for him to look in a book (for instance the printed collections of V.D. Paluskar or Vishnu Narayan Bhatkhande) for a springboard to his memory. He may make a comment about the composition, especially a negative one about the infidelity of the composition to the rag, or about how his father taught that composition, or about how music cannot be learned from books. Usually, however, he silently puts the book away, meditates a few minutes as he muses with the harmonium or sarod, and begins to reconstruct the rag or the composition from his memory. Even if it is from the Seni (from Tansen) gharana, in the main only the words remain from a printed edition.

Khansahib is active as a composer of rags, and has left a legacy of fully constructed masterpieces as well as hundreds of sketches of new rags. Among the rags which he has polished, played in concert, and recorded is the one which is closely identified with him, *Chandranandan*. It is a combination of four rags, *Mālkauns*, *Chandrakauns*, *Nandakauns*, and *Kaushi-Kānṛā*. It typifies one of his approaches to composition, that of artful rag combination. Other of his rags which have been thus generated are *Bhūp Mānd*, *Jogiyā Kalingḍa*, and *Bhairavī Bhatiyār*. Rags which he has both welded together from traditional rags in the literature, but to which he has given additional unique qualities are *Lājwanti*, *Mishra Shivranjani*, *Medhāvi*, *Gauri Manjari*, *Alamgiri*, *Alamalaya*, and *Durgeshwarī*. In addition to these are thousands of rags which he has sketched out in classes, but have yet to be played in concert or on record.

During his stay in Bombay, when Khansahib was active in the Indian film industry, he composed award-winning music for several films, including *Hungry Stones* and *Devi*. He also created the music for the *son-et-lumiere* production at the Red Fort in Delhi. But this style of composition did not fulfill him, and he turned away from it to concentrate on classical music. The art of combining instruments was revived for some time at the Ali Akbar College of Music when he composed many orchestral and dance production pieces for an East-West fusion ensemble called the New Maihar Band. He is often called upon to compose music for other Indian concert artists, and although these compositions may be in light classical genres, they are always touched with his classical sensitivities of tunefulness, rhythmic interest, and profound sense of balance.

As a featured artist in concert, Khansahib does not play to the gallery. He rigorously follows the dictates of his creative instincts and artistic mood. If he senses a new melodic movement in his mind, he will play it, for the very first time, on the stage. If he creates an entirely new pattern, he will play the passage two or three times until he is satisfied with it, often weaving "mistakes" into the fabric of his creation so that the integrity of the composition is assured. In other words, he does not polish a passage backstage for the audience's gratification. He is even careful not to practice a rag in the dressing room and then walk onstage to play something rehearsed. His is a music of "composition on the spot," and he fully trusts in the Creative Spirit of the moment. As a result, his music is always new, sometimes radically different, and sometimes jarring to a conservative's sensitivity; but the concerts are always satisfying at the highest artistic and technical level, and especially so to those who understand the exquisite risks that Khansahib takes. He still presents dhrupad style alap in a serious rag, matched with a composition in tal, no matter who the audience might be. A second rag is likely to be light classical, often a *rāgmālā* (garland, or mixture, of rags), as well as folk melodies from India and the West. Although he invariably begins these light recitals with a mood of *shṛingār* (love and joy) full of popular appeal, sometimes his so-called "light music," permitting as it does the introduction of borrowed notes to a rag, becomes as dramatically modern sounding as its contemporaries, Western art music and jazz.

Khansahib has received awards from governments, universities, and cultural societies the world over. These include five honorary doctorates and, in 1990, the prestigious Padmavibhusan award of the Indian government. In June, 1991, he received a MacArthur Fellowship (United States) for his life's work of "creating, cultivating, and transmitting North Indian classical music." However, he often says that his highest honor came when his father called him *Swara Samrat*, "Emperor of Notes."

Maestro Ali Akbar Khan is the most sensitive, intuitively masterful musician of the age. One can listen to him at any level, at the first encounter or for the five hundredth time, and always come away astounded. There are individual areas of contemplation and vitality which he alone seems to communicate. [His music] is hypnotizing, mesmerizing, ethereal, and mystifying, peaceful, enthralling, and exciting beyond description.

Heuwell Tircuit, *San Francisco Chronicle*

Today Khansahib lives with his wife, Mary Johnson Khan, and three children in San Anselmo, California.

Madina Manjari, Allauddin Khansahib's wife and Ali Akbar's mother.

Manners among Musicians

Since Indian music is rooted in an ancient culture, many norms of behavior have become ingrained in its practitioners. Also, the music, being regarded as a yoga of sound itself, naturally adopts certain of the philosophical ideas from the spiritual sciences and the important way they affect patterns of daily life.

"Is this music a religion, Khansahib?"

"No, not a religion. Nothing to do with that. You don't have to believe in this or that like you do in religion. My father taught that all religions had the right way...but music is beyond that. At the same time, you show respect to music as Nada-Brahma—the language of God. Like you can pray anytime, day or night, but when you are with your father you don't act the same way as when you are out with your friends. Like that, you show respect, you see."

Showing respect is something that comes more or less naturally to everyone, although the particular ways in which it is traditionally done in India may seem different at first. Once learned, these become sensible and effortless.

Head and Feet

The head is considered the top, or highest, aspect of the body, and the feet the lowest. In India, where sandals and bare feet are the rule, the feet can get dirty in the world pretty fast. The head and feet, then, are together a symbol of high and low, pure and impure, and recognition of this is an important part of social manners. The feet are not pointed at people, especially at those loved and respected. When sitting in chairs, we rarely raise the issue; but sitting on the floor, where legs demand to be stretched and extended from time to time, often requires that one always be sensitive to where the feet are pointing. When sitting, fold your legs with your feet underneath you; then, if you need to stretch, be careful not to point them at anyone.

Sitting upright with the back straight (but not rigid) in front of the teacher is considered a suitable posture for attention and learning. Lounging sideways or lying down, for instance, would not be appropriate.

When in a crowded room, one often sees someone entering with the right hand extended downward as if to indicate a path. This is to avoid leading with the feet and showing disrespect to those already sitting there.

One never steps *over* anything respected, be it a book, an instrument, or whatever, and certainly not a person.

If the feet are exceptionally dirty before a lesson, it would be considered proper to wash them before sitting in front of the teacher.

In India, the right hand is kept clean and used for eating. The left one is used for matters of personal hygiene. Gestures of respect, like shaking hands in the West, are done with the right hand, not the left.

Namaskar

Namaskār (or *namaste*) is a gesture with many variations. When used in greeting people of any age, both palms are brought together in front of the chest, and the head is inclined slightly downward. One might also say, "*namaskār*" ("*namaste*"). When meeting someone for the first time, or saying goodbye, it is the commonly used gesture. The meaning of this approximates "God-in-me-greets-God-in-you." Today, of course, the handshake has become a common form of greeting in India as well.

Pranam

Praṇām is used for greeting and showing respect to parents, teachers, and those to whom one wishes to show great respect. In one common form of pranam, one touches the feet of the teacher with the right hand and then touches one's own forehead, sometimes also the heart. It is a way of humbly acknowledging *darshan*, the blessing that comes with being in the presence of (or even catching sight of) a holy person or image. Musicians commonly pranam elder and respected musicians in greeting, before or after lessons and performances. In certain ceremonious forms of pranam, the student or devotee will prostrate himself completely at the feet of the teacher with his head on the ground. This is often mistaken for person-worship, although it is actually a gesture of recognition and a demonstration of humility and respect for the knowledge and tradition that the master embodies.

For Westerners, who tend to be rather self-conscious about these types of gestures, the most important thing is to behave in a manner that feels right, and not feel obliged to do this or that. The discomfort of artificial manners is felt by everyone, and should not intrude in the honesty of relating person-to-person no matter which cultural patterns one may be used to.

Names

These ways of showing respect are also represented in everyday speech. In Hindi, the suffix *-jī* is added to names (Johnji, Raviji, Rashadji, Barbaraji) and to titles (Panditji, Doctorji, Swamiji) and family names (Maji, Didiji, Papaji). It is an easy way to address anyone with an affectionate form of respect, and is even used by itself as a substitute for the name of the person being addressed.

The terms for family relationships—like the Western "uncle," "tio," "grampa," "daddy," "oma," etc.—are also used by musicians to show respect to teachers and elders. The most common are *bābā* (father), *mātā* (mother), *dādā* (elder brother), *dīdī* (elder sister). The latter three are used as suffixes to names as well—Sharadama, Sumatidi, Anniedi, Bruceda, Mohanda. Study with a teacher creates familial bonds. Brothers in the music are often called *bhāī* (or *gurubhai*), and sisters *bahen*, and these terms are also used as suffixes. The suffix *-dev* (god) or *-devi* (goddess) might be used to show extreme reverence—Gurudev, Sharadadevi.

In the old days, the titles *Ustad* (Moslem) and *Pandit* (Hindu) were awarded to musicians by the kings as recognition of their high mastery of their art. They were not so freely used as they are today, when lack of title might mean lack of box office attraction. These titles are also used somewhat more informally to refer to one's teacher. However, older musicians often smile sadly when they hear this or that musician referred to as "Pandit" or "Ustad." They are still remembering the great accomplishment and respect which those titles once represented. Kappelmeister, cantor, and maestro are possible Western equivalents.

The suffix *-sāhib* (pronounced in one syllable, like the Swedish car, Saab) was attached to the names of those Moslem musicians who were titled in the court, as in "Khansahib." Like the title "Ustad," it is more freely used today to show respect, and even is attached to non-Moslem names (albeit with a little smile), as in "Jamessahib" or "Krishnasahib."

Concert Behavior

During concerts, classical musicians appreciate the kind of quiet atmosphere which usually characterizes Western classical concerts. But the musician may wish that the exaggerated formality and distance of Western classical audiences and the glare of the spotlit proscenium stage be lessened somewhat.

They will ask that the lights be kept on in the hall so that the audience can be seen by the artists. They will show appreciation to fellow artists by shaking their heads when they are moved by a musical passage. This appears to be the Western gesture for "no," but is, rather, a method of showing silent appreciation. When hearing lighter music, listeners may respond vocally to a well-turned phrase, crying out *"vāh, vāh," "kyā bāt"* (what a thing), *or "bahut achhā"* (very good). In classical music these vocal displays are reduced to a muted *"ah-hah."* While the performers usually respond warmly to these displays of appreciation, a sense of moderation is necessary; there are always some people who exclaim every minute or so, or otherwise loudly draw attention to themselves and spoil the atmosphere for music.

Knowledgeable listeners may keep the tal with hand claps and waves, but these must be kept silent and unobtrusive lest they distract others or even make it difficult for the performers to hear the rhythm. There is nothing worse than having to sit next to a zealous student clapping the tal loudly, and usually erroneously, during a performance.

Theory of Rag

It is always said that music theory, like grammar in language, can never catch up with usage. One definition of theory is "the words and principles which describe and prescribe musical practice." It is an ancient science in India, and writings on music exist from the beginning of the Christian era in the West. The *Nāṭyaśhāstra*, *Nāradashiksa*, *Dattilam*, *Bṛihaddesi*, and *Saṅgītaratnākara* are treatises of ancient India which reveal a flourishing musical life and establish the vocabulary as well as much of the practical foundations for the modern music. However, there are no musical examples surviving from this ancient period which can fully illustrate the concepts within the treatises. Also, it is generally agreed that the medieval period of Persian and Islamic rule in the North of India brought both new developments and new literature to the music, but the extent and precise nature of these innovations are yet to be identified. So, while it is clear that there is a continuum of ancient values and practices which were modified through the ages, it remains difficult to apply many ancient theoretical terms to modern practice.

Even in recent history, regionalism in language and practice also confounds theory. For instance, the rag *Jaijaivanti*, has many versions, and while it may be agreed by all that it is an evening rag, the theoretical precepts, such as the *ṭhāṭ*, *vādi*, *chalan*, etc., may have a number of variations. It can be an unending, perhaps meaningless pursuit, and many musicians like Allauddin Khansahib could not abide the idleness of such theoretical discussions. There are many stories of the pitfalls of believing too strongly in the importance of theory over practical music.

One beautiful spring evening, a donkey and his friend, the jackal, broke into a farmer's vegetable garden. The beauty of the moon and stars, the friendship of his companion, and the abundance of the garden went to the donkey's head.

"Ah, on a night like this I feel like bursting into song," he said.

"No, no," said the jackal, knowing well what a donkey's voice sounds like, "you'll wake the farmer. And besides, what do you know about music?"

"What do I know about music? What do **I** *know about music?" At that, he recited the names of the thats, the male rags, the names of the important ragas and all their relatives, and on and on. And, to cap it off, he began singing. The braying of the donkey aroused the farmer, and he came and beat the animals and chased them out of the garden.*

No matter how much you know about music, it doesn't make you a musician.

The Panchatantra

The point of the story notwithstanding, some discussion of theory is unavoidable, and plays an especially important role in the teaching of music. All musicians talk about music, especially while they teach, and even their conversations about music on the informal level are, in actuality, theory. In the outline below, which is distilled from a number of sources and has evolved over years of theory lessons and discussion at the Ali Akbar College, the concepts about music can be collected into three divisions: those which relate to aesthetics and extramusical associations; those having to do with the pitches and their movements in the rags themselves; and those which concern the performance of the rag.

Fundamentals to keep in mind whenever rendering a rag

Aesthetic and spiritual principles of rag

1. *guru*
2. *ras* (mood)
3. time or season

Structure of rag

4. *ṭhāṭ*, male rag, or *mela*
5. *arohi-avarohi*
6. *jāti* (*aurav, sharav, sampurṇ*, or mixed)
7. *vivādī* and *varjit svara*
8. *varṇa*
9. *vādī-samvādī* (*anuvādī-sahavādī*)
10. strong notes and weak notes (*bahutva*, and *alpatva*)
11. resting places (*vishrānti sthān*)
12. *shrutis* and tuning
13. *ang* and *sthān*
14. *pakaṛ*, heart of the rag, or *svarūp*
15. *chalan* and *vakra* movements
16. *vidārs*, and typical sequences or harmonies
17. ornaments

Rendering of rag

18. important compositions in rag
19. how to start and finish the asthai and antara
20. source of rag: ancient, modern, pure, mixed, combined
21. style of the rag: dhrupad, khyal, light classical
22. shadows (*chhāyā*) of other rags
23. appropriate matching of rag and tal
24. sequence of the rag in a program or practice
25. appropriate rag for audience
26. *guru*

Guru

Gurū kṟipā bina vidyā koī nahī pāve

This is the refrain of a famous song text dedicated to the guru: "No one can get knowledge without the blessing of the teacher." The classical music of India has always been passed on through the tradition of *gurū-sisyā-parampara,* the age-old chain of teacher and student. It is considered a sacred relationship, and the continuum in the relationship to one's guru stretches to infinity both backward and forward in time. The guru's conception of the rags and tals is the student's most important link to the essence of the music. A performance, and even the practice, begins and ends with the attuning of the musician to that principle.

Guru is next to God in respect and belief.

Time

Each rag has a time of day associated with it, and many have seasonal and festive affinities as well. Rag time references are often based on the *prahar*s (watches), or three-hour time periods. Since India lies close to the equator, there is not as great a seasonal variation in daylight and nighttime hours as in many other parts of the world, and so the rag times can be set against clock-time with greater sureness. Older systems may use one a.m. as the "midnight" hour, so in the following chart one would have to add one hour to the times given. The nature of the sun's yearly time fluctuations has much to do with the mood of many of the rags, especially those in the two half-light periods between night and day known as *sandhyaprakāsh* ("meeting of the light," or dawn and dusk). For these several reasons, the time periods listed below must also be adjusted for seasonal changes. Although each male rag has a season associated with it, the rags for the rainy season and for spring are the ones whose specific seasonal connotations are the most important.

Certain rags, especially ones with light classical traditions, are less confined in their time rendering. Others are more specific: "when the first light of the sun is seen" (rag *Ahir Bhairav*); or "when the first candles (lamps) are lit in the evening" (rag *Purvi*); or "when the sky begins to be red in the afternoon" (rag *Bhimpalashri*). The following general chart lists some of the general tendencies of the timing of rags. The concepts of *ras* (feeling or mood) are discussed in a separate chapter.

The eight *prahars*, or watches of the day and night

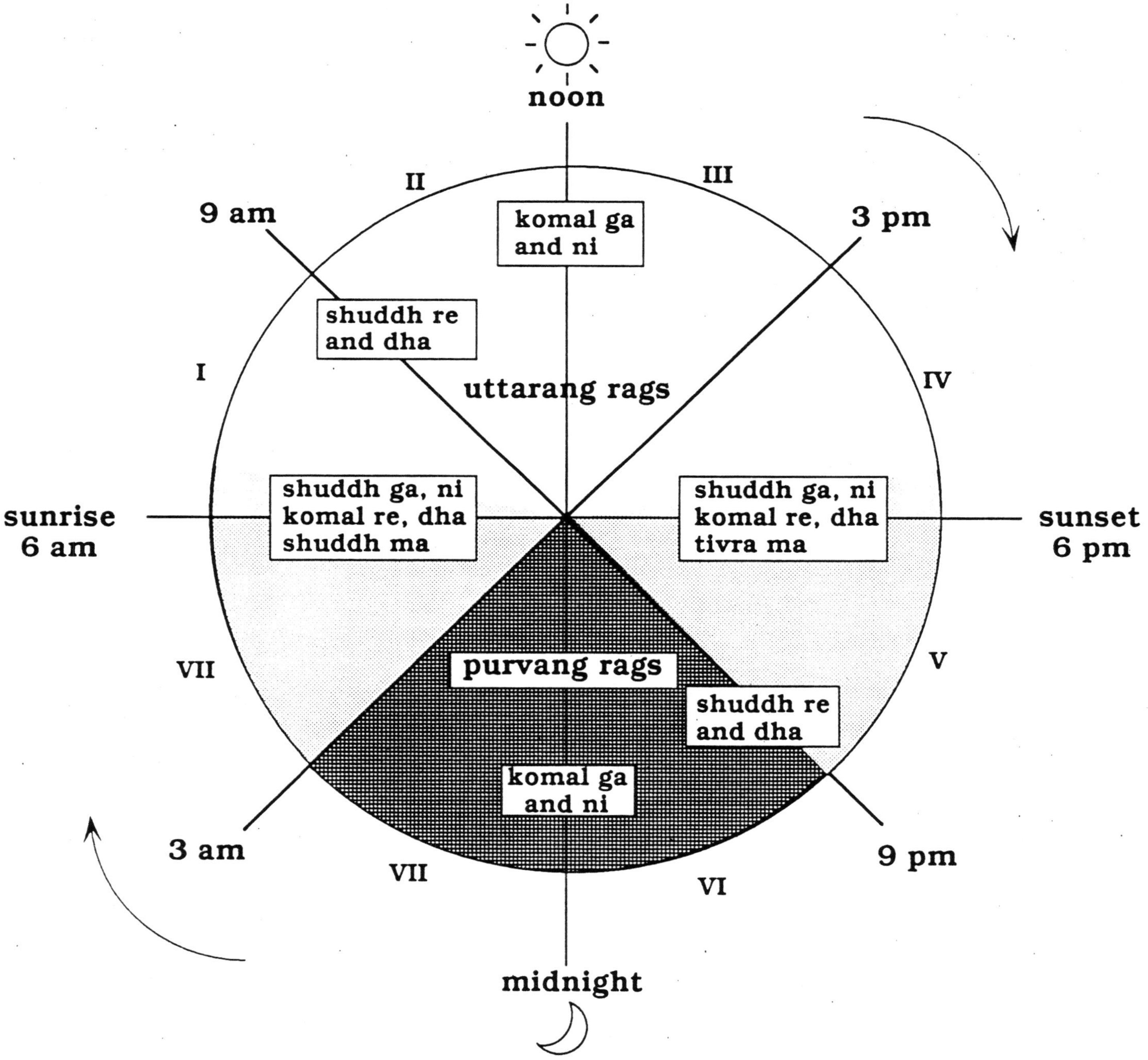

(Adapted from Deva, 1981, and Wade, 1979)

Rag Structure

The rags can be classified and learned through their various structural factors listed as Nos. 4 through 17 (p. 253). The *ṭhāṭ*s and *mela*s (No. 4) are discussed in the following chapter on rag organization. Some rags are very much like scales or modes, and others have many variants from their scale forms. Still others are hardly describable in terms of scale at all. Just as the classification of a rag into a scale may be meaningful in one case and arbitrary in another, the importance of these structural factors varies considerably from rag to rag. In one case the vadi-samvadi relationship will be clearly evident and important to bear in mind; in another it may have a lesser significance. In short, there is no overruling structural framework which governs all rags, and this is why rags must be learned through *bandish*es, or compositions. It is the songs that give the nature of the melodic material of rag, and the abstractions enumerated below (numbered from the chart) may or may not fill out the whole picture. The descriptive phrases listed here are often more important in helping to distinguish one rag from another than they might be in defining what an individual rag actually is. In summary it may be said that the rules of rag are not ends in themselves but guidelines toward fulfilling the artistic potential of the music.

Arohi-Avarohi

"Do you believe in God, Khansahib?"
Pause. Then, smiling, "Well, I believe in ascending and descending."

No. 5 is the *arohī* and *avarohī*: the ascending and descending note patterns, usually simplified to scale form. This is commonly reduced to the pattern as it coheres from middle **sa** to high **sa** (one *saptak*, or octave), although not all rags actually begin on middle **sa** (some begin on lower **dha** or **ni** and ascend to high **re** or **ga**). The ascending or descending pattern suggests the characteristic note motions in a simple form which might be used in fast runs (*tāns*). It includes all the notes in the rag, and both the ascending and descending are described as being in a particular *jāti* (No. 6). *Jāti* means "caste" or "type," and there are three of them: *auṛav* (5-note), *śhaṛav* (6-note), and *sampūrṇ* (full, or 7-note). For the purposes of jati classification, the altered notes are not considered. It is usually said that a rag must have at least five notes, and except for one or two exceptions this is the case. The jatis can be combined (*misra,* mixed) in the following way to make nine in all:

Jati

ascending	**descending**	**Western term**
auṛav	auṛav	pentatonic scale
auṛav	śhaṛav	
auṛav	sampūrṇ	
śhaṛav	auṛav	
śhaṛav	śhaṛav	hexatonic scale
śhaṛav	sampūrṇ	
sampūrṇ	auṛav	
sampūrṇ	śhaṛav	
sampūrṇ	sampūrṇ	heptatonic scale

Vakra Chal

In addition, the jati may be described as *vakra* (curved, zigzag); that is, the ascending or descending pattern may have a crooked motion in it. The descent of rag *Alhaiya Bilāval* is vakra:

Ṡ N D n D P D m G R G m P m G R S

The phrase *vakra chal* (zigzag movement; No. 11), refers to these curved motions in a rag, but since all rags will have curves, these are included in the basic arohi-avarohi pattern only when they are mandatory to the motion.

Enemy Notes

Notes that are not used in the rag are said to be *varjit svar* (prohibited notes; No. 7). Although they are all *vivādī* (enemy notes) which will destroy the rag, there are certain of these notes, different in each rag, which can be used a tiny bit in shadowy ornaments or in passing note motion. The use of these is so subtle that they will never be visually notated, even though they can be faintly heard by careful listening. They lend color, shading, and charm to the rag, but misuse of them will absolutely ruin it, so vivadis must be used with caution.

Vivadi is like the poison, you see. If you drink iodine, you will die. But if you take great care, a tiny drop in the water makes it pure, and then you can drink it.

Varna

Varṇa (color; No. 8) is an ancient term originally associated with describing how a poetic text moves with melody. It is now used to generally describe note motion, or more specifically, "how a note is left or quitted." It is related to the introduction of sharps and flats in Western music, for originally, sharps led upward and flats downward. There are four different *varṇa*s: *ārohī* (ascending), *avarohī* (descending), *asthāī* (or *sthāyī*, standing), and *sanchārī* (moving, changing). If a note has arohi varna, it can be departed from only in ascending motion (like the shuddh **ni** in Khammaj). Likewise, if it has avarohi varna, it is quitted downward, like the komal **ni** in Khammaj. If it has asthai varna, it is neutral and can be left either ascending or descending (like the **dha** or **pa** in Alhaiya Bilaval, above). And if it is sanchari varna, it changes its role like the **ma** in Alhaiya Bilaval: in the first case it descends, for it is skipped in ascent; in the second, it both ascends and descends according to phrase context. This last varna is less certainly defined, and must be learned in each particular instance. Occasionally, a rag will be said to have a lot of ascending or descending varna if their primary phrases move up or down.

Note Hierarchy

Rags commonly have a hierarchy of notes (Nos.9-11). The most important note is called the *vādī*, or "king," and is always described in connection with the *samvādī*, the "prime minister." These two notes will always be a fourth or a fifth apart, and that interval is referred to as *samvād* (consonant). In certain rags, there will be a third note mentioned with governing power, the *anuvādī* (*anu-*, prefix, "along with") and this note may in turn have a samvad a fourth or fifth away, called the *sahavādī* (*saha-*, prefix, "co-"). The other notes, described as strong (*bahutva*, plenteous) or weak (*alpatva*, short-lived) are shown by composition and context, and may not be given in theoretical descriptions of the rag. Weak notes are also said to be *durbal* (weak). The resting places (*vishrānti sthān*) may be shown in the *chalan* (No. 15) and in the composition, but not actually named.

Each rag is like a small state, you see. There is a king, and a prime minister, who sees that the king's work is done. But each state is quite different, too. In this one it is the king who rules, in that one it is his council who makes the decisions. In another, the king sleeps all day and the prime minister collects the taxes and takes all the money. So, therefore, you cannot know the rag just by stating the vadi-samvadi.

Microtones and Shrutis

Very few of the thousands of classes that Khansahib has taught have passed without a reference to playing in tune. For him, it is a metaphor for life itself, and the most important thing about playing or singing a rag correctly. If one were so bold as to ask what the tuning was for a rag, he would probably answer, "Listen to me; I am showing you." He would never give a mathematical ratio description of cents, commas, or fractions. Fifths and octaves are naturally tuned, or "perfect." Other notes are often peculiar to rag. He will usually try to show this relativity of tuning by calling this "*Kāfī* **ga**," or "*Darbārī* **ga**," but would not subscribe to any scientific or mathematic system of tuning. Even though he has the greatest difficulty accepting the harmonium's tempered tuning, he often challenges the students to match their pitch with the harmonium. Moreover, to be *besurā* ("out of tune"), or similarly, *betālā* ("out of rhythm"), he continually teaches, are the cardinal sins of the musician.

When someone wants to sell you something, he gives it another name. The shrutis are like that, you see. Listen to the music, those masters that you respect. Then you will understand about shrutis. From the books and all those names you will get a wrong idea.

Tuning of the pitches of a rag can be very subtle, and the discussion of *shrutis* ("that which is heard," "the ear," "microtone"; No. 12) is too great for a complete discussion here.

The old treatises usually assign twenty-two *shrutis* to the octave, although there have been a number of conflicting discussions as to their placement and number. Tempered tuning, a structural factor in much Western music since the seventeenth century, may be accepted as a beginning guide to the placement of the twelve tones in the scale. In fact, the harmonium, once universally condemned for importing a tragic homogenization of pitch, has now gained a wide acceptance as an accompanying instrument. It is true that much subtlety has been lost with the acceptance of a tempered scale, but on the other hand the voice, and those instruments capable of subtle intonation of pitch, still render microtones fluidly. Those experienced with Western music would agree that there is a great variation in actual systems of tuning according to the many stylistic genres, kinds of instruments, and practices of musicians, even on the "highest levels" of refinement.

I am still learning about the microtones. They reach to your heart and help you feel the rags and the notes. In old theory, they say that there are twenty-two in number, but right now I feel that there are more like twenty-three and a half. There is only one **sa** *and one* **pa**. *Komal* **re**, **ga**, *and* **dha** *all have three. Shuddh* **ma**, *tivra* **ma**, *shuddh* **dha**, *and komal* **ni** *each have two. And shuddh* **re**, *shuddh* **ga**, *and shuddh* **ni** *each have one and a half.*

Specific rags may have notes placed microtonally different than the tempered scale, and these special instances, of which there are a great number, must be dealt with in context. Khansahib may say, "the **dha** is a little flat in *Bhairav*," or "don't make this **re** (in *Bhairavī*) like *Shrī* **re**," in introducing a rag. Other than that, the concept of shruti is always absorbed in the practice of rendering the rag correctly for the student.

My father used to tell me, "Your **re** *in Shri rag is not correct." I thought that he was getting old and was losing his hearing. Then, years later, after I made a recording of Shri, my father came to me and said, "Ah, I see now you have learned the correct* **re** *for Shri."*

Register

The registration of a rag—where it lies high or low in the range—is called the *sthān* (place; No. 13). There are some rags which are developed mostly in the lower register, others in the higher register, and many more which are not confined to one area or another. Each rag is commonly thought of in terms of its *ang* (limb; loosely, "tetrachord"). Occasionally, the words *ang* and *sthān* refer to the same thing. *Sthān* refers to the register in which the rag is most developed. *Ang* will be used more often in reference to the location of the vadi note. If the vadi lies between **sa** and **pa**, the rag is said to be *purvaṅg* (lower limb), and will generally be rendered between noon and midnight. If it is *uttaraṅg* (upper limb), with the vadi between **ma** and high **sa**, then it will be rendered between midnight and noon, that is, in the morning. There are many rags that have either **ma** or **pa** as vadi and could be either *ang*.

Identifying Features

For some rags, there is a particular phrase which identifies that rag. In rags with similar structures, this phrase will be used at critical moments to erase ambiguities arising from other rags which appear in the shadows. If it is short, this phrase is called the *pakaṛ* (catch, grasp), or "heart of the rag" (No. 14). If it takes a longer phrase to capture this identity, that phrase may be called the *svarūp* (feature). In everyday speech, *pakaṛ* and *svarūp* may be used interchangeably.

In presenting the rag for the first couple of times, the teacher will sketch out a picture of the rag's common movements. This is known as the *chalan* (movement), or *sādhāran chalan* (principle or usual movements; No. 15). This sketch can be slightly different each time it is given, for it is an abstract of the rag, and even though it is likened to a road map for the student to follow, it is not fixed in the sense of a composition. The chalan of a master will render the rag, its characteristic features, and *vakra chal*s (curved movements), in a few clear and bold strokes. The chalan of a lesser musician may be full of repeats and ambiguous phrases that may be common to different rags. Often the chalan will have two sections, an asthai and an antara.

Melodic Leaps

It is commonly stated that harmony, in the Western sense, is not heard in classical Indian music. This is wholly misleading, for there are many harmonic elements in rag structure. The way the rag patterns evolve often imply the leaps and intervals of chordal harmony. Sympathetic strings on an instrument may ring out with triadic echoes. It may be said that rendering a rag itself, in its most comprehensive sense, is a working out of a compound, hence contrapuntal, melodic line. The drums may play a counterpoint with the rhythm, and even play some countermelody, too. Thus, harmonic and contrapuntal elements are often quite highly developed, even in many traditional Western uses of these terms. The errors in terminology are a lingering product of well-meaning nineteenth-century amateurs who often made superficial and categorical comparisons of Indian and Western music. Unfortunately, these statements have led to misconceptions which still color many western conceptions about Indian music.

Even though the predominant movement in a rag might be stepwise, there are often sequential jumping patterns from one note to another which can be learned either from the compositions or the chalan. In addition, common *vidār* (*vidārnā,* to fragmentize, to scatter; No. 16) melodic patterns are jagged leaps in the melody which are often introduced as a surprise late in the composition. Since they seemingly overturn the character of the rag, their use must be judicious and calculated lest the rag be shattered altogether.

Pitch sequences, where a phrase will have a natural consequence in an answering phrase, or where an ending pattern will be required, are sometimes dictated by rag structure. In *Iman Kalyāṇ,* this phrase is often used in final cadences to sa:

G -m G R G R S

Ornaments

One important type of ornament (No. 17) is the *āndolan* (movement, wavering). Classical music uses no vibrato in the Western sense of the controlled wavering of each pitch. But certain notes in a rag may be inflected with a very slow up-and-down oscillation. How much movement, and the microtones involved, are supervised by the teacher and should be approached with care, since use of the wrong shrutis will spoil the rag. If there are other ornaments (*alankārs*) which are characteristic to a rag, these should be learned and practiced separately. Often these are strung together in a phrase which reflects a rag's broad note movement.

General Rules

There are a few general rules which most rags follow:

1. A rag must have at least five notes.
2. All rags must have sa.
3. A rag must contain either pa or one of the two mas.
4. Two forms of the same note should not be adjacent (although this principle has some notable exceptions).

Rendering the Rag

From an account of an earlier generation, we have this description of how it was to learn from the great vocalist Pandit Balkrishna Bua in the 1850s:

The students got the talim at the guru's residence in the morning, and more often at night. All of them, the juniors and seniors, learnt together simultaneously. They were not permitted to sit comfortably, but had to sit in the posture of virasana (i.e., kneeling) in a semicircle in front of the guru, seniors to the fore and juniors to the rear. Guruji would teach the chiz (the compositions) but rarely, if ever, tell the name of the raga. It was not in vogue in those days to state the rules of the rag, ascent and descent, vadi-samvadi, etc. Theory, latent in practice, was not analytically conceived as a separate entity to be taught to the students. They learned whatever the teacher taught, and writing the lesson was tabu. No one could ask questions, and if one were so bold as to do so, one courted expulsion from the house. Thus there was always much variation in text, swar, and tal among the students.

B.R. Deodhar

Today, learning the music is the same as it was more than a hundred years ago and no doubt many centuries before that. The rags are not learned through theoretical concepts, but through the compositions which make those concepts manifest. All the subtleties of note balance, chalan, vadi-samvadi relationships, arohi-avarohi, ornaments, etc., are given by the teacher in fixed compositions (No. 18), and of them, there is a great predominance of songs. Hence, the contents of this book. The instrumentalist as well as the vocalist must memorize hundreds of songs in order to develop a feeling for the rag and gain confidence in how to elaborate it. From these songs both the introductory and concluding movements of a rag are seen (No. 19), and its major points of structure, that in ancient times were summarized by the concepts of *graha* (point of beginning), *apnyās* (point of middle prolongation), and *nyās* (point of conclusion).

Rag Purity

Purity in rendering rag is a highly esteemed quality among accomplished musicians. In order to achieve purity, basic source information about a rag should be kept in mind, such as whether it is of classical (*shāstrīya*, scriptural) or modern (*ādhunik*) origin, and whether it is pure of itself, or a mixture of one or more rags (No. 20). A rag without known admixtures is called *shuddh* (pure); two rags mixed together are said to be *mishra* (mixed); three or more rags combined together are *saṅkīrṇa* (blended together). It is important to keep the style of the rag in mind, also, for if it is of dhrupad origin the structural features are likely to be more rigid than they would be in khyal style, and certainly a lot more so than if the rag is a light classical one (No. 21). There are many rags (e.g., *Kāfī* or *Khammāj*) which exist in all three traditions, and the rag concepts are different for each. And, since there are many hundreds of rags from each scale, playing any rag invariably brings out the shadows (*chhāyā*) of other rags with similar note patterns. The student must learn these rags, too, in order to know how to keep the rag pure (No. 22).

Tal

While in the abstract any rag might be set to any tal, the tals also have both a tradition of source (dhrupad, khyal, and light classical or folk) and an inherent tradition of mood (No. 23). Setting the delicate features of a rag full of restless love in a dhrupad tal or a tal with a preponderance of mathematical implications would more than likely sound inappropriate, just as would the contrary—a heroic and tragic rag set to a light and restless dadra tal. The models on how far these limitations can be set are frequently tested, however, and the degree of success can be a test of a musician's mastery. It is a delicate balance in which the composer's and the listener's tastes play a decisive role.

Programming

In preparing a rag for a program, it is important to know how much time is given, what time of day the piece will be presented, and which performances are likely to precede or follow one's presentation. These will often determine what rag is to be chosen, or, if more than one rag is to be played, an acceptable sequence for the compositions (No. 24). Of course, the audience should be considered (No. 25). If it is a learned audience, there will be a wider choice of rags available, usually a greater time limit, and a wider palate of subtleties in the rag presentation.

Concert Format

In presenting a program of classical music, there is a wide latitude for adjusting the length and nature of rag presentation for time, duration, and circumstance. A typically reliable format might be as follows:

Alap-jor in a classical rag followed by fixed compositions in slow, then medium or fast speeds.

Intermission

Short alap and light classical presentation(s).

Guru

In the end, it is the feeling that one gets from one's teacher (No. 26) which predominantly determines the conception of the rag. That flavor lingers in the compostions the musician presents, but the attitude and feelings for the rag, embodied in the guru's playing or singing it, or even talking about it, are fundamental to the way musicians mold the sound, begin and end every performance, and shape their whole vision of singing or playing the rag.

Three generations in a blood line and musical tradition are said to define a gharana, in this case the Baba Allauddin Gharana. Above are Allauddin Khansahib, his son, Ali Akbar, and grandson, Ashish, who is Ali Akbar's son and a distinguished sarod player and musician in his own right.

Classification of Rag

Musicians say that there are about 75,000 rags. Most of these are not in the active literature and are merely hypothetical, but in an ideal sense, they remain always there to be composed or revived by musicians in every age. In practical use, the number is very much smaller, and perhaps only a few thousand rags have been played throughout history. In fact, in any given era, the active number may have been only in the hundreds. A competent musician could have twenty to fifty rags in his functional repertoire, depending on his age, practice, and training. Although he may *know* many more by recognizing their main features, he would not feel ready to render them in public performance. At a certain period of his life, a musician may play a rag frequently, but without practicing it for a while he might well forget many subtleties. This is true with the rags popular with audiences as well. With the practically infinite number of rags beyond his grasp, the musician is properly humbled by the few in his paltry repertoire, and further, must take great pains to render those few purely.

The story is told of the sage Narada who was taken to heaven by Lord Vishnu. They entered a room where there were a number of radiantly beautiful statues but with broken limbs or marred features. "Who has done this terrible destruction?" Narada asked. Vishnu replied, "These are the rags and raginis. By your careless singing and playing, Narada, you have deformed them. Only by strictest attention to the rendering of their forms and feelings can they be properly restored." Narada was thus shocked into humility.

Traditional story

Abstracting musical pitch selections into scales (Latin, *scala*, ladder, stair) is an ancient process common to many musical cultures. In talking of India's rag literature, the scale has never been a wholly satisfactory descriptive device, because the true picture of a rag usually involves more melodic movement in its basic configuration than any scale can imply. And yet, there being a basic foundation of just twelve notes, and those having certain normative combinations, Indian musicians and theorists have often proposed various scale groupings for purposes of classification and learning. Judging from the many different systems of scales proposed through the ages, there has never been even a concensus on which may be the best way. Nowadays there are three systems of scale types that musicians in North India recognize: first, the *parivar* (family), or rag-ragini system; second, the *melakārta* ("collation under the head of the family") system; and third, the *ṭhāṭ* (skeleton or framework) system. All three have strengths and weaknesses, and none portrays the music with complete accuracy; yet, each contributes something unique to the understanding of what is basic and common, and what differs, about scales derived from rags.

The Six Male Rags

In many of the raga-ragini systems, which were first written about in the early middle ages (tenth century and afterwards), there were six male rags, each with six wives (*ragiṇi*s), and each couple had a number of offspring (*putra*s, sons). Some scholars hold the opinion that the original six male rags were pentatonic, even though modern versions of the rags are no longer so, as the following chart shows. Further, there was no general agreement on exactly which six rags were the parent ones, what their pitches were, or which were the wives of each. There were several schools of thought (*mat*s *or math*s, deep study) proposing systems similar in structure but containing different rags .

Rags in the raga-ragini system were related also by aesthetic, emotional, seasonal, time, and other considerations, which made them a feast for painters of *rāgmālā*s in the sixteenth through nineteenth centuries who interpreted poetic phrases describing the rags (*dhyāns*) in miniature paintings full of natural imagery, emotional mood, and poetic imagination. Despite the great beauty and allure of these rag illustrations, it is frequently difficult to match modern versions of the rags with the moods and actions implied in the miniatures. Not only have the rags changed in character and name over the centuries, but it would appear that the painters, who often started from a line of poetry which included the rag's name, constructed their own fanciful genealogies, rather than proceeding from genuinely musical sources. Local variations of the painted rags may have had short or only regional lives. Nevertheless, the rag-ragini system and the ragmala paintings themselves do illustrate two important factors inherent in the music: namely, that melodies are related and collected in families, in which mixtures (intermarriages) are frequent and formally significant; and that the rags have extramusical associations which are an important part of their ethos. The six male rags of the Hanuman math, accepted by many modern musicians, are:

Bhairav	S r G m P d N S
Hindol	S G M D N D S S N D M G S
Megh	S R m P n S
Shri	S r M P N S S N d P M G r P r G r S
Malkauns	S g m d n S
Dipak*	

*Dipak is associated with fire. This fire is usually described as devotional, or oil-lamp light, or occasionally even as raging fire. In this connection, a famous legend of Tansen is related:

Miyan Tansen, the renowned musician of the sixteenth-century court of Akbar the Great, was credited with having such powers with music that he could talk to the birds and animals of the forest, bring rain, as well as change the hearts of gods and men. He was accorded great respect by the emperor himself.

Jealous rival courtiers were skeptical. "If he is so great, let him show that he can light the oil lamps in the great hall with this so-called fire rag, Dipak."

Akbar was reluctantly persuaded to order Tansen to do this, especially since he was made aware that the heat generated by such an effort would be dangerous for the singer's health. Tansen instructed Saraswati, his daughter, to sing Megh, the rainy season rag, in an adjacent wing of the palace. As he then sang Dipak, the oil lamps in the great hall lit of their own accord, and even began to flare up menacingly, and it was only the arrival of rain which prevented the palace itself from burning. The rain cooled Tansen's fevered body, but he fell ill and died shortly thereafter.

Traditional story

Out of respect for this great master, and because of its aura of potential danger, Dipak is rarely, if ever, played. Since Tansen's day, many musicians have refused to even utter the notes. As if purposefully adding confusion to legend, tradition has preserved forms of Rag Dipak in Purvi, Bilawal, and Kalyan thats.

The Melakarta System

In about 1620, the South Indian musicologist, Venkatamakhi, proposed a system of scale types, or *melakårtas*, which included seventy-two basic scales. It was derived from the theories of Ramamatya, a famous musician of Vijayanagar who wrote an important sixteenth-century treatise, the *Svara Mela Kalānidhi*. Venkatamakhi's system, he himself acknowledged, provided for many more note combinations than were then being used in rags. As time went on, more and more musicians of the Karnatak style adopted his method of organization, which is today generally accepted as the basis for the South Indian rag system. Its greatest virtues are its completeness and its allowance for the inclusion of rags which are yet to be composed. Its main weakness is that it does not stem actually from the literature itself, but describes instead a theoretical basis for composition which many musicians feel leans more toward combinatorial mathematics than practical music. However, many Northern musicians recognize these scales to be of real value in organizing the great diversity of the literature.

The seventy-two *melas*, as the scales are known, start from the assumption that every scale has eight tones (the octave), and that each invariably includes both **sa** and **pa**. Half the seventy-two, or thirty-six, are composed with shuddh **ma** and the other half with tivra **ma**. The scale is divided into two tetrachords (groupings of four adjacent pitches), **sa re ga ma**, and **pa dha ni sa**. Then all combinations of the natural and flat forms are systematically ordered. In the South Indian practice, the nomenclature of the notes changes, but the actual pitches of the scales are the same as given below in the North Indian system:

For the lower tetrachord:

S r R m

S r g m

S r G m

S R g m

S R G m

S g G m

Similarly, for the upper tetrachord:

P d D Ṡ

P d n Ṡ

P d N Ṡ

P D n Ṡ

P D N Ṡ

P n N Ṡ

Each one of the six lower tetrachordal arrangements is combined systematically with each one of the six upper ones, making thirty-six; and then the whole process is repeated using tivra **ma**, making seventy-two in all. Each resulting "parent scale" (*janaka rag*) has a specific number in the system as well as an identifying name which is also derived from the ordering of the Sanskrit alphabet. It is enough for the student of Hindustani music to simply understand the basis of the system of the seventy-two melas classification, rather than memorizing the names or number positions.

The Ten Thats

Pandit Vishnu Narayan Bhatkhande, a lawyer by training, is the most prominent musicologist in the first half of the twentieth century in North India. Among his many important contributions to classical music was his organization of the rags into a system of scales known as the ten *ṭhāṭ*s (pronounced almost like English "tots"). The main virtue of his system is its brevity, which is perhaps also its weakness. As classifying the immense literature of North Indian rags into ten scales would be controversial under any circumstances, the ten *ṭhāṭ*s are accepted with reservation by most musicians. Recognizing that the six male rags had too many versions and too many extramusical associations to be useful, and that the seventy-two melas were too theoretical and large a grouping, Bhatkhande chose ten scale types to represent parent frameworks. His conditions were that each scale have all seven notes, the ascending and descending be the same, and that only one form of any note be included in a scale. Out of thirty-two basic mathematical possiblities of note combintaions, he reduced the number to the ten below and named them after the rags which they resembled:

The Ten Thats

Kalyāṇ	S	R	G	M	P	D	N	S
Bilāwal	S	R	G	m	P	D	N	S
Khammāj	S	R	G	m	P	D	n	S
Kāfī	S	R	g	m	P	D	n	S
Asāwarī	S	R	g	m	P	d	n	S
Bhairavī	S	r	g	m	P	d	n	S
Bhairav	S	r	G	m	P	d	N	S
Toḍī	S	r	g	M	P	d	N	S
Pūrvī	S	r	G	M	P	d	N	S
Mārwā	S	r	G	M	P	D	N	S

The *ṭhāṭs* do not have a specific order, although they are given here in this numbering so that the "flatting of the fourths," **ma-ni-ga-dha-re**, can be seen in the first six scales. These also correspond to the "medieval" modes of Western music which are usually identified as *Lydian, Ionian, Mixolydian, Dorian, Aeolian,* and *Phrygian,* and are the *mūrchhanā*s (interlocking scales: see "Exercises") of each other. The latter four have no direct Western equivalents. Five of the *ṭhāṭs* have the names of morning rags (Bhairav, Bhairavi, Asavari, Bilaval, and Todi), and the other five are from evening rags. Bhatkhande stated that the emotional and extramusical content was to be neutral, for there are both morning and evening rags related to many of the individual scales, and he used the rag names for convenience. Many practicing musicians, however, cannot avoid the feelings generated by, say, the rags of the Kalyan family when practicing Kalyan *ṭhāṭ*, and will therefore only practice it in the evening. It is therefore suggested that students observe the morning and evening separation of the five scales in their practice.

In relating to the rags through the *ṭhāṭs*, there are a number of accommodations to be made. The time considerations just mentioned are one. Another is the realization that some important rags do not fit into any one *ṭhāṭ*, but rather are a combination of two or more scales. Transilient rags (ones which omit some pitches) may be related to more than one *ṭhāṭ*: Bhupali (S R G P D S), for instance, relates to Khammaj, Bilawal, or Kalyan—even though in "family" genealogy Bhupali is associated with Kalyan. Similar confusion arises also with rags in which there are more than one form of a note: for example, two **nis** in a rag creates the ambiguity of Khammaj and Bilawal *ṭhāṭs*.

Despite the problems of the system, and the resulting controversies, the *ṭhāṭ* system enjoys a general acceptance among North Indian musicians who see it as a workable basis of reference for collecting and relating the vast literature of rag. Since the *ṭhāṭs* also correspond to the basic fret settings on the sitar, they are very useful for practice on that and other instruments (not to mention the voice), where common pitch and fingering combinations must be systematically practiced. The *ṭhāṭs* also align the notes in straight melodic order, making exercises less cumbersome in their working out.

The memorization of the ten *ṭhāṭs* is usually the first lesson in the theory of North Indian music.

Mood and Effect

Rendering music with feeling is one of the most ancient and common goals of all music. Khansahib has always exhorted his students to "bring life" to the music. He cannot bear to hear a student merely reading from notation. Memorization, even with a few errors, is far better than reading, and if the students were to lapse back into mechanical reading, Khansahib might say, "bring some action," or "more life," or even, "you are playing like a cold fish." He constantly urges with these goading words the necessity to memorize and play from the heart.

Ras

The most important traditional aesthetic concept in classical Indian art and music is that of *ras* (or *rasa*, juice, sentiment). In the *Nātyaśhāstra*, there are eight *rasa*s enumerated:

Shṛiṅgāra	joy and love (erotic and/or divine)
Karuṇa	pathos, compassion, sadness
Vīra	heroism, courage, valor
Hāsya	merriment, laughter
Adbhuta	wonder, surprise
Raudra	anger, rage
Vibhatsa	disgust
Bhayānaka	fear

Bharata, the writer of this fourth-century treatise, stated that a complete dramatic performance should touch on all these emotions and leave the audience with a feeling of *shāntī* (peace). Later theorists include this in the list, which is then commonly called the *nava ras*, or the "nine moods."

The *Nātyaśhāstra* is primarily a treatise on dance and drama, although there are chapters on music as well. But the focus is on theatrical performance, and the *ras* theory should be interpreted with this perspective. Thus, in Bharata's list of the sentiments, music alone—rag, tal, composition, style, etc.—usually conveys only the first four moods of sadness, joy/love, heroism, and gaity and all their related shades of feeling. It can also express peace. Three of the other moods are more dramatic than purely musical: fear, anger, and disgust. In other words, there is no specifically angry rag nor a disgusting one. These feelings are often highlighted in theatrical presentations with the help of musical effects, but seldom by a rag performance itself. *Adbhuta* is not generally used to describe the mood of a rag, either. All rags are "wondrous" in their feeling and atmosphere, but the word *adbhuta* is rather applied to elements of surprise which might occur during a musical presentation. Furthermore, if a note or phrase is designed to come at a particularly satisfying or surprising point in the rag's rendering, or is so produced by the artist, it is often said to be *chamatkār*, "marvelous." One can also speak of the surprise and wonder with which a particular musician might charge the atmosphere.

Since the word *shringar* is most frequently used in the context of its human and erotic romantic feelings, the word *bhakti* (devotion and divine love) may be used to distinguish the emotion of a more serious rag from a lighter one. However, in the poetry of the Sufis, the Bhakti movement, and the Urdu poets, the *shringar* and *bhakti* elements are often mingled: the music reflects and assists in the entwining mystery of human and divine love. Often in the lyrics of the songs, God is addressed as "the beloved," and the inexplicabilities of cosmic love are cast in the words of the interplay and drama of human lovers.

Again, the main classical sentiments attached to the rag tradition are *shringār, bhakti, karuna, hāsya, vīr,* and *shānti*. A musician will usually specify one or several of these moods in describing the feeling that a rag should have. These usually vary from performance to performance, and this can be heard in the variety of moods conveyed by different compositions in the same rag. Since a rag performance frequently presents two or more compositions, there is more than one shade of mood implied in the single rendering of a rag. Obviously, the most effective use of the softer moods is brought out in the alap and the slower sections of the performance.

There are many other words which are used often by musicians to describe the moods of rags—indeed, there are thousands of expressions which would try to capture the subtleties of musical feelings. In the traditional teaching, however, there are a few noteworthy additions to the terms listed above. These are sometimes referred to as the *prakrit* (nature) of a rag. A *gambhīr* (serious, solemn) rag requires a heavier rendering than a *chanchal* (restless, playful) one. A rag full of *tyāg* (renunciation, detachment) would perhaps emphasize devotion to the point of reserving it for one's personal practice or for a select audience.

While the words describing ras are most often used to describe rag, they also apply to tal. The expression of emotion in rhythmic playing is highly appreciated but takes many years of musical study to master. The tal and its theka have important inherent feelings. The way a drummer ornaments and shapes the theka, plays the variations, and controls the speed and dynamics play a very important role in the presentation of mood in a performance. Unfortunately, deviance is often commented on negatively, such as, "the tabla player wanted to run," or "played the wrong type of variation at that point, and the mood was lost."

Common words to describe the emotional nature of a rag:

Bhaktī	devotion
Shṛiṅgār	joy and love (erotic and/or divine)
Karuṇ	pathos, compassion, sadness
Vīr	heroism, courage, valor
Hāsya	merriment, gaity, laughter
Shāntī	peace, restfulness
Gambhīr	solemnity, seriousness
Chanchal	restlessness, playfulness
Tyāg	renunciation, sacrifice
Chamatkār	marvelousness, surprise

There is an old Sanskrit saying which goes, "That which tinges the mind with color is a raga" (*ranjayati iti rāgah*). The whole atmosphere set by the performance of a rag is determined by many factors: the tuning of the tanpura and the notes of the rag; the appropriate selection of rag, tal, and composition; the presentation of the artist; and the receptive abilities of the hearers (the *rasikas*, or "lovers of *ras*"). All these play together to create the desired effect, namely, the "coloring of the mind." Beyond the few words listed above, there are an infinite number of terms which could be used to describe the feelings induced by the rendering of rag, but musicians usually wish the music to speak for itself.

Ornamentation

In the old treatises, ornamentation is referred to as *gamak,* which can be loosely translated as "grace" or "fragrance." It is considered essential to the life of the music and, as the English word "grace" implies, has connotations of ennobling refinement and divine impulse. Even though the word *gamak* can mean any ornament, in modern usage it refers to a special type of ornament described below.

There are two main categories of ornamentation: one is particularly characteristic to a certain rag movement, and the other is a general type which is used in the rendering of the music in various styles. The main ornaments which may define a rag are *mīnd, āndolan,* and *kaṇ. Mīnd,* or *mīr,* is a slide between two notes. In certain rags these slides may be guides to the definition of the rag, for they may give a color to the rag which is beyond just the single notes themselves (for example, the slide shuddh **ni** through komal **ni** to **dha** in Miyan Malhar, and **ni dha pa ma pa** in Kalyan). A *mīnd* might also show shadows of notes never mentioned in the rag's ascending or descending note pattern, but which might otherwise define its color.

Āndolan is the slow wavering of a pitch which usually involves microtones or *shruti*s. It is often maintained that there is no vibrato in Indian music, but this is usually said in distinction to the Western type of vibrato which is intended largely to enhance the harmonic blending of voices or instruments. Many notes (usually not **sa** or **pa**) can use *āndolan* in a rag, but these are particular to each rag and have greatly differing widths of vibration as well as varying speeds of wavering.

The word *kaṇ* (iota, touch) has two usages: on one hand, it is an ornament used in defining the rag itself, and on the other, one used in its exposition. The first *kaṇ* refers to the approach of a note, like touching the high **sa** before playing a komal **ni** on the way to an antara. Here, it is a structural part of the rag, for the **ni** then has a coloring of **sa**. Like the two adjacent vowels in a diphthong, the inflection is different from the separate sounds of **sa** and komal **ni**. Similarly, the approach of **dha** from **ni** in Bhairav, or **ma** to **ga** in Kafi are examples of this structural type of *kaṇ*. In the second context, *kaṇ* used in the course of a rag's exposition is the slight touching of a tone in anticipation of its being brought into full development. Here, it is a pleasing effect rather than a change in the tonal collection of the rag. In this context, it is also called *sparsh* (contact, touch).

Choosing which ornaments are used depends both on the rag and the style. Rags are ornamented according to their particular traditions, and the three main styles of rendering a rag—dhrupad, khyal, and thumri—have particular ways of approaching ornaments and using them in different ways. A dhrupad, for instance, concentrates on the slow and even touch of every note, and usually will not render the faster ornaments at all. Khyal singers may use quick ornaments (*murkī*), but avoid some others, although the gharana tradition of the singer may determine the choices. The light classical singer will use quick ornaments and likely fill the performance with a filigree texture of rapid notes.

Turns and mordents, as they are known in Western music, come under the general description of *alankār* (ornament). Some of the most common are:

SNS SNRS SNRSNS SGRSNS NSRGRSNS

They can be theoretically subsumed under the general pattern of melodic working out of *alankār tān*s, which are described in the chapter "Exercises."

Gamak, as the term is used in modern music, is a way of attacking or repeating a note rapidly with use of its upper or lower neighbor. It is frequently used in the latter stages of a performance to bring out the heroic feeling of a rag, or to augment the excitement of a climax. *Gamak* is also written out in the chapter "Exercises."

The following is a list of some of the more common ornaments. As with similar lists, this terminology cannot be taken as definitive, since many musicians may use these words differently. Where appropriate, an example is notated.

Common Ornaments

sūt (thread): the drawing out of a slide with a slow dragging motion between two pitches.

khaṭkā (knocking): two upper neighbor notes in rapid succession, returning to main tone.

DDP

kampan (tremble): like khatka, but several notes at a time.

PDDDDDP

ghasīṭ (gliding): sliding from one note to another

gitkarī (songlike): a specific ornamental movement:

RGG RGG RGmP

krintan: in instrumental music, pulling off a note from its upper neighbor.

DP

zamzamā: (the name of a famous medieval cannon): in instrumental music, a complex type of krintan.

DPDPmP

ṭip: in instrumental music, the hammering-on of a note with the left hand from a lower neighbor.

PD

Baba Allauddin clowns with some bystanders at the fish market in Maihar.

Once in the market at Maihar, Baba saw a person sitting rather dejected in a corner with a number of dholaks (drums) *to sell but not heeded by anyone. He was touched so much that he took up one dholak and started playing. As a result, a small crowd gathered around him.. Many people threw coins and within a short time a few dholaks were sold. Baba made sure that the money was collected and gave all the coins to the dholak seller and went home happy.*

Nikhil Banerjee

Form

Elemental to the concept of form in classical music are three basic ideas: the rhythmic concepts in *anibaddha-nibaddha* (unmetered-metered) rendition of rag; pitch registration; and the interplay of fixed composition with "improvisation." This word "improvisation" is now so commonly associated with Western harmony that it is not wholly satisfactory to describe the impromptu compositional processes of Indian music. The format of rag presentation is shaped by such diverse elements as the rules and traditions of the rag and tal, compositional style and ornamentation, and the circumstances of rag development in a particular performance. The phrase "on-the-spot composition" is probably better suited than "improvisation," as the latter can imply a freedom beyond the classical restrictions within which the traditional musician must work. Too, there are the factors of style and *gharana*, or particular musical tradition, which play a role in the realization of musical form.

Anibaddh and Nibaddh

A piece of music set to a particular tal is said to be *nibaddh*, or "bound," whereas a piece or section in free rhythm (or without perceptible rhythm at all) is *anibaddh*, or "unbound." *Alāp* and *joṛ* are the primary types of anibaddh music, for there is no tal or meter in these sections, and phrases are of indeterminant length. These movements are of central importance in the dhrupad style. The alap is a rendering of the rag that nowadays is usually thought of as an introductory section of the performance, invocational, in which the rag mood, notes, and salient melodic features are introduced and developed in slow abstract phrases without a recognizable rhythmic pulse. In any later phases of the rag, if the music is rendered in these abstract patterns without rhythmic pulse, performers may refer to them as "alaps," although that word refers particularly to the section of music which precedes a composition in tal. In former times, however, an artist might specialize in playing only alap, and a rag performance can be considered complete with the rendering of this section only. Connoisseurs consider this part of a rag performance to be the most demanding and artful section, and perhaps the most revealing of a performer's maturity.

The *joṛ* (momentum), or alap-jor, is the second part of the alap. In it a regular pulse is introduced, but without specific meter or tal. This aspect of the alap performance is also a speciality of the dhrupad style, as is the alap in general. In a dhrupad performance, the jor will gradually accelerate (sometimes by doubling or quadrupling the tempo) and end with a fast section which instrumentalists call the *jhālā* (sparkling, "welded together").

The various sections of the alap and jor are usually brought to a summation with a phrase which is called the "alap sam" or the *mohṛā*, and sometimes informally, *nikās*, (exit). Although the music before and after this short phrase has no fixed meter, the mohra introduces a temporary feeling for a metrical downbeat which demarcates the end of the section. Tonally, the mohra will return the rag to the neutral note middle **sa**, at which point the prior melodic tension is resolved and new melodic development can be added. The pitches will vary from rag to rag, but the basic melodic contour of the mohra will be:

+

— Ṇ Ṇ S R — S —

ta na tom

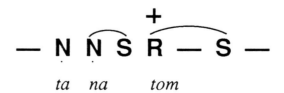

A second aspect of formal design is pitch register. Old Sanskrit treatises catalog sections of the ancient *prabandha gīta*, or sectional song, which, in addition to tempo, may have been distinguished by differences in where they lay in the general pitch register. Some of the names are still used in one form or another, such as *udgraha, melapaka, dhruva, ābhoga, antarā*. Several modern words derive from these older forms, and perhaps inherit some of their formal definition as well.

Asthai

The *asthāī* or *sthāyī* (refrain, standing, fixed) is the main part of a composition in rag which shows the structure of the rag's melody in its principal pitch registration. For the great majority of the rags, this is the middle saptak from **sa** to **ni**. There are exceptional rags in which the asthai might show higher **sa** and even a little above, or descend into the register below middle **sa**. Often the asthai is a pair of lines which complement each other melodically. All the same, the important features of the rag in its own home register must appear in the asthai in order for it to be acceptable as representing that rag. For this reason, the asthai part of the composition is of paramount importance in detailing the features of a particular rag, and a musician "knows" a rag only after he learns many asthais in that rag by heart. Of critical importance in the composition of the asthai are the point of starting (*graha*), the places of standing and emphasis (*vishrānti sthān, apnyāsa*), and the ending note (*nyāsa*).

Antara

The *antarā* was a middle section of the long sectional song, the word meaning "interior" or "between." Nowadays, this term refers to the second part of a composition in which the rag is rendered with an approach to high **sa** from below, emphasizing it by prolongation, or ornamenting it by repeating this approaching melodic figure with some variation, and then extending the composition into the higher register. Like the asthai, the most critical compositional features of the antara are how it is begun and ended. Its return junction to the asthai also takes special care. Because of its limits in pitch range to the highest reaches of voice or instrument, and its lesser function in delineating the melodic features of the rag, the antara is sometimes given less attention in the khyal styles of composition. Very occasionally in slow khyals it may be even omitted altogether. On the other hand, some of the older vocal compositions have a more elaborate text for the antara than the asthai, and sometimes one hears even two or more antaras. Occasionally the antara will include the name of the poet, typically in the last line.

Additional Composed Sections

A fixed composition is normally considered "complete" if it has an asthai and antara. In light forms of composition, especially in *bhajan* (hymn, devotional song), there might be more than one asthai and antara. In the dhrupad style, there are frequently two additional sections known as *sanchārī* (moving, changing) and *ābhog* (expansion, completion). In the sanchari, the composition returns to the register of the asthai, usually presenting the composition with a different emphasis in melodic contour which consequently gives a contrasting feeling. For instance, the sanchari will frequently start from the note **dha** (sometimes **pa** or **ni**) and approach the heart of the rag from above. The abhog, which follows the sanchari directly, is in effect another antara, again going to the upper register. In the composition of alap, the performer may use the structures of sanchari and abhog in both the alap proper and even in the jor and jhala. They are usually very brief sections, used like recaps of the asthai and antara.

A dhrupad is like driving on an old road through a city: you have all the bends and curves, the small bridges, the stoplights. You must drive slowly, but you see the beauty of that area. Khyal is like the freeway: maybe you get to the center of town very fast, but often you don't get any feeling for that city. Everywhere the freeways are the same, you see.

Fixed Composition

While it is true that Indian classical music is well known for its spontaneity and improvisatory spirit, there are many elements which are fixed both in performanance and, especially, in the learning of the music. There exists an immense literature of fixed compositions in all styles for both voice and instruments. These compositions are typically in asthai-antara form, and some of the dhrupad compositions will include an extension called the sanchari-abhog.

As stated before, a musician "knows" a rag not by being able to recite the theorectical features, such as ascending-descending, vadi-samvadi, etc.; rather, a rag is primarily learned by the memorization of a great number of compositions in it. Some of these compositions are traditional, handed down orally through the years, while others are newly composed by teachers for their students. Engaging in this latter process of composition, if the rag itself is a traditional one, teachers not so much "compose" as "reassemble" materials from their own storehouses of compositions, materials that even they themselves might have partially forgotten. A teacher may remember only the first line or perhaps the whole asthai, and therefore have to compose the rest—a whole new antara, for instance. To the student, who will have no idea which parts are new and which are old, these compositions will seem as if set in stone, and have the same authentic values as any older ones. In this manner, along with each composition, the teacher transmits a mental experience to the student, a dynamism extending far beyond any notational representation. This is why learning one composition with the same notes from two different teachers, even two in the same tradition, can be an experience as different as night and day, and this is why it is said that a student must stay with one teacher in order to learn anything at all.

On-the-spot Composition: Sectional Additions

Typically, the asthai-antara composition will be given in one sitting, although a teacher may spend uncounted hours in subsequent sittings in order to refine details and "bring the mood." Added to this composition will be sections which are also fixed for the student's learning, but have the sense of "impromptu composition invented on the spot." These, too, follow compositional models, some of the names of which are *vistār* (expansion), *tān* ("expanded tones," usually thought of as "rapid pattern"), *laykārī* ("playing with the rhythm"), and *bolbāṇṭ* ("divisions of the words") or *boltān* (variations using words of the lyric). It is not uncommon for these impromptu forms to be combined as they are composed, especially as the composition progresses. The various sections will be delineated in the following chapters describing the individual styles, but here it is most important to note that many of the stylistic features of one genre are imported into another—for instance, techniques of dhrupad into khyal and instrumental music. Indeed, because so many features developed in dhrupad are found in other styles, this older style has assumed the position of an older parent in the classical tradition.

Dhrupad

He who has the strength of one hundred water buffaloes, let him sing dhrupad.

Traditional Saying

Form and Style

We come now to the aspect of style in rag presentation. The words "form" and "style" are sometimes considered together, and even used interchangeably, but they refer to two different aspects of music. We shall use the word "form" to refer to compositional sectioning and repeat schemes, and "style" to refer either to the major classifications of vocal and instrumental composition, such as dhrupad, khyal, or thumri, or to their many variations which have been influenced by gharanas, historical periods, and personal innovations. Hence, one can speak of a *stylistic* difference between the treatment of the same *formal* sections (e.g., asthai-antara) in dhrupad, khyal, and thumri. Composition in these three basic styles is also different, as is the realization of rag structure, ornament, tal, text, and "improvisation."

From the oldest currently-practiced vocal style, dhrupad, derive several of the basic formats for the layout of a rag in performance. These have in turn been adopted and converted by the khyal, thumri, and instrumental styles. Dhrupad is a style with many ancient forerunners. It employs both the *anibaddh* and *nibaddh* (metrically free and in meter) qualities of performance which are described in the earliest writings on music. Indeed, partly because of their bearing virtually the oldest practiced classical traditions, the dhrupads are regarded as having a sacred quality transcending the present and going back in time. Thus, among musicians there is a certain reverence and devotional attitude towards dhrupad. Because of the rigor of its tradition and the meticulous care shown in its performance, it is said to have maintained and passed on to the present era the oldest knowledge of the movement of the rags—more so, perhaps, than the other styles, where the composition may have either the informal feeling of a spontaneously composed piece, or may melodically concern itself only with some small detail of the rag's movement.

A dhrupad is like the Gregorian chant—sacred and sung with a sober and serious mood and with even weight to the notes....like you are carrying a very full glass of water, you see: if you move quickly, you will spill the water, and like that you spoil the dhrupad. Those musicians that were great in the old times, they all sang dhrupad, even though they also played vina, sursringar, or rabab.

Dhrupad Alap

In Sanskrit, *ālāp* means "narration" or "conversation." In a vocal rendering in dhrupad style, abstract syllables are sung to give shape and texture to the sound. Besides simply *ah*, there is usually a random ordering of *ta na ri re ra nā nom tom*. These are said to be the syllables remaining from the disintegration of sacred mantras such as *ananta hari om* ("Infinite God Om"), and *om tumhī narāyaṇa harī* ("Om, Thou only Vishnu, God"). These have become abstract, losing their specific meanings, and are now collectively referred to as "nom-tom syllables." The artist begins the alap by slowly unfolding the rag, revealing it note by note and then in longer phrases, painting its character, mood, and feelings. In this beginning movement there is no meter, or perhaps it would be more precise to say that there is no evident meter, for the length of the phrasing is abstract and in free gestures of varying lengths. It can be compared to a sort of narrative exposition, one in which full sentences might be interspersed by phrases with only adjectives and no verbs, as in poetry. Because of this abstract quality and lack of fixed metrical content, the alap is at the same time easier to begin and yet more difficult to sustain than other styles. In order to render the alap in a full sense, the artist must have a storehouse of ideas about the movements of the rag, imparted by the teacher in many ways, but usually through the learning of fixed compositions. Such compositions form the essence of this book, and learning them by heart gives the best approach to understanding what a rag really is and how it might be rendered in the abstract. This abstraction of alap embodies, in a sense, a blended decay of that body of learned literature which, in the mind of the artist, engenders also the selection process of composition in the rag. This is another reason why the word "improvisation," when describing the process of playing or singing in this tradition, is not fully applicable. Hence, the rendering of a full alap reveals the maturity of the artist and his command of the material. If it is done well, it is a fulfilling and complete picture of the personality of the rag which gives a sense of the balance and proportion of the rag structure as well as an engaging overview of its charm and detail. If it is done poorly, it may well distort the delicate balance of the notes and become tedious with repetition and chopped-up phrases; at worst, it would reduce the rag merely to its scalular properties, a hodgepodge of ascending and descending phrases.

For all its abstraction, however, the alap does proceed according to structure and follows several variable formats. An artist might create an alap with many sections, but no two alaps would ever be the same. Moreover, instrumental alaps differ from vocal ones, although both share similarities in structure.

The asthai-antara form usually prevails throughout. A section in the rag's home register (*asthāī*, or *sthāyī*) is presented and varied using the notes up to **ni** and, occasionally, higher **sa**. A contrasting section (*antarā*) using the notes from **ma** or **pa** to high **sa** emphasizes this high note, and then is followed and completed by sounding the other notes of the high register, finally returning down to the middle **sa**. The way these sections are structured must follow the course of the rag as it is prefigured in the literature of fixed compositions: where the phrases and sections are begun, which notes are held out, which notes are used in combinations, where the phrases and sections end, etc., are all patterns to be learned in their metrical forms from the fixed literature of dhrupad compositions in tal.

If appropriate to the performer's mood and allotted time, a *sanchārī* (changing, moving) and *ābhog*(extension, completion) may be rendered, both as whole sections following the asthai-antara, or as structural elements in ensuing sections. An instrumentalist may use the highest extremes of his instrument in this latter section. These four formal divisions—asthai, antara, sanchari, abhog—may be also used by the artist to structure later and much briefer sections of the rag.

Jor

Following the first section, or alap proper, the artist then begins the *joṛ* (momentum), where rhythm is introduced, still without fixed meter. The jor is usually described as slow, medium, or fast, with the medium twice the tempo of the slow and the fast four times as fast. In practice, all the intermediate speeds are employed; they proceed in gradual order from slow to fast and generally divide the beat into binary divisions. In these jor sections, there is great variation in development between rags, between artists and schools, and between individual performances. It is the area where the specialities of technique in ornamentation or instrumental inflection are developed. Each section will end with the *mohṛā* ("sam of the alap") rhythmic figure incorporated into the invention of the jor, and the whole alap may well end with this figure repeated three times, as a tihai. Instrumentalists may incorporate a jhala section at the end of the jor proper, or proceed directly to a *gat*.

Dhrupad Composition

It is usually said that the dhrupad style emerged in the medieval court of Raja Man Singh Tomar (1486-1525) at Gwalior. But it was not a static form which just suddenly appeared, for it had been developed out of the old sectional song form known as the *prabandha gīt* ("bound song"). The twelfth century *Gita Govinda* of Jayadev is a long devotional poem in stanzas set to such sectional songs. The music of these songs is long since lost, save for the names of the rags which are given before each canto. The dhrupad inherited the sectional quality of this style of song, shortened it and cast it in four divisions, asthai-antara-sanchari-abhog. Some dhrupads omit the latter two sections. The word *dhruva* means "fixed" or "true" and was used in the *Nāṭyaśhāstra* to describe a type of sectional theatrical song. *Pada* means "verse" (literally, foot), so a *dhruva-pada* is a song in which the verse is set, and in which the text has a leading role. Additionally, its melody, formal order, and ornamentation are also more or less immutable, so that the element of fixed composition in dhrupad is paramount. Dhrupads are rendered in quite the same way each time, just as one would expect from performances of notated compositions in the Western tradition. While the words normally follow the tal structure in dhrupads, some compositions, known as *laṇgḍā* ("lame") dhrupads, are freer with the tal structure while keeping to the syllabic rhythm of the texts.

Tansen

In the sixteenth- and seventeenth-century courts of the Great Moghuls, Akbar, Jehangir, and Shah Jehan, the dhrupad was at its zenith; but even during the era of princely courts in the eighteenth and nineteenth centuries and into modern times—when the khyal style became more popular—the dhrupad style has maintained its role as a watershed of the music. Miyan Tansen of the court of Akbar the Great is remembered as the greatest of the dhrupadiyas, and indeed, as a father of modern Hindustani music. His compositions are still sung and treasured, and his musical lineage (*parampara*) continues today.

Bani

After Tansen, there came to be identified various major styles of rendering dhrupad, called *bānī*s (or *vānī*s, customs), something like the gharanas of khyal. The origins and use of the banis are not clear. Some scholars hold that they are the personal styles of the descendents of Tansen, while others maintain that they arose through regional stylistic developments. These ideas are not mutually exclusive. Modern dhrupadiyas might well use all the banis in their rendering of rag, but it was also said that each bani emphasized a particular mood or technique. Although there remains dispute over which affect characterized which bani, it is usually agreed that a dhrupad composition rendered in *shuddh* (pure) bani is without stylistic alterations, ornaments, or affectations (this bani is also referred to as *Dāgar* bani, from the distinguished dhrupad family of that name). *Gohar* (*gobahāra* or *gaur*) bani emphasizes calmness and peace in slow slides; *khandar* bani generates excitement through gamak and has been influenced by instrumental techniques; and *nohar* (or *naubahāra*) bani features dramatic leaps within the rag to create wonder and surprise.

Bolbant

The expansion of a dhrupad composition is typically executed with *bolbāṇṭ* (word division), also referred to as *bol banāna*, which means literally "to create (with the) word." Generally, this latter term is used to describe the development of thumri style, discussed below. A bolbant is formed by creating new, spontaneously composed rhythmic patterns of composition using the text of the song. The invention should follow the natural division of the word (*pad*) into its longer or shorter syllables. The bolbant might retain long phrases from the composition, but it more commonly uses a short phrase of four or five words which repeats with newly created rhythms and melodies. These melodies also must follow the rag and, as importantly, should extend the sense of the mood and movement of the composition itself. The rhythmic development of these bolbants has traditionally followed the mathematical patterns of halving, doubling, tripling, etc., the metric pulse, and each may end with a *tihai*, a phrase repeated three times which returns the composition to the sam or beginning point of the asthai. The composition of bolbant is a rigorous and exhilarating feature of dhrupad which, like the dhrupad style itself, is rarely heard today.

Tal in Dhrupad

There are a number of old tals which are common in the dhrupad style, but one tal, chautal (12 beats) so predominates that it is sometimes called "dhrupad tal." The distinguishing feature of the drumming style in dhrupad is the use of the pakhawaj (barrel-shaped drum) and the limited use of the *theka*. The singer is expected to keep track of the rhythm cycle through the use of the *kriya*, the hand gestures, and not rely on the drummer to do so with the theka pattern. The drummer, in turn, plays in a freer style but endeavors to match with his stroke patterns the mood and rhythmic sense of the composition. In the bolbant section he is called on to imitate on the spot the freshly composed patterns of the singer (or instrumentalist).

Other Dhrupad Forms of Composition

There are other songs in dhrupad style which may be sung in place of, or directly after, the larger compositions in chautal or other slow tals. One particular style is called *shādra*, or *chhādra* (e.g., *shasha dhara*, in Bhairav, or *tuma samāna* in Todi in this book). These have a devotional text and are set in slow jhaptal. They usually have two parts and may have bolbant expansions. Other dhrupad songs follow that format as well, particularly fast songs in *sulphak tal* and *teora* (*tivra*) tal.

Dhamar

A *dhamār* (*dhammār*) is a song or composition in the fourteen-beat tal of that name. These are often sung after a dhrupad composition, hence another title of the genre, *dhrupad-dhamar*. The mood is somewhat lighter than the dhrupad, and the main group of these compositions celebrates the love play of Lord Krishna with his consort, Radha, and the other milk-maids of Vrindavan. Many are about the spring festival known as Hori (Holi) in which the playful spraying of colored dyes accompanies festive singing and dancing. The note movement, rigor of the text, and ornamentation of dhamar is less strict than dhrupad, the mood a little less serious, and the ras *sringar* (love) more emphasized, all of which may approach the style and feeling of khyal. Melismas, where several notes are sung to one syllable, are very rare in the dhrupads themselves (except occasionally in the last line of a section), but are much more common in dhamar. A typical structure would be for the artist to render a dhamar in two parts, asthai and antara, and then some bolbants. Sometimes vistars (short phrases of abstract alap-type rag development), boltans, and tans are sung today in dhamar, revealing perhaps the influences of the khyal style.

Tarana

The concluding item in a performance of dhrupad may be a *tarānā*, the words of which are composed of syllables from drumming, dance, nom-tom (alap), and a few particular to the tarana itself. All are meaningless and used for their rhythmic expression, with the possible exception of a few words originally derived from the Persian devotional lyric, "ya la li, ya la loom." Used primarily in the antara, these probably originate in "ya illah, il-allah," the Islamic exclamation of faith and praise. Most taranas are medium to fast in tempo and may feature added tans in sargam. Khyal singers also sing taranas and usually develop it in the same manner as a chhota khyal.

Some Main Features of the Dhrupad Style

—Devotional mood most important (*bhakti ras*)

—Developed in the Middle Ages from ancient compositional genres

—Preceded by long nom-tom alap

—Nibaddh compositions based on a fixed poetic text of two or four stanzas: asthai-antara, sanchari-abhog format

—Fixed compositions centrally important; these embody the oldest ideas of rag and tal

—Further developed by bolbant, short rhythmical compositions based on the song text, composed on the spot; no tans

—Restricted use of melisma; each syllable of the text clearly articulated with one or two notes (exception: final line of a section)

—Tals structure shown by hand motions (*kriyas*); accompanying drum is pakawaj

—Main instruments of this tradition are rudra vina, Seni rabab, sursringar, and surbahar

KHYAL

The early history of khyal is also difficult to trace with any accuracy because of the lack of written evidence both of the music itself and secondary sources about the practice. Its origins lie in the tremendous mixture of ideas and cultures which occurred in the Middle Ages in North India from the thirteenth through the eighteenth centuries. The diverse combination of Hindu-Moslem aesthetic and religious cultural elements was colored by the influence of music from many regions, extending from Persia to all corners of the Indian subcontinent. Oral tradition maintains that the roots of khyal are in the contributions of the Sufi poet-musician Hazrat Amir Khusrau of the court of Sultan Allauddin Khilji at Delhi toward the end of the thirteenth century. Oral tradition also acknowledges the contributions of the courts of Jaunpur and Sultan Hussain Sharqi in the fifteenth century, and again of khyal singers in the court of the seventeenth-century Moghul, Shah Jahan. But it is not until the eighteenth-century court of the Moghul Emperor Mohammad Shah at Delhi that the style we now call "khyal" emerges as recognizable and traceable. Within the khyal are admixtures of former styles, such as the *rupak ālaptī* of the prabandh git tradition, the *qavvālī* devotional songs of the Sufis, and the many compositional techniques which are found in dhrupad and dhamar.

At the close of the eighteenth century, when regional courts were asserting their political independence after the decline of the Moghul central court at Delhi, styles of singing khyal developed on regional lines and family traditions known as *gharānās*. The courts of Jaipur (later associated with Alladiya Khan), Agra, Lucknow, Rampur, and Gwalior lend their names to several musical styles. Included, too, are Kirana, Sahaswan/ Rampur, Patiala, and Indore, which have also become famous names among the many khyal gharanas. It is usually said that three generations of musicians in one style are necessary to start a gharana. Each gharana controls its own inherited repertoire of rags and techniques of rendering the khyal, which can vary widely in terms of performance formats, types of variations (tans and vistars), tempos, and the qualities of the compositions themselves. Now, with the acceleration of recording and the relocation of the musicians to the major cosmopolitan centers, the individuality of the gharanas has become somewhat blurred. However, since a classical musician's training still usually involves the rigor of long practice under the close eye of a single master, the idea of the stylistic unity which gharana implies is still, in the main, intact.

The Nature of Khyal

The word *khyāl* (sometimes transliterated *khayāl*) comes from the Persian word meaning "fantasy," "imagination," and "idea." The most prominent feature of the khyal is the way that it combines the free imagination of the performer within the nibaddh, or metrical, structure of tal. For this reason, khyal is sometimes thought of as a liquid which takes the shape of its container (the tal). This fluidity employs the impromptu composition-on-the-spot of *vistār* (or *bistār*, expansion), *boltān*, and *tān*. These formal processes and techniques, described below, have many antecedents in the dhrupad style, and are manifested differently in the different gharana styles; so much so, in fact, that it would be hard to generate one verbal picture which would satisfy the many aspects of style found in khyal.

The modern khyal singer usually renders a performance of a rag in two parts, in slow (*vilambit*) and then in medium-fast (*drut*) tempos. Two compositions are commonly chosen to be the bases for these expositions called, respectively, the *baṛā* (big) khyal and the *chhoṭā* (small) khyal. The composition itself is known as the *chīz* (object, thing), and will usually be comprised of two stanzas, forming an asthai and antara. The subject matter of their lyrics is normally less weighty and strictly devotional than the dhrupad texts, and is often about *shringār*, love. Like much of the world's poetry, but specifically the Urdu and Hindi devotional/love lyrics, these texts have a meaning which can be interpreted on a human and a divine level at the same time. The language of khyal is Hindi, and the singer's emphasis does not fall so rigorously on the poetic or metric values of the text as it does in dhrupad; further, regional or archaic poetic constructions in the wording may make the literal meaning obscure, even to the performer. The general sense of the lyric, though, is known to the singer, who is usually more attuned to its general mood. What is often most important is the intrinsic sound of the text as its verbal syllables are prolonged.

Once, while he was singing, a famous khyal singer forgot the words to the antara. He just sang his address at that time, but in such a way that no one could tell. The wording of some khyal singers can be like that, you see.

The alap, which is vital to the rendering of dhrupad because of the balancing of its abstract (*anibaddh*) qualities against the fixed nature of the composition in tal (*nibaddh*), is hardly ever found in khyal style. Instead, after a few warm-up phrases (sometimes called a "pre-chiz alap"), the singer begins the bara khyal. Within the framework of the slow tempo, the abstract phrasing of the alap is incorporated into the rendering of the asthai-antara of the khayal, and instead of a *mohṛā*, or cadential phrase, the short introductory phrase of the khyal chiz itself serves as a point both of ending and departure for the inventions. This short introductory phrase is called the *mukhṛā* (face, introduction) and leads to the sam, or downbeat.

The binding quality of the tal in khyal can be very loose. Unlike the dhrupad singer, khyal singers do not keep the clap and wave patterns of the tal as they sing. Rather, the keeping of the tal is entrusted to the tabla player. Because of the clarity between the open and closed sounds made by the tabla (treble drum) and the baya (bass drum), it is easier to show certain patterns for the tals on this drum pair than on its older brother, the barrel-shaped pakawaj. The distinctive patterns of strokes which identify particular tals are known as *ṭhekās*, and the idea of theka has become a strong force in the development of khyal and hence classical music in general. Musicians, including those who do not play the tabla at all, learn to distinguish the sounds of the common thekas in order to maintain their place in the rhythm cycle.

Chhota Khyal

The chhota khyal is sung in a medium to fast tempo, and is older than the bara khyal. The extremely slow tempos of the latter are a more recent innovation, and are not sung by all the khyal gharanas. The rhythmic vitality of the chhota khyal is sometimes akin to that of the fast dhrupad. The accents of the words are often dynamically exciting in the ways they are set against the tal, just as in the faster dhrupads. Lyrics of many of the antaras of the chhota khyals are longer than those of the asthai, and may include the name of the poet in their final lines. Abstract and alap-like bistars, boltans, and fast tans are also sung in the fast tempos, in much the same manner as they were in the framework of the slow tempo, tailored, of course, to the more frequent occurrence of downbeat.

Vistar

The word *vistār* means "expansion" or "enlargement," and refers to the first part of the elaboration of the khyal which is sung immediately after the chiz, or fixed song. The vistar will use the text of the chiz, or use the abstraction and prolongation of its syllables or, many times, simply use *ah*.. This latter method is called "singing *ākār*." Vistars will be composed on the spot on models given by the teacher, presenting the essence of the rag in its melodic phrasing and mood. Normally the *mukhṛā* of the composition, the short lead-in phrase of chiz, will be used as a theme for return and departure in the presentation of the vistars. Many vistars will have no definable meter, but will rather follow the logic and sense of the moment in coordinating with the rhythm of the tabla and theka. The vistars will be composed with a careful ear toward presenting the rag in the correct manner of its unfolding, and will follow the form of asthai-antara in the development of the rag.

Boltan

The literal meaning of the word *tān* is also "expansion," or "protraction," but usually the word refers to musical variations which are rhythmically active or in a fast tempo. In this latter sense, a jazz musician might call a tan a "riff" or a "run." There are many and various types of tans. A *boltān* is one which uses words in its inflection. Similar to the *bolbāṇṭ* in dhrupad style, a boltan will use the words of the khyal chiz to generate melodic and rhythmic patterns. Generally, there is not so rigorous an attitude toward the rhythm as a dhrupad singer might display, but rather the gliding and slurring of the song words in boltan style will effect an easy lilting rhythm. Of course, this and all facets of khyal presentation varies greatly with the gharana, the nature of the rag or composition, the ability and training of the performer, and the demands of the moment. These, after all, are the essence of the khyal.

Types of Tans

In summary, the style and type of vistars and tans which are in the repertoire of a mature khyal singer are immense, and depend on the many factors which characterize a particular gharana, a particular performer, and the rag and chiz being rendered, as well as the circumstances of its performance. Some of the many types of tans are:

drut	fast
sargam	using the names of the notes as words
vakra	with crooked movements
chhuṭ	with abrupt jumps and turns of phrases
gamak	with shaking, using the neighbor notes
alankār	using a repeated melodic figure on different pitch levels
sapāṭ	with a full sweep of the entire range of the rag
bidār	with wide and unexpected leaps
phirat	with unexpected combinations of phrases
ulṭā	turning the rhythmic accent "inside out"

Ali Akbar Khansahib, here in class in San Rafael, California, often composes and teaches both vocal and instrumental music with the harmonium. Photo by Faustin Bray.

Light Classical Music

The term "light classical" is used to denote music which borrows ideas from the classical styles, but does not strictly adhere to the rules and constrictions implicit in rag and tal. Primarily, light classical music is associated with the voice, but there are highly developed instrumental idioms as well. An important aspect of light styles is the combination of voice with instruments deriving from folk traditions. Some of these styles may be virtuosic to the highest degree, requiring years of practice to achieve that feeling of effortless filigree in ornamentation. Mostly, they are derived from *deshi sangit*, folk and regional music which is sung and played by the people in celebrations, religious observances, and festivals. But there are also many ghazal, bhajan, and qavvali singers of great refinement who have immense popularity. Some light classical music can be found in Indian film songs which play a very important role in the daily life of hundreds of millions of people in many parts of the world, and artists in this field are as lionized as rock stars in the West. Most light classical music does not share that kind of popularity, but is still a vigorous and vital aspect of the presentations of classical musicians; nearly all their concerts feature music from these styles, usually as concluding items.

The structure of light classical melody depends primarily on the more straightforward rags—that is, rags whose ascending and descending forms are simple seven-note patterns: Kafi, Khammaj, Bhairavi, and to a lesser extent, Kalyan. One hears a few important derivative rags as well, such as Kirwani, Tilak Kamod, Pilu, Desh, Gara, Pahari, Manj Khammaj, Mand, and Jogiya (although any complex structural or melodic relationships which these rags may have on their own are usually disregarded). Rags with two **gas**, **dhas**, or **nis**, are favored. Borrowed notes and a touch of Western-style harmony are common interpolations, and even a mixture of other rag patterns. Rags so altered are properly called *mishra* (mixed), but are often not so identified by name. Quick ornaments (*murkī*) are typical of light classical styles.

Drumming

The importance of drumming in Indian folk music is reflected in the rhythmic accompaniment of light classical music. It is mostly in duple or triple meter, which are generally referred to as the tals *kaharwā* (eight beats) and *dādrā* (six beats). There are a great variety of thekas (drum patterns) for these tals, as there are a great variety of drums and regional styles of playing them. Seven- and occasionally five-beat rhythms are also common. The more refined styles may use slower tals of fourteen and sixteen beats. All are usually played on tabla, but also are heard on the barrel-shaped folk drums, *khol*, *ḍholak*, and *nāl*. Folk drumming is often highly virtuosic, and performing excellence in these light styles can be financially rewarding, especially in the film industry.

Thumri

There are many vocal genres which are cultivated by classical musicians and other specialists. One of the most important of these is called *ṭhumrī*. Although there are assuredly antecedents to this style, it was at the nineteenth-century court of Nawab Wazid Ali Shah in Lucknow where thumri received special character and development as an adjunct to Kathak dance. It is filled with *shṟiṅgār* ras in a *chanchal* (restless) mood. A short text of two to four lines was usually composed about the *ras līla*, the amorous play of Lord Krishna with the Gopis, especially with his chief consort, Radha. The lines are repeated with new music, sometimes with an asthai-antara form. An important aim in the thumri is the new shades of meaning which the artist can bring from a single line of text by vocal inflections and melody changes—a process known as *bolbanānā*. It is a highly ornamental form, with a lot of melodic filigree and tiny quick turns (*murkī*) and shakes. It is not easily taught; in fact, it is usually said that "thumri is learned, but not taught." Thumris are set in a slow tal such as *chāchar* or a sixteen-beat *dīpchandī* with occasional lively drum interludes (in duple meter) called *laggī*s. There are now several different broad styles of singing thumri, the most prominent being the Punjabi, Purabi (Lucknow, literally "east"—that is, of Delhi), and Benares styles. Because of the importance of the text, sometimes people say that thumri cannot be played on instruments. It is a moot point; the parallel style that is highly cultivated by modern instrumentalists uses the whole musical vocabulary of thumri without the lyrics.

Tappa

A rarer but highly cultivated light classical vocal genre is the *ṭappā*. Like the thumri, tappa is based on a few short lines of love poetry in chanchal mood, with quick note movements. It is said to have been developed in the late eighteenth century by Mian Shori, also of the court at Lucknow. The main characteristic of tappa is the continual use of tans, or fast note runs, in the development of the rag. The early development of khyal borrowed from this feature of tappa, and although the tappa's sweetness and character are unique, the modern khyal has taken over part of the presentation of this style. As a result, tappa is heard more and more infrequently today.

Bhajan

A *bhajan* is a devotional poem set to music and is sometimes just called a "hymn." Its lively drum accompaniment and melodic filigree does not sound much like the Christian hymn, but the poetry upon which it is based is often comparable. Among the many Bhakti poets of North India who wrote the initial body of this vast devotional literature in the sixteenth and seventeenth centuries, the names of Ravidas,

Surdas, Tulsidas, Nanak, Kabir, and Mirabai are most often heard. Their poetry is set over and over by hundreds of composers, and when one hears a particular "bhajan of Mira," for example, it is the text and not necessarily the music which is being referred to. But bhajans are sung in every religious and social context, and a particular group of people may identify a certain text with a specific melody. In a concert presentation, a bhajan may have two or three lines of asthai melody, with a similar pattern for an antara, and these may be repeated and embroidered in a number of patterns by the artist. Often a poet will put his name in the final line of a bhajan with a moral or devotional aphorism, as does Tulsidas:

> Somehow, says Tulsi, O you who send mercy,
> let me find at your feet a refuge of peace.
>
> *Songs of the Saints of India*

Ghazal

The *ghazal* (*gazal*) is a light classical song style based on a genre of classical Urdu love poetry. This Urdu word derives from an Arabic one whose meaning implies "a conversation between lovers," but present is a characteristic ambiguity as to whether the love is human or divine. Like the bhajan, a ghazal may feature only a few melodic lines which are repeated and embroidered as the declamation of the text, all important in this style, may demand. The lines of a ghazal are couplets, and often tell a short story or series of episodes in the poet's love life. There is a strict rhyme scheme, and the first line of the couplet may pose a situation satisfied by the second. Typically in dadra or kaharwa tal, the ghazal may have starts and stops in the rhythm to accord with a given performer's interpretation. Audience interaction with the ghazal singer is common, and there may be loud vocal demonstrations of appreciation for the effective delivery of the various couplets, many of which will be well known. Ghalib, Mir, Sauda, and Mir Hasan are the most famous classical poets of this tradition.

Qavvali

The *qavvālī* is a Moslem devotional song in Urdu, generally sung by a small ensemble which may be divided into solo and choral parts. The soloist will melodically embroider the verse, and the chorus will repeat the refrain, more or less the same way each time. Like a ghazal, the metered rhythm may stop and start, according to the performer's declamation. The typical qavvali is sung in an intense, emotional style in the higher registers of the vocal range, and effective expression of poetry or music are rewarded by the audience with exclamations of pleasure, praise and disbelief, and sometimes gifts of money.

Other Light Forms

There are so many folk and light classical regional songs that their characteristics cannot be described here. These include lullabies and children's songs and rhymes, devotional songs, marriage songs, songs for feasts in the calendar, and a great number of love songs in regional languages. They go by a variety of names, including *kirtan, kajrī, nātya sangit, dhun, gīt, dādrā*, etc. Although they may or may not borrow the melodies and rhythms of the classical styles, they lend their vitality to the music of serious vocal and instrumental performers and form a regular feature of their classical programs as concluding numbers and encores.

A virtuoso violinist, Baba Allauddin played left-handed, and yet strung and tuned the violin in the Western fashion, GDAE, such that the higher notes were furthest from his bowing hand.

Instrumental Music

The style of presenting classical music has been changing over the last two hundred years, and the evolution of instrumental music has been dramatic. The stylistic syntheses of Allauddin Khan, technical changes in the instruments' construction, the advent of the microphone, the modern concert format, and the worldwide expansion of the audience are some of the principle reasons. It used to be said that vocal music was the basis of all Indian music, and while it may be true in a cosmic sense, on the practical level instrumental music has had its own integrity for thousands of years. Many vocal styles, for instance the nom-tom alap, tarana, and many types of tans, have been strongly influenced by instrumental styles of rendering rag. Despite this, it is common practice to group instrumentalists with vocal traditions, and many of the well-known names in instrumental music have also been established singers. In the past, those instrumentalists who had training in dhrupad styles of vina and rabab also had extensive vocal training. This is less true of khyal and thumri styles, but it was rare for any instrumentalist not to have knowledge, if not intensive training, in these vocal genres. Today this statement still applies, even though acquiring vocal mastery is difficult.

Before the twentieth century and Allauddin Khansahib, the mainstays of classical instrumental music in the Seni gharana were the *beenkars* (players of the *rudra vīṇa*) and *rababiyas* (*rabab* players) who played in the dhrupad *ang* (branch or "style") and/or the *gat-toṛa* tradition. In alap, the dhrupad-style instrumentalists follow the compositional procedures of their vocal counterparts, for example, asthai-antara-sanchari-abhog, but to it are added sections unique to the particular instruments. The instrumental alap is decribed as being "in twelve, eighteen, or twenty-two parts," but in modern performance, these are not enumerated so much as acknowledged as the reservoir of techniques to draw upon. In the case of the vina, a rich catalog of left- and right-hand movements has been inherited from ancient times, many of which were listed in the thirteenth-century *Saṅgītratnākara*. On both the vina (or *bīṇ*) and rabab, the right-hand technique is highly developed, and several of the formal sections can be described in terms of it. For instance, *laṛī* (chain, string), the technique of playing rapid tremolo strokes of the right hand to prolong a note, has a number of variations:

laṛī jhālā	interpolating chikari strokes in a *laṛī*
laṛī lapeṭ	bringing melodic variation through *mīnd*
laṛī guthāv	interpolating bol patterns into the *laṛī*

The entire scope of the concluding section called *jhālā* (sparkling, cymbal; also, "fused together"), which is characterized by rapid strokes of the high drone strings, can also be developed through interpolating other right and left hand techniques, such as *tān*, *tār paran*, *laṛī*, *ṭhok*, and *gamak*. *Paran* (*paṛhan*, recited) describes a manner of playing (or composing) from pakawaj drumming, and *tār* (string) *paran* is a compositional specialty of the rabab, as are many of the rhythmic bol patterns which are characteristic of its type of plectrum strum.

Gat-tora

When the sitar and sarod began to emerge as the chief instruments of the classical tradition in the later eighteenth century, they adapted many of these older instrumental techniques and further developed the style of solo playing known as the *gat-toṛā* tradition. Sitarist Masit Khan is credited with the innovation of a sixteen-beat bol pattern in medium tintal which bears his name, the *masītkhāni gat* :

	3	+	2	o
diri	**da diri da ra**	**da da ra, diri**	**da diri da ra**	**da da ra**

This style of composition, originally in a medium tempo but now rendered more slowly, is an adaptation of an old song rhythm found in much world music, notably the Lutheran chorale, itself an older song form.

A *gat* (Sanskrit, going) is a composition for instruments (or drums and dance), whose rhythmic patterns are defined by bols, that is, right-hand instrumental strokes. The gat also functions as the main theme of the instrumental rendering of the rag, and is treated like the A section of a rondo form which is returned to again and again throughout a performance: A B A C A D A.... Common modern concert procedure features a short tabla solo upon the return to the gat, for the gat is fixed and provides the framework of the tal against which the tabla player can play variations. In pakawaj accompaniment styles, a drummer is likely to play continuous paran with the instrumentalist, as might be heard in the performance of a dhrupad. In previous eras, gat styles were sometimes named after famous practioners (e.g., *Ferōzkhānī gat* and *Razakhānī gat*), but in modern times there are so many variations of gats, especially since the fusions and innovations of Allauddin Khansahib, that these terms are rarely used.

The *toṛā* (plucked; "a bouquet of notes") are the variations in the rag which are also defined by bol patterns, which are the episodes (B C D...) of the rondo-like form. In former times, an alap might be played on surbahar or surshringar, and then the player would either change instruments or yield the stage to a performer of gat-tora on sitar or sarod. In certain gharanas, this is still the pattern. The instrumental style of gat-tora playing is one of the characteristic features of North Indian classical instrumental music for strings, and players are judged on their ability to render tightly woven, clearly thought-out, and inventive patterns in this style.

The term *gāyakī ang* (singing style) is used to describe the adaptation and performance of khyal vocal styles on instruments. The realization of a masitkhani gat is in fact most often done in gayaki ang, no matter who the player. But the term is otherwise used to describe the melodious sitar style of Vilayat Khan and many others he has influenced. In this style, there is a concentration on a khyal-style "gat" (i.e., a *chīz*) with pregnant pauses in the exposition followed by short, melodious, and often powerful tans in a virtuosic style. In the Seni

and often powerful tans in a virtuosic style. In the Seni Allauddin gharana, a similar gayaki ang is combined with playing styles of the dhrupad ang: there is greater emphasis on longer tans developed from bols, and the pauses between shorter tans are not as dramatically heightened with silence.

Possible Format and Outline for a Modern Instrumental Presentation

ALAP:

- I. **Alap**—sectional movement without audible rhythmic pulse; each section finished with a shorted metered return to **sa** called the *mohṛā*
  - A. **Asthai**—in several sections, each exploring a certain melodic area of the rag, unfolding the rag's tonality and balance
  - B. **Antara**—a movement to high **sa** and above
  - C. **Sanchari**—a quick recapitulation of the asthai in one longer span of phrases, usually beginning in **dha** or **ni** in the low or middle register
  - D. **Abhog**—joined to the sanchari, begins like the antara and quickly explores the very highest (and or lowest) extremes of an instrument's (and rag's) registers
- II. **Jor** —introduces rhythm but with no fixed meter, although a duple feeling is usually implied
  - —may unfold in asthai-antara-sanchari-abhog form as described above
  - —may repeat this scheme in medium and fast tempos
  - —often jor is played entirely with only downstrokes (da) of the right hand, i.e., without either bols or diris if strictly imitating dhrupad vocal style
  - A. **Tans**—mixed tans with slides and gamaks
    - —boltans: tans created primarily from rhythmic patterns of the right hand
    - —*ekāra* tans: rapid patterns with one right hand stroke per note
  - B. **Lari** —a section of protracted tones, drawn out with right hand tremolo (diri-diri)
    - —may be combined with bols (*guthav*, braided), slides (*lapeṭ*, winding, turning), or lari-jhala
    - —may follow asthai-antara (sanchari-abhog) development

C. Jhala—*thok jhālā*: a chikari stoke followed by three quick strokes; this and later jhala sections may be developed with asthai antara (sanchari-abhog) formal sections or mixed with tans and laris described above
—*siddh* jhala: pattern in duple rhythm with a melody string pluck followed by three quick strokes of the chikari strings
—mixed jhalas, often accelerating
—ends with *mohrā*, perhaps extended or elaborated

Gat

The gat is the entire section of composition which is in tal, although only the fixed composition is actually the "gat" itself. It is accompanied by tabla or pakawaj.

Ideally, the gat should fully figure those melodic and rhythmic features of the rag which may have only been suggested during the alap. It then comes as a fulfillment of the rag development. Further, the shape of the chosen composition should heavily influence the structures of the expansions of the gat—the vistars, tans, laris, boltans, and jhalas. Broadly speaking, this is known as *baḍhāt* (increasing, growing): all development proceeding from and growing out of the fixed composition. Typically, gats are paired in slow and faster tempos, and are followed occasionally by medium or very fast gats. But one gat is considered complete in itself and may be played for a long time, depending on the invention and stamina of the player. After a compositional section, outlined below, the instrumentalist will play the first line (gat) and maintain it while the tabla player plays his solo (which, at its most artful, emerges out of the rhythmic content of the tan played by the instrumentalist). Because of the desire to present and maintain the mood of the rag in softer sections, tabla players often restrict their solos to later stages in the rag's development. The following list of items is subject to radical shifts of ordering, according to the circumstances of the performance. The slow gat may accelerate to a medium tempo in sections, or continue at a slow pace throughout:

I. Slow gat

A. Entry of tabla

—normally waits for one full cycle of the instrumentalist's playing of the gat

—enters with *uthān* (to blossom, build); a sparsely stroked introductory movement (one to three cycles) which builds to a small introductory climax on the downbeat *(sam)*

B. Vistars

—first few may highlight the *mukhṛa* (opening phrase of the gat) by embellishing the principle movements of the gat melody in short tans in the same rhythmic movements as the gat

—second stage may develop the rag by phrase as in the alap, but ideally without exact duplication of those alap movements

—some introduction of rhythmic variation in vistar style

—usually in asthai-antara form; the antara may be precomposed

—sometimes sanchari-abhog added

C. Rhythmic tans

—may highlight or use as their compositional basis, peculiar instrumental techniques: *krintan, zamzama, gamak, bols,* etc.

—*layakari*: composing extended tans with different rhythmic ideas; well constructed tans will use rhythmic figures economically and inventively, and entire tans in different *lay*s are common (*deṛh, tigun, chhaigun,* etc.)

—*peshkar*: the introduction of a short rhythmic and melodic theme which is returned to again and again after short, and often rapid, tans in virtuosic style

—*tihai*s: a composition in three identical sections (palas) which leads dramatically to sam or the beginning of the gat. Short tihais are a regular feature of the middle and ending sections of rhythmic tans.

—*chakradar tihai*: a longer tihai made up of three interior tihais, each of which may have an introductory movement. These complex forms may be highly mathematical and are usually precomposed.

—*sath sangat*: the composition of short tans in which the drummer plays along, imitating the rhythmic patterns simultaneously; these usually are short but may end with a longer tan and tihai; this section is often very playful, full of *hasya ras.*

—*lari*s and *jhala*s as in alap and jor, but with tihais and tans interspersed

II. Fast gat The ending sections of a slow gat are often drawn out over many cycles of the tal. The following fast gat may present several cycles of composed material with it, each well bound by the tal metrically, thus affording a contrasting relief to the extended feelings of the materials preceding it. An antara may be composed in similar style, and attached directly. The fast gat accelerates in section, ending in the presto tempo of the jhala.

—fast tans, each within one cycle of the gat
—*tora*: boltans which are "bouquets" of notes presented with tightly composed right-hand plucked patterns, ending with a tihai
—slow vistars which may use "alaps" (abstract phrases) in the slower styles of earlier movements
—layakari tans
—lari tans
—very fast gat
—jhalas
—*sawal jawab* (question and answer): usually at the very end of a performance, an antiphonal section in which rhythms and figures are stated by the instrumentalist and answered by the drummer; ends with halving the length of the phrases until one beat in length
—closing section: often fixed or highly modeled, a short section of tightly composed and repeated melodic figures which precede the final tihai
—final tihai, often a chakradar, and often ending on the high **sa**

Mohammad Wazir Khan of the Rampur gharana, guru to Allauddin Khansahib and one of the last of the great Seni Beenkars—vina players who traced their blood descent from Tansen.

History

We adore that Supreme Being of the form of sound which is the one bliss without a second, and the light of the consciousness in all beings that has manifested itself in the form of the universe. By the adoration of sound are also adored the Gods Brahma [the Creator], Vishnu [the Preserver], and Shiva [the Destroyer], for they are the embodiments of sound.

Prayer from the *Sangitaratnakara,* 13th C.

Oral history among the musicians maintains that the classical music of India is a tradition five thousand years old. One of the implications of this sweeping statement is that the music of ancient times was in some way similar to the music of modern times, and that there is something timeless and unchanging in the fundamental concept of the music. Also, intuitive and spiritual dimensions are at work here, and neither can be underestimated in its importance to modern music. When musicians sing or play, they are attempting to tune themselves to the infinite, and many of the differences which characterize musical styles over the ages are infused with just that sense of ancient constancy. This aspect—an awareness of the eternal in music—is part of the concept *Nāda-Brahma,* the understanding of sound itself as a divine aspect of cosmic reality. Any detailing of historical developments in music in the face of this infinity of *nād* is likened by practicing musicians to ant scratches in the sand: mere surface ripples, and not so significant except perhaps to us other ants.

Until late in the nineteenth century there was no systematic investigation of music history, although there are a good number of Sanskrit theoretical treatises dating from ancient and medieval times. But there were few attempts at chronological ordering until the twentieth century, and even now the dates of many of the developments in music history remain cloudy. These problems are inherent in the oral tradition, which has not even preserved a written record of the music itself. Although the names of the theoretical concepts, such as the musical forms, scales, melodic features, and microtones, are there in great abundance in the old treatises, the necessary illustrative music is not, and so the exercise of reconstructing past music and charting its course of development is vaporous at best. Practicing musicians deride as rainbow chasers musicologists who would wish a more specific history, and musicologists chide them back for their ill-read and fanciful view of their tradition.

In these pages it will be impossible to give more than an outline of the long and multi-faceted history of the classical traditions. The purpose of this chapter is to collect in its seven sections the formative contributions of these eras of music: Prehistoric, Vedic, Buddhist, Hindu, Medieval, British, and Modern.

Pre-History (4000-1500 BC)

The prehistoric study of India presents a curious duality. In the normal sense of the word "prehistoric," the antiquity of culture in India dates back to the Stone Age settlements of the Deccan peninsula. Settlements have been dated from 4000 BC, and language and culture studies show that a mix of many Asian, African, and Mediterranean ethnic groups inhabited the subcontinent. The interesting other side of the word "prehistoric" is that in India, where the population heads toward the billion mark in the twenty-first century, there are still a number (perhaps even millions) of tribal people who live a life closely akin to a neolithic style. And although times are rapidly changing in India too, tribal styles of dress, dance, and music still play an influential part in coloring modern culture.

The cities of the Indus Valley cultures which are still being excavated in modern Pakistan date from 3000 BC. Findings show that these cities were advanced in architecture and traded extensively, especially with the Mediterranean cultures. Very few artifacts of musical life have turned up, but a flute and a statuette of a dancing girl attest to some artistic activity. There are a few remains of these peoples' script, but they appear to deal mostly with business affairs and have yet to be deciphered; their language may be a relative of the Dravidian languages of South India. There are no clear reasons for the disappearance of this sophisticated early culture. Most likely the Aryans, who rode fiercely out of the central Asian hills, annihilated them in their march into the Ganges Valley.

Vedic Period (1500-500 BC)

The Aryans began to settle in India around 1500 BC. Their sacred literature was the collection of hymns and incantations known as the *vedas* ("divine knowledge") named respectively the *ṛig*, *sāma*, *yajur*, and *atharva vedas*. Even though this Vedic culture produced an abundance of philosophical literature and the foundations of the great Indo-European language, Sanskrit, there were philosophical and cultural injunctions against writing down the actual Vedas themselves, and they have lived as a part of oral tradition for more than three thousand years (although Vedic manuscripts do exist from around 1500 AD). Although the other three Vedas were and are chanted primarily on one tone elaborated by its upper and lower neighbor notes, the *Sāmaveda* was sung with all seven tones, and is considered one of the origins of the musical system. The hymns of the *Sāmaveda* are mostly musical elaborations of the texts of the *Rigveda*, and the tunes may have been adopted from a wide variety of sources, some perhaps pre-Aryan in origin. There came to be a codification of the singing practices, and a system of hand and body gestures to aid in the teaching of the *Sāmaveda*. One of the earliest texts describing these features is the *Nāradashikshā*, a collection of instructional verses on Vedic presentation.

The *Atharvaveda* and the *Yajurveda* are ritual blessings and sacrificial formulae used as consecrations to sanctify weddings, harvests and other auspicious occasions. In them, a highly systematic permutation of the syllables of the text was worked out (*vikriti,* disordered), perhaps as an aid to memorization. If, for example, the syllables of one of these verses are labeled a b c d e..., then possible vikriti patterns might be:

ab bc cd de...
abbaab bccbbc...
ab ba ab bcd dcb bc cedf fedc cd defgh hgfed...
ab yz bc xy cd wx de vw ...
etc.

Thus, these *vikriti* patterns can be seen as a precursive model of the permutation of syllables in the language of drumming.

The Vedic and later the Puranic periods also introduce many of the gods and epic characters for the pantheon which still populates the song literature: Brahma, Vishnu, Shiva, Saraswati, Durga, Indra, Rama, Krishna, and numerous others, although many of these deities have gone through an evolving identity process through the ages. The events of *Rāmāyana* and *Mahābharata* epics date from this era, although they were not written down until many centuries later. In the *Rāmāyana,* Hanuman, the monkey god, teaches the hero, Rama, the names of the pitches **sa re ga ma pa dha ni** in the forest. From earliest times, then, the great epics have always been recited and dramatically staged with music.

Buddhist Period (500 BC-300 AD)

The performances of these sacred dramas, like Brahmanic society in general, must have become somewhat degenerate, for just as the two great reformers of the sixth century BC, Mahavira (founder of Jainism) and Gautama the Buddha, sought to rectify the seeker on the religious path, so a person who called himself Bharata later wrote a major treatise called the *Nāṭyaśāstra* in order to correct excesses in the art of performance. Although scholars have disagreed on the date of this treatise (many now assign it to the first centuries of the Christian era, perhaps as late as the fourth century), it describes the era which precedes it, now loosely called the Buddhist period. Political control during this era was by a number of dynastic empires, such as Magadha, the Mauryans, and the Kushans. In

326 BC, Alexander the Great made inroads into the Indus Valley from Greece, and there is some speculation that after this time, as in sculpture, there was a commingling of Greek and Indian ideas about music theory. The great king of this period was the Buddhist Emperor Asoka (273-232 BC), who was one of the first rulers to extend his political power almost entirely throughout the subcontinent, thus outlining modern India as a nation.

The *Nāṭyaśhāstra* (treatise on the dance-acting) speaks of the art as *saṅgīt* (sung together), which was comprised of dance, drama, and music. The science of dramatic arts, from its aesthetics to production to facial and hand gestures, comprises the bulk of this study, but there are several chapters on music. These form the foundation of classical music theory, and have been the subject of commentary for the next fifteen hundred years, for nearly every subsequent theorist cites the *Nāṭyaśhāstra* as a starting point. Bharata describes two scales, called the *sā grāma* and the *mā grāma*, and the microtones (*sruti*s) which distinguish them. He constructs a mathematical experiment on a vina to illustrate the difference between the two. These scales are sometimes compared with the modern rags Kafi and Bageshri, but although Kafi (*ṭhāṭ*) is agreed to have been the original natural scale, the nature and placement of the srutis has since had a vast and controversial literature devoted to it.

Bharata classifies instruments into the four categories which are today the basis of the Sachs-Hornböstel system of organology: *tata* (chordophones), *suṣhira* (aerophones), *avanaddha* (membranophones), and *ghana* (idiophones). He categorizes melody types called *jāti*s by their important notes and starting and ending points. He enumerates the moods (*rasa*s), and the structures of *tala*s, and classifies types of fixed composition (e.g., *dhruva*s) by their texts. He speaks of ensemble music as being the common practice at theatrical performances.

At the same time, in South India the Tamil poetry and literature tells of a flourishing musical system. The names of the musical features are different, but many of the concepts seem to be similar to those of Bharata.

It is never assumed that Bharata himself invented all his theory, but rather that he codified what was already ancient practice in his time in order to rid the stage of contemporary abuses. The vastness of his descriptions is unfailingly impressive, although the vagueness of his terminology is all too often confusing. Nevertheless, the *Nāṭyaśhāstra* is still revered as "the fifth Veda" because it is the seminal treatise of the performing arts as the instruments of divine expression.

Hindu Period (300-1300)

With the Gupta dynasty's rise to power in 320 came the era now called the "Golden Age of Sanskrit." Astronomy, mathematics and science were highly regarded, and sculpture, philosophy, and literature flourished. In the fifth century, writings of the still celebrated dramatist and poet Kalidasa, as well as in the *Kāmasutra* of Vatsayana, there are allusions to a flourishing musical life as well. Iconographic evidence of the abundant sculpture of the period shows a rich variety of drums, wind, and string instruments, as well as dancing and orchestras.

There are later references to a number of musical treatises, now presumed lost, which may have been written in this era, but the most important existing one is the *Bṛihaddeshī* of Matanga from around the seventh century. In it is one of the first uses of the word *rāga* to describe perhaps what Bharata had called a *jāti*, that is, a melodic type. Many kinds of composition are mentioned, and he describes also a vina with movable frets, which suggests that the tonic may already have been considered as fixed by this time. Another treatise of the tenth century, the *Sangit Makaranda*, ascribes times and genders to certain rags.

The most important treatise of this great classical period was written near its end, and summarizes music theory from ancient times. During the later centuries of this era, the Arabs had begun making military incursions into North India, and the climate there was probably too agitated for Hindu musical speculation. In the thirteenth century, an accountant named Sarangadev from Kashmir went to live and work at the southern court of Devgiri (later renamed Daulatabad, near modern

Aurangabad) in Maharashtra. There he wrote the *Saṅgītaratnākara* (*The Ocean of Music*), the final classic summary of ancient music. In it are descriptions and theoretical commentary about raga, tala, ornamentation, aesthetics, instruments, compositions, and tans, with even some musical examples. In the ensuing turbulence of medieval India, it became the beacon which many authors looked to as their theoretical bible.

Medieval Period (1300-1700)

The establishment of Moslem hegemony over North India after 1300 had profound influences in the musical practice. In the court of Sultan Allauddin Khilji (1296-1316), there were two musicians who played an important role in what was to become a reshaping of the tradition. The first, Amir Khusrau was a musician-poet of Turkish lineage who served in a court dominated by Persian customs, and who commented with marvel on the music of his adopted land: "Indian music, the fire that burns heart and soul, is superior to the music of any other country." At this court, he heard the second musician, Gopal Nayak, a Southern singer from whom Khusrau is said to have learned by hiding behind curtains during the Nayak's practice and performances. Khusrau's spiritual teacher was the Sufi Nizamuddin Auliya, later to be revered as a saint of the Islamic spiritual tradition which exalts music as an expression of mystic love. These three elements—the indigenous classical style of Gopal Nayak, the Persian influences brought by Amir Khusrau, and the devotional mysticism of Sufism (and later the Bhakti Movement) expressed through music—became three of the main features of a new direction in Indian music which is now called Hindustani music in contradistinction to the Carnatic style of South India. Both traditions still flourish, based on the same musical vocabulary but realized in different styles and languages, with different instruments and compositional forms.

The spiritual revival known as the Bhakti Movement spread into the North from South India during the fourteenth through the sixteenth centuries and had a great impact on the music. One of the first of the northerners to extol the ecstatic feelings of love which characterize the literature and music of this movement was the Bengali poet Jayadev, who wrote the *Gītagovinda*, "The Song of Krishna," in sections (cantos), each of which is to be sung in a designated rag. The poets Tulsidas, Surdas, Mirabai, Nanak, and Kabir were all a part of this spiritual revival which has left a legacy of sung devotional poetry that is still being set to music. The Sufi movement also both inspired and partook of the feelings of the Bhakti Movement—a mystical fusion of Hinduism and Islam and a conscious rejection of the formalism and sectarianism of both.

Under the Rajput rulers of Mewar and Gwalior, music flourished, and Raja Man Singh Tomar (1480-1517) of Gwalior is said to have first developed the dhrupad style of singing. Based on an older multisectional song form called the *prabandha gīt* ("organized song"), the dhrupad was a four-sectioned song whose usually devotional text extolled the gods, music, kings, or nature. It was to come to full flower in the splendor of the Moghul courts.

The Moghul dynasty, founded by Babar, and including Akbar, Jehangir, and Shah Jehan, lasted from 1526 to 1857, and at times controlled nearly all of modern India. Under Akbar the Great (1556-1605), there developed a fusion of Hindu and Moslem cultures which blossomed in the dhrupad singing and playing of his great court musician, Miyan Tansen. "There has not been a singer of his like for a thousand years," wrote Akbar's chronicler, Abul Faz'l. Tansen was the composer of many modern rags, including the famous Darbari Kanra, Miya ki Todi, Miyan ki Malhar, and Miyan ki Sarang. He played, too, on the rabab and founded the musical lineage called the Seni Gharana, which has included so many of the great names of music in the era since his time. Tansen was one of Akbar's "nine jewels" and an important figure in the court.

One day Akbar asked that Swami Haridas, Tansen's teacher, be brought to court so that he might hear him. Tansen told the emperor that they would have to go into the forest to hear him, since his teacher would not come for anyone. Even at that, Emperor Akbar had to disguise himself as a servant first, and it was only by Tansen's intentionally singing a rag incorrectly that the old man finally sang to rectify the error. "I sing for men," Tansen later explained to his royal patron, "but Swamiji sings only for God."

There exist dozens of treatises on music written in medieval times, both in Persian and Sanskrit, and this was the formative era for Hindi, the language of the Bhakti poets; henceforth, Hindi/Urdu would be the language of Hindustani classical song. Treatises of that time concentrate on attempts to organize what was becoming a widely disparate practice, and most of them attempt to reinterpret the ancient music as it was presented in the *Saṅgītratnākara* rather than adequately describing contemporary practice. A favorite new topic was gathering the rags into genealogies, headed by a male rag, and connected with family relationships (the *parivar* system): wives, sons, grandsons. These were often fancifully accompanied with descriptive meditative poems on each rag (*dhyāna*s) which were in turn painted in miniatures. A collection of these was called a *rāgamala* (garland of rags), and were produced by the hundreds well into the eighteenth century. The later medieval writers refer to four *mat*s (opinions) which are now usually remembered for their parivara systems of rag classification: Somesvar Mat, Bharat Mat, Kalinath Mat, and Hanuman Mat. The origin and authority of these systems are disputed.

One of the main features of the treatises of the sixteenth and seventeenth centuries is a new empiricism which seeks to classify rags according to the principles of their scale construction. This began with the Southern writer Ramamatya whose *Svara Mela Kalānidhi* (c. 1550) began the musicological schism between Northern and Southern schools. Instead of totally accepting the ancient ideas about theory, Ramamatya based his classifications on what he observed. He said that there were twelve notes with eighteen srutis, and that the rags could be gathered into collections of scale types. This scientific model became the basis for musical theory in the South but, even though imitated by several Northern writers, did not gain wide acceptance elsewhere.

The most extensive classification of rags was that of the South Indian Venkatamukhi, in whose *Chaturdandi Prakāshika* (c.1620) the 72 melakarta system is proposed which became the theoretical basis for the organization of Carnatic music. The Northern musicologist Pundarika Vitthala wrote three treatises in which he followed Ramamatya's models, but his theories

ries were not widely accepted, and it was not until the twentieth century that this style of musicological sytematization was generally adopted with the theories of Bhatkhande.

The musicians of the medieval period were the founding fathers of the modern style of rendering the music. The contributions of Amir Khusrau and Tansen may themselves be difficult to prove on the level of personal achievement, but it is clear that from their era come the rags and forms of composition which are still in practice. Indeed, some scholars believe that even the fixed **sa** and presence of the drone instruments were among practices established during this time. From the miniature painting, it can be seen that the tanpura, vina, and many other instruments can be identified as the forerunners of those which are in common use today.

British Period (1700-1947)

Aurangzeb, the last of the Great Moghuls, died in 1712, but under his rule the course of music history began to change. In his strict interpretation of Moslem orthodoxy he banished music and musicians from the court.

Hoping to impress the emperor with their outcast plight, the musicians staged a mock funeral procession and paraded past the palace. Aurangzeb looked out the window and asked who was dead. "Your Excellency, it is Music, which has died under your edict." "Fair enough," he is said to have calmly remarked. "Bury it deep enough so that no one will be able to hear it!"

In England, the East India Company had been founded in 1600 to put its arm in the sea trade with the Dutch and Portuguese and, later, the French. Originally, there were no thoughts of empire and political maneuvering was between the rival nations and with local rulers for trading privileges. These privileges included fortified seaport facilities, and in this manner the British founded what were to be the modern cities of Bombay, Calcutta, and Madras. Militarily, the British put an end to French commercial rivalry in 1757, but with the decline of Moghul power beginning under Aurangzeb and the fragmenting of that vast empire, the British had already begun to fill a power vacuum, leading to their total control after the supressing of the Sepoy Rebellion in 1857.

Although many seventeenth-century court musicians had begun to look for employment beyond the splendors of the central courts of Delhi and Agra, there was a notable exception: the Delhi court of the emperor Mohammad Shah (1719-1748) once again patronized the arts in royal Moghul style. His famous court musician was Niamat Khan, who is still remembered by his poetic name *Sadāraṅg* ("all colors") which he used in his compositions. He was a rudra bin player who also sang dhrupad, but he is most famous for initiating the popularity of the khyal style by teaching it to his students, even though it is said that he himself did not perform it at court. The khyal is said to have existed since the days of Amir Khusrau when it was associated with *qavvālī*, a style of Moslem devotional singing. Later, the fifteenth-century Jaunpur court of Sultan Sharqi is also credited with khyal innovation. But only during the eighteenth century did this style ascend to the predominance that it holds today as the prime vehicle for vocal rag presentation. Niamat Khan's contribution to khyal was probably that he introduced into it elements of dhrupad, and perhaps refined its once exclusively fast tempo and short song (*chhoṭā khyāl*) qualities into a more dignified and slower exposition of rag (*baṛā khyāl*).

One Khusrau Khan, a younger relative of Niamat Khan, popularized the sitar, a new combination of the bin with Persian elements; and hence, as Allyn Miner comments, "the same family, the same musical environment, and the same Delhi public were directing the course of musical innovation." After the sack of Delhi by the Persian Nadir Shah in 1739, the Moghul court itself was no longer the central umbrella under which artistic life flourished. Patronage passed to the great houses and country estates of the amirs, the wealthy courtiers, and landowners. Although Delhi continued to hold central importance for style, since it was cosmopolitan and held the old traditions, the courts at Lucknow, Rampur, Jaipur, Benaras, and Gwalior began to play an increasingly vital role in the nurturing of music. The innovations of Delhi, which included the new singing style, the khyal, also influenced instrumental styles and branched out to the neighboring court cities where these innovations took on their own regional characteristics. The sitar took the place of the bin, the sarod developed from the several types of rabab, and the sarangi and tabla became the chief accompanying instruments. Many *gharanas* were founded around the turn of the nineteenth century. These schools of playing and singing handed down—through blood lines, more often than not—particular styles and techniques, compositions, and versions of their rags.

When the British declared Queen Victoria Empress of India after the Rebellion of 1857, a center of musical activity had been the regal court of Avadh (Oudh) at Lucknow. While the deposed king took some of his musicians and dancers with him to Calcutta, others went to Bombay—for there was beginning to be wealth enough in the cities to support the arts; still others found employment at neighboring courts, notably Rampur, which by the end of the century, employed some five hundred musicians and dancers. It was to be one of the last of the magnificent courts to patronize music.

Calcutta was the center of British and Indian intellectual activity in the nineteenth century. Colleges, founded there largely to educate Indians to work in the civil service, began to research and preserve the national cultural heritage. From Calcutta came the first writings which unveiled India's cultural legacy to the world. William Jones published the first Western investigation into Indian music, *On the Musical Modes of the Hindoos,* in 1784. He also founded the Asiatic Society of Bengal, which was to publish a great number of articles and translations of Sanskrit literature. Later, Capt. Augustus Willard's *A Treatise on the Music of Hindostan* (1834) attempts to describe the music from an observer's standpoint, whereas Jones had confined his discussion to what little was available of the Sanskrit literature. In general, the nineteenth-century scholars from the West were tremendously excited by the richness of India's past, but paid little attention to the music of the day which they saw as being in a state of great degeneration.

In Hindoostan, music arrived at its greatest height during the flourishing period of the native princes, just a little before the Mohammedan conquest, and the subsequent depravity and decline since then, closed the scene with utter catastrophe....At present most native performers of this noble science are the most immoral set of men on earth...

Capt. Augustus Willard

The task of righting the fallen image of music was one of the lifelong projects of the Bengali scholar Saurindra Mohan Tagore (1840-1914), who collected the early English writings on music in his *Hindu Music from Various Authors* (1874). Tagore also founded schools for music in Calcutta and is known for his writings of Indian music as well as the first Indian book on world music. By the beginning of the nineteenth century, a more balanced viewpoint about music began to emerge. A.H. Fox-Strangways visited India twice in the early 1900s and published his *Music of Hindostan* in 1914. Two years later, Vishnu Narayan Bhatkhande introduced his controversial theories to the first All-India Music Conference with these words:

> *I have tried to redeem our music from the hands of illiterate artists whose method of teaching is unscientific inasmuch as it is unsystematic, and consequently unappealing and unacceptable to the educated student, and also unnecessarily long and tedious and incapable of permanent results.*
>
> V. N. Bhatkhande

It is no wonder, then, with such an attitude he offended many musicians, often the very ones whose help he needed in collecting his six-volume collection of the song literature, *Kramik Pustak Malika* ("graded book garland"), published in stages from 1917 to 1936. The musicians frequently gave him corrupt versions of the songs and rags as a result. Bhatkhande's Western bias for a "scientific attitude" is also evident, and created skepticism for his theory of the ten *ṭhāṭs* (scales) which, though simple and easily assimilated, has been attacked as providing a misleadingly simple basis for the study of rag. Nevertheless, Bhatkhande founded schools, collected and published the literature, and assembled a modern theory for teaching the music which, controversial though it remains, is widely used.

Another pioneering musician was Vishnu Digambar Paluskar (1872-1931), who not only founded schools and published the song literature, but championed the cause of the practical musician. An exponent of the Gwalior gharana, he was among the first to present public concerts of classical music. For this he was heavily criticized by those who felt he was casting the great pearls of a refined court tradition before the swine of an uneducated public. His concept of theory was to classify rags according to their characteristics and traditional family associations, which was in part a rejection of Bhatkhande's more rationalistic theories. Paluskar trained dozens of important artists and teachers and established the Gandharva Mahavidyalaya, a group of music schools throughout India.

The most important and influential instrumentalist of the early twentieth century was Allauddin Khan of Maihar. The intensity of his bearing, his virtuous behavior, and his phenomenal mastery of technique and literature were legendary. He revitalized old rags and tals, and amalgamated the techniques of playing, fusing classical styles and introducing into light music many classical insights and practices. His orchestra music was pioneering, and he redesigned the sitar and sarod and a number of other instruments in order that they could accommodate his wide sense of instrumental style. Finally, his training of a galaxy of instrumentalists of the highest caliber, including his son Ali Akbar, his daughter Annapurna, and grandson Ashish, as well as Ravi Shankar, Nikhil Banerjee, Panalal Ghosh, and Timir Baran, are among the great legacies of this genius.

There is no doubt that Allauddin Khan made a revolutionary change in the playing style of classical instrumental music without shaking off its traditional roots. What he actually did was to shake off the monotony, which was then prevalent, by adding a new stimulant with a scientific outlook. He fetched beautiful gems from different styles and synthesized a new one which enlarged the horizon of North Indian classical music.

Ajoy Singha Roy

Modern Period (since 1947)

The modern period of the history of India's music actually began with the changes of the past century, and yet is demarcated decisively by the political Independence of India on August 15, 1947. The old social order that had been in decline for many years was left behind and the "world's largest democracy" created. Court patronage of musicians, for most already a thing of the past, was ended once and for all. Gravitating to the larger cities, musicians relied on national radio, films, and later television for employment, and classical music circles arose in these cities to sponsor concerts and festivals. Recording and broadcasting changed the required length of the programs; and microphones, necessary in the larger halls, altered vocal and instrumental techniques. As the subtleties and variations of esoteric rags was lost on the mass audiences, artists cut down severely on the number of rags in their active repertoire. Recordings spread the literature and styles of all gharanas, so the former distinctions between the styles of these schools became less apparent. Tabla players, formerly relegated to the secondary position of accompanists, found themselves elevated in the public eye and drawing applause for their musical contributions. The star system favored certain artists over others, and indeed made some of them commercial commodities. Musicians traveled abroad to Europe, the United States, Japan, Australia, and Asia to appear before new audiences and train thousands of foreign students.

How these dramatic sociological changes will affect the music itself is not easy to see. The speed of modern society means that the artists will have to contend with more economic pressure, yet will enjoy less leisure to create and practice. The langorous tempo of court life is losing its grasp on the feeling in the music. Already there is widespread lament for the decline of certain aspects and refinements of the classical tradition. But the fundamental nature of the music, *Nāda-Brahma,* cannot be altered and will continue to be realized in many different styles.

"Will bringing this music to the West alter it, Khansahib?"
Pause.
"Well," he smiled, "they can't change Rag Bhupali."

Treatises

The following is a brief summary of the content of some of the major treatises from ancient times until 1813. This summary is divided into three sections: Ancient, Earlier Medieval, and Later Medieval. Much of the modern practical music theory is based on that of the Medieval periods, although many of the later theorists still tried to orient their thought to the ancient texts, especially the *Sangītaratnākara*. This summary is based on the writings of Nijenhuis, Powers, Bhatkhande, and Grieg.

I. Ancient Period (to 1300)

1. *Nāradasiksha*, first century BC, is a treatise on Saman Vedic chant which includes sections describing the pitches, scales, and ritualistic practices of music.

2. *Nātyaśhāstrā* by Bharata, fourth century, is the seminal treatise on dance, drama, and music; it sets forth rules on aesthetics, classifies instruments, and describes musical theory and performance practice, the latter especially as it relates to drama.

3. *Daṭṭilām* by Dattila, fourth century, is closely related to the *Nātya Shāstra*, though it deals extensively with Gandharva music, which was less attached to dramatic performance.

4. *Bṛihāddeshī* of Matanga, eighth century, repeats much of Bharata's material, discusses philosophical bases of music, and indicates that the word *rāga* had come into use.

5. *Sangitmakaranda*, tenth (perhaps thirteenth) century, describes extramusical associations of rag: times of day and male/female classifcations.

6. *Saṅgītaratnākara* by Sarangadev, thirteenth century, is the last major treatise of the ancient era, which gathers together and sums up what was known about music before the Moslem cultural presence in North India. Its extensive survey of philosophical and musical practice was to be a beacon for musicologists throughout the Middle Ages.

II. Earlier Medieval Period (1300-1600)

1. *Sudhākara* and *Kalānidhi* are two commentaries on the *Saṅgītaratnākara,* the second of which, by the South Indian Kallinātha, ca. 1450, seems to confirm the establishment of the concept of a fixed tonic.

2. The Jain treatises of the fourteenth century, *Saṅgīta-samaya-sara* and *Saṅgītopanishat-sāroddhāra* also review the *Saṅgītaratnākara;* the second treatise discusses the concept of theka, and is the first to describe an established *parivar* (six male rags) system of rag classification.

3. *Saṅgītarāja,* from Rajasthan, 1453, reiterates much of the *Sangītaratnakara* but also includes parivar classification.

III. Later Medieval Period (1500-1813)

1. *Svārамelakalānidhi,* by Ramamatya of Vijayanagar in South India, 1550, is the first to present the new style of "enlightened" rag classification, which takes issue with both the ancient and the fanciful parivar systems, and classifies rags instead by parent scales based on intervallic structures.

2. *Chaturdaṇḍi prakāshika* of Venkatamakhi, ca. 1620, developed Ramamatya's ideas into the seventy-two melas, the basis of the South Indian rag classification system.

3. *Sadrāgachandrodaya* and *Rāgamāla* by Pundarika Vitthala are from the late sixteenth century. Vitthala was a South Indian who traveled North where he integrated Ramamatya's concept of scales with those of the North Indian iconographic parivar systems.

4. *Rāga Taraṅgini* by Lochana Kavi from the end of the sixteenth century, includes a positioning of the shrutis and thus demonstrates that Kafi (dorian) was still considered the natural scale. Kavi presents a *ṭhāṭ* system of twelve scales with seventy-five derivative rags, and gives the times of perfromance for the principal rags.

5. *Saṅgīt Darpana* of Damodara, 1625, describes the *Hanuman-math* system of a thirty-six basic rag-ragini parivar system with iconographies.

6. *Hridāya Prakāsha* and *Hridāya Kautuka* by Hridaya-narayandeva, 1660, discuss placement of microtones and advocates twelve *ṭhāṭs*, which he says are a "collection of notes capable of producing ragas." In explaining vadi-samvadi, Hridaynarayanadeva says that each raga must have at least five notes, and gives a short phrase (lakshana) to decsribe several rags. He notes that Rag Dipak has fallen out of use.

7. *Tuhfat al-hind* by Mirza Khan is a seventeenth-century compilation on music and other arts written in Persian. It includes a summary of theoretical ideas from the *Saṅgīta-ratnākara* as well as contemporary sources.

8. *Saṅgīt Parijāt* by Ahobala, from the latter half of the seventeenth century, was translated into Persian in 1724. Ahobala, like Vitthala, was a South Indian who came North, but he includes a few Southern ragas in his collection. Ahobala describes one hundred twenty-two ragas, and calls Kafi the natural scale.

9. *Saṅgītsār* by Pratap Singh, from the late eighteenth century, is a vast compilation of old and new materials, quoting the *Saṅgītaratnākara*, but also acknowledging the introduction of many medieval and Persian additions to music practice and theory.

10. *Naghmāt-i āsafī* of Mohammad Reza, 1813, revises the parivar system and recognizes Bilawal as the natural scale.

Language and Lyric

The language of the texts sung to North Indian classical music is in that sprawling collection of dialects called Hindi. Hindi is the national language but is not the language spoken all over India. In fact, there are many sayings about the profusion of languages in India, such as, "Every hour that you walk in India brings a new language." Moreover, there are so many dialects of the major languages that the same words often change entirely over regions and time. This has wreaked havoc with the purity of song texts, for most of them have been passed on orally. Short vowels become long, *v*s become *b*s, nasalizations come and go, aspirated letters appear and disappear, and poetic shades of meaning are transformed, obfuscated, and sometimes lost altogether.

There are two major language groups in India, the Sanskrit-based of the North and the Dravidian of the South. The major modern Indian languages derived from Sanskrit are Hindi (with its Persianate sister, Urdu), Bengali, Punjabi, Gujarati, Marathi, Nepali, Oriya, and Sindhi, several of which are written in different scripts. These bear a similar relationship to one another as the Western Romance languages do through their derivation from Latin. The most important Dravidian languages are Tamil, Telegu, Malayalam, and Kannada, also written in different scripts. The largest single language group is, however, the Hindi-Urdu fusion of the North, which is the mother tongue of more than 150 million people and is taught as a second language in schools all over India.

Hindi is the modern form of a language called "Hindvi" and "Hindoostanee" by the British in the eighteenth century, which included a multitude of dialects and eventually Urdu. Like other Indian languages, Hindi is characterized by the word order subject-object-verb; uses postpositions (instead of prepositions); and makes a distinction between dental and retroflex sounds. Its ancestor, the Indo-European language Sanskrit, became crystalized in about 400 BC, and the first grammar of any language, Panini's famous 4000 verses on the rules of Sanskrit, were composed in the period immediately following. But the spoken language continued to evolve, and three families of Prakrits, or regional languages, can be recognized: Maharashtri which became modern Marathi, Magadhi which became modern Bengali, and Sauraseni which became modern Hindi.

In medieval India this third branch developed two major literary languages. Tulsidas wrote his version of the *Rāmāyana (Rāmacharitamānasa)* in the dialect of Avadhi (named for the region of Avadh, or Oudh, around modern Lucknow). This was an important milestone, being one of the first times this major sacred work was presented in a North Indian language other than Sanskrit. Many other devotional lyrics were also cast in this dialect and are still sung today. Another major branch of the Sauraseni Prakrit developed in the area of Braj in the Doab region where the rivers Jamuna and Ganga flow together. This is the region held sacred to Krishna, and innumerable devotional song texts were written in this dialect, Braj Bhasha. The most renowned Braj poet was the blind Surdas, hundreds of whose song lyrics are still regularly sung and are still being set to music. Besides its association with this master poet and his subject, Lord Krishna, the language of Braj is also preferred by singers because it softens some of the hard conjunct letters of Sanskrit and modern spoken Hindi by separating them with short vowel sounds.

The original language of the Moghul court in Delhi and Agra was Persian, which later evolved into Urdu, a combination of Arabic, Persian, and Hindi. The grammatic construction of modern Urdu and Hindi are the same, and there is an immense shared vocabulary, so much so that the language of North India is often called Hindi/Urdu, even though Urdu is written in Arabic script and has a different flavor in its purest forms of pronunciation. Urdu is the language of the ghazal, a popular form of love/devotional poetry which is both recited and sung.

Hence, within the body of poetry which comprises the song lyrics there are many influences at work, not the least of which is the continual dynamic of the oral tradition, which interprets the sounds of languages in the way the ear picks them up. This is true of songs learned at the same time by two different students of the same master, as well as the effects of time on the memory. It is often difficult under these circumstances to reproduce an accurate translation of certain lyrics, for as long as the general sense is understood, literal translation is frequently not sought after. This, of course, does not apply universally, for there are the relatively established texts of the great Bhakti poets such as Surdas, Tulsidas, Kabir, Mirabai, Guru Nanak, and Ramdas, not to mention the famous ghazals of Ghalib, Mir, Sauda, and Mir Hasan, all of which live as independent poetry. Nevertheless, even within the pure literary tradition there are many versions and recensions of the classic poetic texts.

The translations presented in this book are primarily the work of Ali Akbar Khan and the musician-scholar Biresh Roy of Calcutta.

Glossary

ābhog	आभोग	*the fourth section of a dhrupad composition* (lit., *extension)*
ādhā	आधा	*half the original tempo* (lit., *half)*
ādhunik	आधुनिक	*a twentieth -century innovation to the music* (lit., *modern)*
ākār	आकार	*the broad ā sound, "ah" (ä, as in "father"), used in singing vistars and tans*
alankār	अलंकार	*ornament; or a specific type of melodic ornament worked out with permutations of the notes*
ālāp	आलाप	*the introductory movement of a rag in dhrupad style, including alap and jor; loosely, any melodic phrase rendered in abstract rhythm*
alpatva	अल्पत्व	*the scarcity or lesser duration of a note* (lit., *smallness)*
anāgat	अनागत	*a tihai or cadential phrase which ends before sam* (lit., *not attained)*
āndolan	आंदोलन	*the slow wavering of a note, or controlled vibrato, articulated according to the particular precepts of a rag* (lit., *movement)*
aṅg	अंग	*loosely, tetrachord; the range of the rag where the vadi-samvadi lie* (lit., *limb*)
anibaddh	अनिबद्ध	*not bound by meter*
antarā	अन्तरा	*the second part of a composition emphasizing the high* **sa** *and the other notes in the high register* (lit., *between)*
anuvādī	अनुवादी	*with the sahavadi, a secondary tonal center in a rag* (lit., *repetition)*
apnyās	अपन्यास	*an ancient term designating a note capable of being prolonged in a rag*
ardha-	अर्ध	*prefix meaning "half," used in half-beat tals*
ārī	आड़ी	*any triple rhythm* (lit., *oblique)*
ārohī	आरोही	*ascending*
ās	आस	*the halo of atmospheric sound which is produced by an instrument, especially the tanpura* (lit., *enclose, surround)*

asthāī, sthāyī	स्थायी	*the part of a fixed composition in the main register of the rag* (lit., *refrain)*
āṭhgun	आठगुन	*eight times the original tempo*
ati	अति	*an adverb suggesting extremeness, e.g., ati-tara, "very high register"; ati-komal, "very low pitched," etc.* (lit., *very)*
atīt	अतीत	*a tihai or cadential phrase which ends after the sam has passed* (lit., *elapsed)*
auṛav	औड़व	*pentatonic, a jati of five notes*
avarohī	अवरोही	*descending*
āvarta (-n)	आवर्त(-न)	*one rhythmic cycle of a tal* (lit., *revolution)*
baḍhat	बढत	*the natural progression from slow to fast in a rag; the process of expansion which pays particular attention to the constant relationship of vistar and chiz* (lit., *increased)*
bāj	बाज	*style, used particularly in reference to instrumental styles*
bahutva	बहुत्व	*the prevalence of a note in a rag* (lit., *plenitude)*
bandish	बंदिश	*a fixed composition for voice or instrument* (lit., *bound)*
bānī	बानी	*one of four main styles of rendering dhrupad*
baṛā	बड़ा	*big; as in the bara khyal, i.e., slow khyal*
barābar	बराबर	*the original speed of a composition; loosely, any duple rhythm* (lit., *even)*
baṛhat	बढ़त	*a technique of vistar in which melodic material is derived from the original composition* (lit., *extended)*
bāyān	बायाँ	*the left-hand or bass drum of the tabla pair* (lit., *left)*
bedam	बेदम	*composed without a gap between phrases* (lit., *without breath)*
besurā	बेसुरा	*out of tune*
betālā	बेताला	*out of rhythm, off the tal structure*
bhajan	भजन	*a Hindu devotional song; a hymn*
bhakti	भक्ति	*devotion*
bhāv	भाव	*emotion, feeling, expression*

bīnkār	बीनकार	*a player of the rudra vina* (also, *beenkar)*
bol	बोल	*the name for the word in a song lyric; the right-hand stroke for an instrument; also, the words of a tabla or dance composition* (lit., *word)*
bolbanānā	बोलबनाना	*the elaboration of the lyric in thumri style; loosely, to compose using the text of a lyric*
bolbāṇṭ	बोलबांट	*an extending section of the vocal dhrupad style which features new melodic and rhythmic compositions with the text* (lit., *division of the words)*
boltān	बोलतान	*an extending section of a khyal performance in which vistars are articulated with the song words; an instrumental tan inflected with bols*
chakradār	चक्रदार	*a type of tihai in which a tihai itself is repeated thrice, or nine statements in all*
chalan	चलन	*the characteristic way of note motion in a rag; a thumbnail sketch of those movements; sometimes called "sādhāran chalan"* (lit., *usual movement)*
chamatkār	चमत्कार	*said of a note or phrase introduced in a surprising or wondrous way* (lit., *marvel, wonder)*
chanchal	चंचल	*a style (prakriti) of playing rags with light classical flavor* (lit., *restless, unsteady)*
chaturang	चतुरंग	*a type of vocal composition using four types of lyric: sargam, poetry, tarana lyric, and drum syllables* (lit., *four parts)*
chaugun	चौगुन	*four times as fast as the original speed*
chhādrā	छाद्रा	*same as* shādrā
chhand	छंद	*the grouping of a rhythmic pulse; hence, the syncopated accent pattern which results* (lit., *rhythm)*
chhāyā	छाया	*shadings of other rags which are near to a rag which is being rendered* (lit., *shadow)*
chhaigun	छैगुन	*six times as fast as the original speed*
chhoṭā	छोटा	*a chhota khyal is the faster composition and movement in a khyal recital* (lit., *small)*

chhūt	छूत	*a tan which jumps suddenly, especially to another octave* (lit., *stitched)*
chikārī	चिकारी	*the high drone strings on an instrument, used for rhythmic articulation* (lit., *high pitched)*
chīz	चीज़	*in khyal style, the fixed composition* (lit., *thing)*
dādrā	दाद्रा, दादरा	*a genre of light classical vocal music in the tal of the same name*
dāyān	दायाँ	*the treble drum of the tabla pair* (lit., *right)*
ḍeṛhī	डेढ़ी	*one and a half times the original speed; loosely, any triple rhythm*
deshī	देशी	*folk and regional music* (lit., *of the country)*
devanāgarī	देवनागरी	*the alphabet of Sanskrit and Hindi*
dhamār	धमार, धम्मार	*a fourteen-beat rhythm cycle, and a song genre of dhrupad style*
ḍolak	ढोलक	*a barrel-shaped folk drum*
dhrupad	ध्रुपद	*the older style of rendering classical music vocally*
dhrupadiyā	ध्रुपदिया	*one who is proficient in dhrupad*
dhun	धुन	*a folk melody*
drut	द्रुत	*fast*
dugun	दुगुन	*double the speed of the original tempo*
dunī	दुनी	*generally used to indicate a fast tempo, but literally, double*
durbal	दुर्बल	*describing a weak note in a rag*
ekārā tān	एकारा तान	*an instrumental style of playing a fast tan by means of one right-hand stroke per note*
farmaishī	फ़रमाइशी	*request: a special type of chakradar composition in which the third, sixth, and ninth statements of a tihai come to sam; a relative of such a mathematical composition*
gamak	गमक	*in the heroic mood, a specific type of rapid repetition of a note* (lit., *grace, ornament)*
gambhīr	गंभीर	*solemn or serious; describing the nature* (prakrit) *of a rag's performance style*

gaṇḍā	गंडा	*the thread tied around a disciple's wrist in the initiation ceremony of bonding with a guru*
gāndharva	गांधर्व	*an ancient branch of celestial music, later identified with* marga sangit, *"music of the spiritual path"*
gat	ग़त	*a fixed composition for instruments in which the melodic or rhythmic patterns are defined by bols; the main theme(s) of an instrumental rendering of rag*
gatkārī	ग़तकारी	*to play variations on the gat*
gat-toṛā	गत-तोड़ा	*traditional style of rendering a rag on plucked instruments with the developmental emphasis on bols, or right-hand strokes*
gāyakī	गायकी	*vocal style; also, the particular instrumental style of sitar master Vilayat Khan and his gharana*
gharānā	घराना	*family, clan; the collective musical family and teaching lineage of a particular teacher, and hence in the style of that family*
ghasīṭ	घसीट	*vocal sliding from one pitch to another* (lit., *gliding)*
gazal	ग़ज़ल	*a light classical vocal genre composed with the Persian/Urdu love lyrics of that name (*also, *ghazal)*
gīt	गीत	*song*
gopī	गोपी	*one of the milkmaid companions of Lord Krishna*
graha	ग्रह	*the initial note of a composition*
grāma	ग्राम	*scale; one of three ancient scale forms described in the* Natyasastra
hāsya	हास्य	*the ras of humor, comedy*
horī, holī	होली	*a Hindu spring festival celebrated with the spraying of colored powder, dancing, and singing songs to Lord Krishna; a song genre in dhamar from this festival*
jāti	जाति	*in ancient music, a melodic variety of scale which was a precursor to rag; in modern rag theory, the number of notes in ascent or descent (5, 6, or 7)* (lit., *type)*

jawārī	जवारी	*the buzzing sound produced by the flat bridge which especially characterizes the sound of the tanpura and sitar* (lit., *glimmering, jewel-like)*
jhālā	झाला	*the final fast movement of an instrumental rendering of a rag featuring rapid repeated chikari strokes* (lit.,*sparkling, cymbal; also, "welded ")*
joṛ	जोड़	*the second movement of the alap portion of a dhrupad style performance, characterized by unmetered rhythm*
jugalbandī	जुगल्बंदी	*an instrumental performance with more than one melodic soloist; usually a duet with tabla accompaniment* (lit., *tied together)*
kaidā	क़ैदा, कायदा	*a theme and variations for tabla featuring limited strokes and prescribed permutations* (lit., *confinement, restriction)*
kampan	कंपन	*the ornamental shaking of a note* (lit., *trembling)*
kaṇ	कण	*in rag structure, the touching upon a neighbor tone in the approach to a note; or, anticipation by touching a note before it is fully intoned in the rendering of a rag* (lit., *iota)*
kāndān	कानदान	*family; the blood descendants of a musician*
karuṇ	करुण	*the ras of sadness, compassion*
khālī	खाली	*empty; an unstressed division of a tal, often beginning the second half of the cycle, shown by a wave of the hand and indicated by an* **o** *in print*
kharaj	खरज	*another word for* **sa**; *or, the lowest* **sa** *string of an instrument*
khaṭkā	खटका	*a type of murki, involving the fast repetition of a note* (lit., *knocking)*
khyāl, khayāl	ख्याल	*the prevailing genre of classical vocal music* (lit., *fantasy, imagination)*
khyāliyā	ख्यालिया	*a specialist in khyal singing*

kīrtan	कीर्तन	*a genre of Hindu devotional song*
komal	कोमल	*flat, a note lowered one half step* (lit., *soft)*
krintan	क्रिंतान	*pulling off; an ornamental technique for the left hand in instrumental music*
kriyā	क्रिया	*the pattern of claps and waves which delineates a tal* (lit., *action)*
kuāṛī	कुआड़ी	*a rhythmic pattern based on five*
laggī	लग्गी	*a lively and rhythmic style of light classical drumming, often spotlighted in a performance of thumri*
laharā	लहरा	*a repeated melody, usually of one tal cycle, used for keeping tal in drum solos and dance performances*
lakshaṅgīt	लक्षणगीत	*a song in which the lyric describes the characteristics* (lakshan) *of the rag*
laṛī	लड़ी	*a string tremolo technique to extend the duration of a note* (lit., *string, chain)*
laṛant	लड़ंत	*a musical "duel" between the instrumentalist and drummer* (lit., *opposition, fighting)*
lay (laya)	लय	*speed, tempo; also, the speed relative to the original tempo*
laykārī	लयकारी	*a style of composition based on rhythmic variation*
madhya	मध्य	*middle;* madhya lay *is medium tempo*
mandrā	मंद्र	*the lower saptak or register* (lit., *deep)*
mārga	मार्ग	*classical music as a yogic and spiritual path, as opposed to* deshi *(folk music)* (lit., *way, path)*
mat	मत	*school of thought, opinion, sect*
mātrā	मात्रा	*beat; the duration between two beats*
mel, mela	मेल	*a scale or scale type, used primarily in reference to South Indian* melakartas (lit., *combination)*
mīṇḍ, mīṛ	मींड, मीड़	*sliding from one pitch to another; deflection of the string in left-hand instrumental technique* (lit., *glide)*

mishra	मिश्र	*mixed or combined*
mohṛā	मोहड़ा	*the sam of the alap; also informally called the nikās*
moharā	मोहरा	*a small drum composition used to bring a solo to a conclusion or lead back to sam, usually with a tihai*
mūrchhanā	मूर्छना	*the generation of new scales by beginning on successive degrees of a scale* (lit., *modulation)*
murkī	मुर्की	*a small, quick ornament*
mukhṛā	मुखड़ा	*the introductory and main phrase of a composition* (lit., *feature, introduction)*
nāda	नाद	*sound, especially in its cosmic, sense (Hindi,* nād)
Nāda Brahma	नादब्रह्म	*the philosophical premise that sound is a manifestation of the divine; "the language of God"*
nakkāṛā	नक्काड़ा	*kettledrum; or a type of stick-drum pair often played with* shenai
naugun	नौगुन	*nine times the original speed*
nibaddh	निबद्ध	*a compositional section in meter (tal); also, fretted* (lit., *bound)*
nikās	निकास	*informally, the phrase used to conclude a section of dhrupad style alap: "ta na na tom"* (lit., *exit)*
nyāsa (nyās)	न्यास	*the note upon which a rag or composition can end*
ochhār	ओछार	*a small introductory alap* (lit., *superficial); also,* uchchhār *(from verb, "to utter")*
pad	पद	*the lyric of a dhrupad composition* (lit., *verse)*
pakaṛ	पकड़	*the key phrase which identifies a rag; "the heart of the rag"* (lit., *catch)*
pala	पल	*one of three phrases of a tihai* (lit., *moment)*
palṭā	पलटा	*a general word for exercises (or tans), especially those in alankar style* (lit., *turn)*
paṇḍit	पंडित	*a learned man in Hindu society; a teacher; a title awarded to a respected musician*

paramparā	परंपरा	*the tradition of passing on musical learning from guru to disciple, and the chain created thereby* (lit., *tradition)*
paran	परन	*a style of composition in the pakawaj tradition*
parivār	परिवार	*family; rag-ragini geneologies of the medieval period which assembled rags into families headed by a male rag*
pānchgun	पांचगुन, पचगुन	*five times the original speed*
pashtu	पशतु	*a folk tal of seven beats from the Punjab*
paun	पौन	*three-quarter speed*
peshkār	पेशकार	*a theme and variations type of composition presented in the context of a larger solo for instruments or drums* (lit., *presented)*
phirat	फिरत	*a type of tan using unexpected successions of notes* (lit., *turned, wandering); also the ability to perform such tans*
prabandh	प्रबंध	*bound; the prabandha git was a forerunner of dhrupad*
prahar	प्रहर	*three-hour period of time in which a rag is optimally performed*
prakār	प्रकार	*type; a kinship term for rag families, e.g., Todi prakar, Kaushi prakar, Kanra prakar, etc.*
prakr̲iti	प्रकृति	*the general demeanor or mood of a rag, e.g., serious, restless, etc.* (lit., *nature, demeanor)*
pūrab	पूरब	*an old name for the instrumental style of nineteenth-century Lucknow, or the thumri style from Benaras; "east of Delhi"* (lit., *east)*
pūrvāṅg	पूर्वांग	*a rag whose vadi is in the lower half of the octave, from* ***sa*** *to* ***pa***
putra	पुत्र	*in the old rag-ragini system of classification, the third generation of rags* (lit., *son)*
qavvālī	क़व्वाली	*an Islamic devotional song in light classical style, usually in a call and response form of verse and chorus*

rāgiṇī	रागिणी	*a female rag, or secondary rag, in the old rag-ragini-putra system of classification*
rāgmālā	रागमाला	*garland of rags; a light classical performance in which short phrases from different rags comprise the vistars; a genre of medieval miniature painting in which rags are fancifully depicted according to verbal descriptions called* dhyāns *("meditations")*
ras, rasa	रस	*emotion or mood* (lit., *sap, juice)*
rasika	रसिक	*one who understands ras; one who has a cultivated taste for the appreciation of fine art or music*
riyāz	रियाज़	*practice*
sādhanā	साधना	*devotion and spiritual practice*
sādhāran	साधारण	*common, ordinary, as in sādhāran chalan,"usual movement"*
sahavādī	सहवादी	*a note consonant with the* anuvadi, *making a secondary tonal axis in a rag* (lit., *auxiliary)*
sāhitya	साहित्य	*the text of a song* (lit., *literature)*
sam	सम	*the first beat of a tal, hence the final downbeat of a musical phrase*
sampūrṇa	सम्पूर्ण	*a jati of seven notes; heptatonic (Hindi,* sampūrṇ, *complete)*
samvādī	समवादी	*the "prime minister" note of a rag* (lit., *consonant)*
sanchārī	संचारी	*the third section of a dhrupad composition* (lit., *moving)*
saṅgati	संगति	*a general word for the lesser notes in the tonal hierarchy of a rag* (lit., *followers, company)*
saṅgīt	संगीत	*the ancient word for the combined performing arts of singing, instrumental music and dance (including theater)* (lit., *sung together)*
sandhyāprakāsh	सध्याप्रकाश	*twilight or dawn, or the rags pertinent to those times* (lit., *meeting of the light)*
saṅkīrṇa	संकीर्ण	*a rag made from the commingling of more than two rags* (lit., *mixed together, combined)*
sapāṭ	सपाट	*a tan which ascends and descends in straight patterns* (lit., *plain, flat)*

saptak	सप्तक	*a group of seven; the octave; pitch register*
sārgām	सारगाम	*singing the names of the note; a composition in which the words are the names of the notes*
sāth saṅgat	साथ संगत	*the melodic soloist and the drummer improvising at the same time* (lit., *with accompaniment)*
sawāl jawāb	सवाल-जवाब	*question-answer; a call and response section near the end of a performance wherein the drummer imitates the rhythm of a passage played by the solo instrumentalist*
shādrā	शाद्रा	*a slow/medium dhrupad-style song in jhaptal*
shānti	शांति	*the ras of peace*
ṣhāṛav	षाड़व	*a jati of six notes; hexatonic*
shāstrīya	शास्त्रीय	shāstriya sangīt *is classical music* (lit., *scriptural)*
shenāi	शहनाइ	*a double reed instrument*
shṛiṅgār	श्रृंगार	*the ras of romantic love, or joy*
shuddh	शुद्ध	*pure; a natural note*
shruti	श्रुति	*microtone; the smallest increment of musically utile pitch differentiation* (lit., *ear, Veda)*
sparsh	स्पर्श	*the ornamental touching of a note* (lit., *touch)*
sthāyī	स्थायी	*refrain; the part of a fixed composition in the home register of a rag* (lit., *permanent)*
sur	सुर	*tone; a musical note*
sūt	सूत	*ornamental series of notes glided over* (lit., *thread)*
svar	स्वर	*a musical note; pitch* (lit., *vowel, sound)*
svarūp	स्वरूप	*a collection of notes which reveal the identity of a rag similar to, but usually larger than, the* pakar (lit., *feature)*
tāl	ताल	*clap; rhythm; rhythm cycle*
tālī	ताली	*a numbered division of a tal receiving a clap*
tālīm	तालीम	*instruction; especially long-term musical tuition*
tān	तान	*a musical passage, often fast, appended to a fixed composition* (lit., *extension)*
ṭappā	टप्पा	*a style of light classical music featuring continual rapid tan movement*

tār (tāra)	तार	*the register above high* **sa** (lit., *string, high-pitched)*
tarānā	तराना	*a song genre in which meaningless rhythmic syllables are used as the lyric*
ṭhāṭ	ठाट (थाट)	*one of ten modern basic scale patterns; the pattern of fret settings on a sitar* (lit., *framework, scale)*
ṭhekā	ठेका	*rhythmic stress; the basic pattern of drum strokes which identifies a tal*
ṭhumrī	ठुमरी	*a light classical vocal style, developed from Kathak dance, which emphasizes expressive filigree melodic variations*
tigun	तिगुन	*three times the original tempo*
tihāī	तिहाई	*a rhythmic (or melodic) cadence, or ending phrase in three parts leading to sam or the beginning of the composition* (lit., *one-third)*
ṭip	टिप	*hammer-on, a left-handed ornamental movement in instrumental technique* (lit., *bounce)*
tīvra	तीव्र	*sharp; a note raised a half step* (lit., *pungent)*
toṛā	तोड़ा	*in instrumental composition, a "bouquet" of rag phrases which are arranged and defined by bol patterns* (lit., *plucked)*
ṭukṛā	टुकड़ा	*a short fixed composition for drums usually ending in a tihai* (lit., *piece, fragment)*
tyāg	त्याग	*the mood of sacrifice or renunciation*
ulṭā	उल्टा	*a tan which turns itself inside-out* (lit., *reversed)*
ustād	उस्ताद	*a Moslem title meaning "master;" hence, a classical music teacher*
uṭhān	उठान	*the introductory compositions in a tabla player's solo or entry in instrumental accompaniment* (lit., *blossoming, to build)*
uttarāṅg	उत्तरांग	*a rag having its vadi in the upper half of the octave, from* **ma** *to* **sa** (lit., *upper limb)*

vādī	वादी	*the "king" note of a rag*
vādya	वाद्य	*musical instrument*
vakra (chal)	वक्र	*motion in an ascending or descending pattern which follows a curved, zig-zag path* (lit., *crooked)*
vandanā	वंदना	*invocational song*
varjit	वर्जित	*a note absolutely avoided in a rag* (lit., *prohibited)*
varṇa	वर्ण	*one of four qualities of note motion:* sthāyi, *stable;* aroha, *ascending,* avaroha, *descending; and* sanchārī, *moving, or changing according to context* (lit., *color)*
viāṛī	विआड़ी	*a rhythmic pattern based on seven*
vikṛit	विकृत	*altered (note); i.e., either* komal *or* tivra
vibhāg	विभाग	*division; a structural section of a tal*
vidār	विदाड़, विदार	*leaping from note to note in an unpredictable and surprising manner* (lit., *fragmentize)*
vilambit	विलंबित	*slow tempo*
vīr	वरि	*the ras of valor, heroism*
viṣham	विषम	*as in sam-visham bandish, a composition so composed as to land on the downbeat one time, and miss it the next* (lit., *odd, difficult)*
vishrānti sthān	विश्रांति स्थान	*a note that can be rested upon in a rag* (lit., *resting place)*
vistār	विस्तार	*the section of a rag's rendering following a fixed composition* (lit., *extension, elaboration)*
vivādī	विवादी	*dissonance; an "enemy" note to a rag, sometimes barely touched upon for effect*
zamzamā	ज़मज़मा	*a type of instrumental ornament executed by the left hand alone; a vocal ornament resembling this effect*

Bibliography

A selected list for additional reading:

Basham, A. L.
1975 A Cultural History of India, Delhi, Oxford University Press.

Bhatkhande, P. V. N.
1971 "A Short Historical Survey of the Music of Upper India," *Journal of the Indian Musicological Society ML5 I 4151*, 2/4 (1971), 1-43.

Bhatkhande, V. N.
1984 Music Systems in India, A Comparative Study of Some of the Leading music Systems of the 15th-18th C's., Delhi, S. Lal and Co.

Bhattacharya, J.
1979 Ustad Allauddin Khan and His Music, Ahmedabad, B.S.Shah Prakashan.

Bor, J.
1987 The Voice of the Sarangi, Bombay, National Center for the Performing Arts.

Bose, N. K.
1960 Melodic Types of Hindustan, Bombay, Jaico Publishing House.

Deodhar, B. R.
1973 "Pdt. Vishnu Digamber Paluskar in His Younger Days," *Journal of the Indian Musicological Society* 4/2 (1973), 21-51.

Dhar Chowdhury, Sisirkona
1982 "Acharya Allauddin Khansahib," *Journal of the Department of Instrumental Music,* Calcutta:Rabindra Bharati University, v. 2.

Deva, B. C.
1973 An Introduction to Indian Music, New Delhi: Publications Division, Ministry of Information and Broadcasting, Government of India.

Deva, B.C. (cont.)
1974 Indian Music, New Delhi, Indian Council for Cultural Relations.
1981 The Music of India: A Scientific Study, Delhi, Munshiram Manoharlal.

Gautam, M. R.
1980 The Musical Heritage of India, New Delhi, Abhinav Publications.

Hawley, John, and Jurgensmeyer, Mark
1988 Songs of the Saints of India, New York: Oxford University Press.

Jairazbhoy, N. A.
1971 The Rags of North Indian Music, Middletown, Connecticut, Wesleyan University Press.

Miner, A. J.
1981 Hindustani Instrumental Music in the Early Modern Period:A Study of the Sitar and Sarod in the Early 18th and 19th Centuries [to be published 1992]

Neuman, D.
1980 The Life of Music in North India, Detroit, Wayne State University Press.

Nijenhuis, E. t.
1974 Indian Music: History and Structure, Leiden, E.J.Brill.

Popley, H. A.
1966 The Music of India, New Delhi, YMCA Publishing House.

Powers, Harold
1980 "Music of India," in Sadie, S., ed, New Grove's Dictionary of Music and Musicians, New York: MacMillan, v. IX, 69-97.

Ranade, A. D.
1984 On Music and Musicians of Hindoostan, New Delhi, Promilla and Co.

Roy, Anjana Debnath
1980 Contribution of Ustad Allauddin Khan to Classical Music, MPhil thesis, Delhi University.

Sangeet Natak Academi
1984 Who's Who of Indian Musicians, New Delhi, Sangeet Natak Academi.

Shankar, R.
1968 My Music My Life, New York, Simon and Schuster.

Shringy, R. K. and P. L. Sharma
1978 Sangita Ratnakara of Sarngadeva, Varanasi, Motilal Banarsidass.

Slawek, S. M.
1987 Sitar Technique in Nibaddh Forms, Delhi, Motilal Benarsidass.

Tagore, S. M.
1965 Hindu Music from Various Authors (1882), Varanasi, Chowkhamba Sanskrit Series.

van der Meer, W.
1980 Hindustani Music in the 20th Century, New Delhi, Allied Publishers.

van der Meer, W. and J. Bor
1982 De Roep van de Kokila, Den Haag, Martinus Nijhoff's.

Wade, B. C.
1979 Music in India: the Classical Traditions, Englewood Cliffs, N.J., Prentice -Hall.
1984 Khyal, Creativity within North India's Classical Music Tradition, Cambridge, Cambridge University Press.

Sources for Indian music publications and recordings:

Ali Akbar College of Music Store
215 West End Ave.
San Rafael, CA 94901
(415) 454-6264

Au Bout du Monde Muziek
Singel 281
1012 WG Amsterdam
The Netherlands

Motilal Banarsidass
Bungalow Road,
Jawahar Nagar
Delhi 110 007

Munshiram Manoharlal
54 Rani Jhansi Marg
New Delhi, 110 055

Original Music
418 Lasher Road
Tivoli, New York 12583

South Asia Books
Box 502
Columbia, MO 65205

Index of First Lines

Index